Facilities Management

D0549347

Also of interest

Better Construction Briefing
Peter Barrett & Catherine Stanley
0-632-05102-7

Total Facilities Management
Brian Atkin & Adrian Brooks
0-632-05471-9

Building Maintenance Management
Barry Chanter & Peter Swallow
0-632-03419-X

EU Public Procurement Law
David Medhurst
0-632-03813-6

Facilities Management

Towards Best Practice

Edited by

Peter Barrett
MSc, PhD, FRICS
Professor of Management Systems in Property and Construction
University of Salford

b

**Blackwell
Science**

© 1995 by
Blackwell Science Ltd
Editorial Offices:
Osney Mead, Oxford OX2 0EL
25 John Street, London WC1N 2BL
23 Ainslie Place, Edinburgh EH3 6AJ
350 Main Street, Malden
    MA 02148 5018, USA
54 University Street, Carlton
    Victoria 3053, Australia
10, rue Casimir Delavigne
    75006 Paris, France

Other Editorial Offices:

Blackwell Wissenschafts-Verlag GmbH
Kurfürstendamm 57
10707 Berlin, Germany

Blackwell Science KK
MG Kodenmacho Building
7-10 Kodenmacho Nihombashi
Chuo-ku, Tokyo 104, Japan

The right of the Author to be identified as
the Author of this Work has been asserted in
accordance with the Copyright, Designs and
Patents Act 1988.

All rights reserved. No part of this
publication may be reproduced, stored in
a retrieval system, or transmitted,
in any form or by any means, electronic,
mechanical, photocopying, recording or
otherwise, except as permitted by the UK
Copyright, Designs and Patents Act 1988,
without the prior permission of the copyright
owner.

First published 1995
Paperback reissue 1998
Reprinted 1998, 2000

Set in 10/12.5pt Palatino
by Setrite Typesetters Ltd, Hong Kong
Printed and bound in the United Kingdom
at the University Press, Cambridge

The Blackwell Science logo is a
trade mark of Blackwell Science Ltd,
registered at the United Kingdom
Trade Marks Registry

DISTRIBUTORS
Marston Book Services Ltd
PO Box 269
Abingdon, Oxon OX14 4YN
(*Orders*: Tel: 01235 465500
            Fax: 01235 465555)

USA
Blackwell Science, Inc.
Commerce Place
350 Main Street
Malden, MA 02148 5018
(*Orders*: Tel: 800 759 6102
                  781 388 8250
            Fax: 781 388 8255)

Canada
Login Brothers Book Company
324 Saulteaux Crescent
Winnipeg, Manitoba R3J 3T2
(*Orders*: Tel: 204 837 2987
            Fax: 204 837 3116)

Australia
Blackwell Science Pty Ltd
54 University Street
Carlton, Victoria 3053
(*Orders*: Tel: 03 9347 0300
            Fax: 03 9347 5001)

A catalogue record for this title is available
from the British Library

ISBN 0-632-05043-8

Library of Congress
Cataloging-in-Publication Data

Facilities management: toward better
    practice/edited by Professor
    Peter Barrett.
        p.   cm.
    Includes bibliographical references
    and index.
    ISBN 0-632-03941-8
    1. Real estate management.
    2. Facility management.   1. Barrett,
Peter, professor.
HD1394. F23 1995
658.2-dc20   95-1293
                                            CIP

For further information on
Blackwell Science, visit our website:
www.blackwell-science.com

Contents

Introduction

Facilities management must be one of the fastest growing professional disciplines in the UK. As a profession it is, however, very much in its early stages. There are many examples of exemplary individual actions on specific issues, but there is not much in terms of a body of knowledge facilities managers can call their own.

This book endeavours to bridge that gap, by taking models and ideas from a wide range of sources and linking them to extensive case study material drawn from practising facilities managers. It is intended to be helpful to a facilities manager with a particular problem, whilst at the same time introducing a broad range of connected issues which will allow the facilities manager to enhance his general service as well as address the immediate problem. Simple packaged solutions are not given, but instead the emphasis is on: advice about the nature of the type of problem, the techniques and processes that can be used and examples of how other facilities managers have addressed similar problems. In other words the intention is to complement the facilities manager's own expertise and local knowledge so that *he* can derive a good solution.

There are many definitions of facilities management. For the work underpinning this book quite a focused view was taken, namely:

> 'An integrated approach to maintaining, improving and adapting the buildings of an organisation in order to create an environment that strongly supports the primary objectives of that organisation.'

This stresses the physical infrastructure rather than support services such as portering. These other aspects are not excluded and do arise at various places, but the emphasis is on the buildings and their use.

It should be clear from the definition that key aspects of facilities management are taken to be:

❑ an integrating role in which management issues predominate over technical matters;
❑ a service justified and orientated towards making a positive contribution to the primary business.

It is in these areas that the future of facilities management lies. It is stressed in the first two chapters that facilities management currently tends to be seen as a low-level cost centre. This does not have to be and much of the advice given is aimed at providing facilities managers with the knowledge, skills and ammunition to fashion facilities management into a high-value activity of strategic importance within their organisations.

The book is divided into three closely interrelated parts. Part 1 is made up of two chapters dealing with facilities management practice. First, current practice is illustrated through case studies leading to an overview of the full range of demands facing the facilities manager. This is linked to good practice examples. The second chapter concentrates on the dynamics of moving from the current position to enhanced facilities management provision.

Part 2 turns to a number of key facilities management issues which require more in depth examination than could be provided in Part 1. Three areas are included, namely: user needs evaluation, contracting out and using computer-based information systems.

Part 3 provides extensive advice on two enabling capabilities that are essential if facilities managers are to reach their full potential. One chapter concentrates on managing people through change, the other covers decision making. These capabilities are highly relevant at various points in all of the previous chapters.

As stressed before this material is intended to be useful in practice. A long introduction would be inappropriate. The future of facilities management is very rosy. It is hoped that this book will accelerate progress on the journey from *facilities* manager to facilities *manager*, both by improving the performance of the individual readers and by contributing to the development of a shared knowledge base for the profession.

Acknowledgements

This book is the result of a collaborative effort between a team of people from both industry and academia. Half of the input came from industry, but the other half was provided by the Engineering and Physical Sciences Research Council and the Department of the Environment through the LINK CMR programme and this support is gratefully acknowledged. A grant was also received from the Royal Institution of Chartered Surveyors which greatly facilitated the work.

The research that led to this book was carried out in a wide range of areas and the following industrial partners all contributed in different ways, by providing, variously, material, information, access to situations, advice and ideas:

❑ Barclays Property Holdings Ltd
❑ Chesterton International plc
❑ Cyril Sweett & Partners
❑ Ernst & Young
❑ Nuffield Hospitals
❑ The Royal Institution of Chartered Surveyors

Of particular note is Dr David Owen's input to Chapter 4 on Contracting-out, which is derived substantially from his doctoral work which was associated with the project.

Many organizations were involved beyond the main partners, especially in providing the case study material in Chapter 1. Thanks are due to these organizations, despite their anonymity.

The LINK programme provided the team with a group of advisors, whose views were very helpful, expecially in the early stages of the project. Those principally involved were Professor Derek Croome and Richard Rooley. Additionally, Peter Pullar Strecker, the programme co-ordinator, was a constant source of wise counsel.

A key decision early on was to create a Local Practitioner Group of facilities management practitioners to comment on the output of our work as it emerged. This proved invaluable and we are greatly indebted to this group led and co-ordinated by Bob Davey within the AFM (now BIFM) structure.

Several members of staff within Salford University made helpful contributions. In particular John Hudson's advice in the areas of briefing and IT deserve mention.

Last, but by no means least, I must express my own gratitude to Martin Sexton and Catherine Stanley, who were the research assistants on the project and who carried out the great majority of the fieldwork and wrote much of the material which now appears as this book. More specifically, principal credit goes to Martin for Chapters 6 and 7 and to Catherine for Chapters 1 and 3.

Many people have been involved. I should like to thank them all for not only creating this book, but also for making the process so enjoyable.

Acronyms

BMS	building management system
CAD	computer-aided design
CAFM	computer-aided facilities management
CIS	computer-based information system
HVAC	heating, ventilating and air conditioning
IT	information technology
M&E	mechanical and electrical
MTC	measured term contract
PABX	private automatic branch exchange
POE	post–occupancy evaluation
QA	quality assurance
TFM	total facilities management
TQM	total quality management

Part 1

Facilities Management Practice

Chapter 1
Current Good Practice in Facilities Management

1.1 Introduction

1.1.1 Scope of the chapter

The aim of this chapter is to encourage facilities managers to assess their facilities management systems to see if there is room for improvement. A number of case studies are presented which provide real life examples of existing facilities management organisations. The case studies do not necessarily demonstrate good practice, indeed in some cases they show how not to do it. They are just intended to show the wide variety of approaches that can be employed. Following the case studies, a summary section makes suggestions for good practice. However, the suggestions should not be followed to the letter, they are intended purely to stimulate the facilities manager into thinking about the different possibilities. No two facilities departments are likely to be identical as they will be designed to meet the needs of their parent organisations.

1.1.2 Summary of the different sections

❏ Section 1.1 – Introduction.
❏ Section 1.2 – Different models are presented allowing facilities managers to identify their organisation with a particular model. Each model is accompanied by a pointer to a particular case study in the next section, that provides a real life example(s) of that model.
❏ Section 1.3 – Case studies are used to illustrate how different organisations operate within the different models.
❏ Section 1.4 – This section draws conclusions from the case studies, stating where the problem areas in facilities management may lie. The section goes on to consider suggestions for good practice within facilities management.
❏ Section 1.5 – A generic model is presented that shows how an ideal facilities management department would operate.

1.1.3 How to use this chapter

The material in this chapter can be used in a number of ways:

- ❑ It can be read sequentially.
- ❑ You may be able to identify with a specific model and go straight to the appropriate case study.
- ❑ You may be particularly interested in a specific area, such as the structure of the facilities department and hence may wish to compare across the case studies (to make this easier each case study follows the same format).
- ❑ You may find a useful reference within the text and decide to go straight to another chapter.
- ❑ You may wish to go straight to the suggestions for good practice.

1.2 Facilities Management Models

1.2.1 Context

Experience has demonstrated that facilities management departments vary considerably from one organisation to another. This is due to the fact that they have developed in response to the particular needs of their organisation. Despite these differences most facilities departments generally fall into one of five categories:[1]

- ❑ office manager
- ❑ single site
- ❑ localised site
- ❑ multiple site
- ❑ international.

As these models focus primarily on location, and therefore indirectly size, this is only one method of classifying facilities departments. However, location is probably the major factor that will affect how a facilities department is organised.

  Facilities managers may want to try to identify their organisation with a particular type and then go on to read the associated case studies to see if there are any similarities. It should be noted that the models are not core business specific and so even if the case study is of a different organisational type, the facilities manager should still find some similarities.

1.2.2 Office manager model

In this model, facilities management is not usually a distinct function within the organisation, instead it is often undertaken by someone as part of their general duties, such as the office manager. There are two possible reasons for this. In the first instance, the organisation is located in just one building, which is too small to warrant a separate facilities department/manager. Alternatively the organisation may be located in a leased building and hence will not want to devote personnel resources for facilities management in a building that they have no real control over. Any necessary facilities work is likely to be undertaken by consultants or contractors on a needs basis. Hence, facilities management in this case is primarily conducted through the administration of service contracts and leases. Any facilities related activities are likely to be reactive, rather than proactive.

Case Study 1: Small manufacturing firm
The firm specialises in innovative equipment for the healthcare industry. The organisation is located in a factory unit that was built three years ago, specifically for them. As the building is so new and relatively small, facilities management is not a distinct function and hence facilities related activities are undertaken by the office manager, as part of his general duties.

1.2.3 Single site model

This model applies to organisations that are large enough to have a separate facilities department, but are located at just one site. Consequently, it is the most straightforward example of a full-service facilities organisation. In this category, organisations tend to own the buildings that they occupy and therefore are prepared to spend more time and money on them than in the previous example, hence the establishment of a separate department to deal solely with facilities issues. These organisations will probably use a combination of in-house and contracted services, however, the balance of the two will vary from organisation to organisation.

Case Study 2: Independent day school
The school provides co-education for over 1000 pupils. It consists of buildings of various ages, with some over 100 years old, grouped together on one site. Facilities management is the responsibility of the bursar, assisted by a small facilities team who deal mainly with the maintenance of the buildings and associated grounds.

Case Study 3: Commercial organisation's headquarters
The headquarters provide office accommodation for 600 people in a building located in a business park. A separate facilities department has been established to deal just with this site due to the large number of people housed there. Three full-time facilities staff are responsible for the co-ordination of a number of contracted functions.

1.2.4 Localised sites model

This model is generally applicable to organisations who have buildings on more than one site, most often within the same metropolitan area. Typical examples would be an organisational headquarters with branches located nearby or a university with several sites. However, the same principles could easily apply to an organisation with just a couple of buildings in different parts of the country.

The idea of decentralisation comes into play with this model, as it is probable that simple operational decisions can be made at the lesser sites, while problems are passed back to the headquarters. Complete decentralisation is unlikely in this case due to economic constraints. This model will probably have a combination of in-house personnel and consultants/contractors in order to deal with the time-distance factors involved. The more decentralised the organisation, the more probable it is that external personnel will be used. In all cases, however, the headquarters will provide policy, overviews, budget control and technical assistance.

Case Study 4: Professional group
The group operates from two locations; an old headquarters building in London and a regional office in a new business park located at some distance from the capital. The facilities team consists of a facilities manager based in London, who is concerned with general facilities policies and two assistant facilities managers, one in each building, who are responsible for daily operations.

1.2.5 Multiple sites model

This model is applicable to large organisations that operate across widely separated geographic regions, probably nationally. In this model the major headquarters is primarily concerned with policy and providing guidance to subordinate regional headquarters. The principal functions are allocating resources, planning (both tactical and strategic), real estate acquisition and disposal, policy and standard setting, technical assistance, macro-level space planning and management, project management and overview. Operational issues tend to be de-emphasised, apart from when they relate to the major headquarters itself, and are dealt with at regional level.

Case Study 5: Private healthcare group
The group has 32 hospitals located around the country. Facilities management exists at four levels: board, corporate, regional and hospital. The facilities director assisted by the corporate level provide guidance on general facilities policies. The latter also oversee new/refurbishment work. The regional level undertakes a co-ordinating role and the hospital level covers daily operations.

Case Study 6: Historic property group
The group acts as the managing agent for over 350 historic properties, so it can actually be considered as a professional facilities management firm. Many of the properties are open to the public. The group has a three-tier management system: regional, local and site-based. At present most services are provided in-house, but there are plans for privatisation in some areas.

1.2.6 International model

This model is very similar to the previous example, but applies to large international organisations rather than national ones. The facilities department located at the headquarters will again act as policy maker and resource allocator, whilst the regional/national offices will be primarily self managing and responsible for operational activities. It should be remembered, however, that allowances will have to be made to accommodate possible differences between the countries involved, such as legislation and language.

1.3 Case Studies

1.3.1 Overview

The following case studies provide real life examples of a number of facilities management organisations. The case studies demonstrate that facilities managers employ a variety of different approaches to similar situations and problems. However, the case studies do not necessarily demonstrate good practice, indeed in some cases they positively show how things should not be done.

Whilst conducting the interviews for the case studies, a standard checklist was utilised so that comparisons could be made later across the organisations. This checklist was derived from a generic model which demonstrates how an ideal facilities management department would operate if designed from scratch and covers both operational and strategic facilities management. (The model is discussed in detail in section 1.4.4.) The checklist expanded upon the following basic themes:

❑ FM structure
❑ management of FM services
❑ meeting current core business needs
❑ FM and external influences
❑ strategic FM.

Consequently to enable comparisons to be made across the case studies the same headings are used throughout.

1.3.2 Office manager example

Case Study 1: Small manufacturing firm
The firm specialises in innovative equipment for the healthcare industry. The organisation is located in a factory unit that was built three years ago, specifically for them. As the building is so new and relatively small, facilities management is not a distinct function and hence facilities related activities are undertaken by the office manager, as part of his general duties.

Background
The organisation is a small manufacturing firm that produces specialist technical equipment, particularly for use in healthcare. The firm is actually part of a larger group with five other sites located around the same city. The group as a whole are very customer driven and new products are developed in line with the latest requirements. Hence, this particular building was erected three years ago to house a new product. Even though the firm is part of a larger group it actually operates as an autonomous unit and so for the purposes of this study can be regarded as a separate entity. The building itself is a typical 'shed type' factory unit, with the majority of the floorspace dedicated to manufacturing and the remainder taken up mainly by offices.

Facilities management structure
The scope of facilities management is naturally limited within small organisations, particularly in non-office situations like this factory where changes to layouts etc. are minimal. In this case therefore facilities management corresponds basically to maintenance considerations. A full-time facilities manager would be inappropriate and so facilities linked operations form just part of the office manager's general duties. Similarly there is no point in employing in-house staff to actually carry out occasional maintenance activities and so the majority of these functions are contracted out, including HVAC and plumbing. However, the organisation employs a full time electrical engineer, who is responsible for both the building and the production machinery. Cleaning is also retained in-house as it is necessary every day.

Management of facilities management services
In this particular organisation, the role of the facilities manager (office manager) is relatively straightforward, basically it is his responsibility to ensure that all maintenance work is carried out as necessary. In the case of the contractors this involves checking that they carry out regular servicing as laid down in their contracts. In addition, if any failures or problems occur, it is his duty to arrange for them to be corrected.

Meeting current core business needs
The fact that this is a manufacturing firm means that it is likely to have different expectations, as far as facilities management is concerned, to organisations whose work is predominantly office based. Most of the

machinery is in fixed locations and does not need to be moved very often and so most facilities requests will concern technical failures, such as the ventilation system not working. In this particular situation formal procedures for assessing current core business needs are not really necessary, if problems occur people will go directly to the office manager to get things sorted out. However, there are certain areas within the building that are not related to production, which the facilities manager feels could be improved, such as the rest areas and the cafeteria, hence, he is planning to ask the staff if they are satisfied with these areas.

Facilities management and external influences

Even small organisations are not immune from external influences and this firm is no exception. The organisation's insurance company recently conducted a risk assessment of the firm and as a consequence a new condition of their insurance was that a disaster recovery plan was drawn up. So the office manager had to devise a contingency plan, stating what the firm would do in case of power failures or fire.

The office manager is also responsible for health and safety within the organisation. However, the subject actually gets very little attention and he relies mainly on junk mail to keep him informed.

Strategic facilities management

In an organisation of this size, certain strategic facilities considerations are likely to be automatically linked to the core business strategy. For example, the introduction of a major new product line in this organisation normally involves building a new factory. Also in this case the hierarchy is very flat and so the facilities manager is involved naturally in the strategic decision-making process.

Comment

At the moment facilities management as a whole is actually quite a minor consideration in this organisation. However, small organisations such as this one, will probably have to abandon such a laissez-faire attitude in the future as further legislation relating to facilities and workers' environments is introduced. As this occurs, organisations will be forced to take a more professional attitude towards facilities management and actually plan how they are going to deal with these new requirements, without totally disrupting the core business.

1.3.3 Single site example 1

Case Study 2: Independent day school

The school provides co-education for over 1000 pupils. The school consists of buildings of various ages, with some over 100 years old, grouped together on one site. Facilities management is the responsibility of the bursar, assisted by a small facilities team who deal mainly with the maintenance of the buildings and associated grounds.

Background

The focus of this case study is an independent co-educational day school. The population of the school comprises approximately 200 junior pupils, 900 seniors, 80 teaching staff and 30 administrative staff. All of the school's facilities are located on one site and there are a number of different buildings of various ages, with some dating back to the previous century.

The school is not large enough to warrant a totally separate facilities department and so facilities are the responsibility of the bursar. He is assisted by a small in-house team who are solely employed to attend to facilities issues.

Facilities management structure

In this school, all non-educational services are controlled by the bursar and are divided into two main areas: facilities and general office services. The facilities section is directed primarily at building maintenance and includes the following functional units, which are retained in-house due to the constant demand for these services.

❑ engineering – mechanical and minor electrical work (one engineer);
❑ groundwork – upkeep of grounds (head groundsman and four assistants);
❑ joinery – minor joinery work (head joiner and assistant);
❑ caretaking – security, movement of furniture (head caretaker and two assistants).

Other facilities related services are contracted out due to their specialist nature or fluctuating demand, such as cleaning and major building work.

Management of facilities management services

In-house services   Each of the in-house functional units are responsible for carrying out work in their own area of expertise. Once a week the bursar meets separately with the heads of each of the different units to discuss formally any outstanding work and new requirements. However, the bursar probably sees the units almost every day on an informal basis. In addition, all four functional units are encouraged to work very much as a team and are in constant communication, sorting out any minor discrepancies between them. The first three functional units work to a maintenance/refurbishment schedule, which is reviewed half termly. However, where repair work is not urgent the school tries to accommodate work during the holidays to minimise disruption.

Contracted services   With contracted services that need to be carried out on a regular basis, such as cleaning, the contractor works to a detailed specification compiled by the bursar. Regular checks are carried out to ensure that the work is consistent with these requirements. If the contractor fails to comply then the bursar can implement the three month exit clause built into the contract.

While minor building work is dealt with in-house, major projects are contracted out. The school engages the same architect for all major works as a good working relationship has been established over recent years. Thus the school finds it easier to brief for new projects as the architect is already familiar with how the school operates. In addition, the architect is assured of an almost constant stream of work, as an increasing number of major projects are required each year in order to satisfy changing educational requirements. Major electrical work is dealt with in a similar manner, as a local electrician is permanently on call, who is also engaged during major building projects.

Meeting current core business needs

As with many organisations, there are a number of different factions at the school whose opinions have to be taken into consideration when the school is assessing current core business needs. In this case, such groups include:

❏   the board of governors
❏   the headmaster
❏   the staff
❏   the parents.

To ensure that the facilities department is meeting the requirements of these groups, a series of briefing and feedback procedures have been established.

Once a term, prior to the main governors' meeting, two sub-committees are held; a finance meeting and a facilities meeting. Each meeting is attended by five governors, the headmaster and the bursar. At the facilities meeting various building issues are discussed, ranging from proposed classroom alterations to the progress of ongoing building work. The bursar takes the minutes, which are distributed to the governors prior to the main meeting, so that topics causing concern can be raised and problems resolved.

The headmaster likes to keep acquainted with facilities developments through informal discussions with the bursar. However, at present this is very difficult to arrange as other school matters are taking precedence. In order to rectify this, the headmaster and the bursar are planning to formalise arrangements and hold weekly meetings specifically to discuss facilities issues.

Once a week a staff meeting is held which is attended by the headmaster, the bursar, the administration staff and the teachers. People are free to raise any issue relating to the school that they feel needs to be discussed, including facilities topics. However, staff do not have to wait for this meeting to report problems, as people are encouraged to contact the bursar direct to request that certain tasks are undertaken. By utilising both formal and informal methods, the bursar is thus able to obtain constant feedback on facilities issues.

As parents pay for their children to attend this particular school, the headmaster feels it is important to keep them up to date on school developments. Parents are sent a newsletter once a term which keeps them informed of all school activities, including any plans for new buildings or refurbishments. On major issues parents are given the opportunity to voice their opinions. Recently parents were sent a questionnaire which presented them with a number of possible options for future school developments. On this occasion they voted for the school to build a new IT language building, as this was seen as a major selling point for the school. A parent association also exists which meets once a month. This is attended by the headmaster who will refer any facilities problems to the bursar as necessary.

Facilities management and external influences
The bursar is responsible for ensuring that all legislation relating to facilities is complied with. This is obviously quite an undertaking for one person and so the bursar has to rely, to a certain extent, on other people to keep him informed of changes. The contracted caterers, for example, are responsible for ensuring that they comply with all the relevant current legislation and to inform the bursar of new developments. Perhaps more interestingly, the bursar also makes use of external contacts who are not working for the school. He has developed a strong working relationship with the local fire service, who carry out fire inspections in the course of alterations to check that current standards are met and who also advise informally on potential changes in the law. In this way the bursar can plan refurbishment work with the new changes in mind.

Sometimes facilities managers working in small organisations may not be aware of new developments in the facilities management field. In order to ensure that this is not the case, the bursar has joined the British Institute of Facilities Management. Through this membership he receives literature on new services and ideas. He also attends local meetings of the group, where he has the chance to discuss different approaches and problems with other facilities managers who can identify with his situation.

Strategic facilities management
Until last year there had been no real link between facilities considerations and the core business strategy. Facilities management was seen very much in terms of maintenance and daily operations. As long as the facilities were maintained to a high standard and problems dealt with as they arose, the school could concentrate on its core business of education and consequently saw no real need for a facilities strategy, however, the school has been forced to rethink the importance of its facilities due to a number of external forces.

Firstly, over the last few years the educational establishment has undergone major changes with the introduction of the national curriculum. The school has been forced to consider how it will meet the new requirements that have been imposed on it. For example, new subject areas have been introduced which the school now has to offer. This will have both physical and financial implications, as additional space will need to be found to accommodate the new subjects and new teachers will also be required. Therefore, the school had to decide whether it could utilise existing classrooms or build new ones.

Secondly, the school is independently run and so it has to attract pupils in order to maintain an income. Increasing competition in private education means that the school now has to try harder to get new pupils. As a consequence, the school not only has to provide a high standard of education, but has to back this up with modern first class teaching facilities. The school had to decide whether this could be achieved by upgrading some of the buildings or whether new ones would be necessary.

Thirdly, the school had always offered a boarding option in addition to daily attendance, but last year the number of boarders at the school dropped so dramatically that this mode of attendance was dropped. Consequently the boarders' building became vacant and so the school suddenly had extra space to play with. This had two major implications for the school: firstly refurbishment work could be carried out more easily as the space could be used as temporary accommodation; secondly, taking account of the extra space, the layout of the school could perhaps be rearranged so that departments were located more logically and new specialist areas created.

The combination of all these three factors meant that the school had no choice but to consider how its facilities should be used in the future. Hence, the school has since developed a core business strategy which covers the next ten years and a corresponding facilities programme.

The latter was achieved in the following manner. Initially a building condition survey was carried out of the whole school. This identified which buildings could be refurbished and which should perhaps be demolished. From this the bursar produced a facilities strategy that established ideally in which order the buildings should be refurbished. At the same time the bursar worked with other staff members to produce a new layout for the school which took the latter into consideration, as well as the core business strategy. Finally a ten year programme was drawn up which details exactly what building and maintenance work needs to be carried out so that the new layout can be achieved.

Comment

Even though the school is too small to warrant a full-time facilities manager, the facilities systems are actually quite well developed. Communication is the key to efficient and effective services in this organisation. Both formal and informal communication networks are utilised to ensure not only that the work is done, but that the user's needs are met. Strong links have also been established with external consultants so that the school is fully aware of new developments relating to facilities management.

As regards strategic facilities management, this was really seen as an unnecessary complication until external pressures actually forced the school to consider how their buildings contributed to the overall success of the organisation. Now that the school has studied their future options they have come to realise that the rationalisation of their buildings may help them to gain a competitive edge and thus facilities management may be about more than just maintenance. Consequently facilities implications are likely to be assessed when considering core business strategies from now on.

1.3.4 Single site example 2

Case Study 3: Commercial organisation's headquarters
The headquarters provide office accommodation for 600 people in a building located in a business park. A separate facilities department has been established to deal just with this site due to the large number of people housed there. Three full-time facilities staff are responsible for the co-ordination of a number of contracted functions.

Background

This is a large commercial organisation. A subsidiary group has been established which is responsible for property related issues. The latter has three main divisions, with the following responsibilities:

❏ property: investment, development, acquisition/disposals;
❏ professional services: managing agents, refurbishments, valuations, rent reviews;
❏ facilities: house management in headquarters buildings.

The facilities department therefore is concerned solely with the day-to-day running of the headquarters, while the property division is responsible for strategic planning.

Facilities management structure

Facilities management within this particular organisation covers a wide range of activities, however, the organisation has chosen to contract-out the majority of these functions and so the facilities department consists of an in-house management team of only three people who ensure that the various contractors complete their duties. Broadly speaking these contracted-out functions can be divided into two areas: building/maintenance and general/office services (Table 1.1).

Table 1.1   Contracted-out functions

Building / maintenance	General / office services
❏ Mechanical and electrical (M&E) maintenance ❏ Grounds maintenance ❏ Building contractors ❏ Furniture alterations ❏ Office moves and changes ❏ Cleaning ❏ Day janitorial service ❏ Waste disposal	❏ Security ❏ Office administration ❏ Reception ❏ Telephones and switchboard ❏ PABX ❏ Mail room ❏ Newspapers ❏ Taxis ❏ Press control ❏ Catering

Management of facilities management services

The in-house facilities management team are responsible for ensuring that all of the above activities are completed as agreed in the relevant contracts. The contracts vary according to the activity, some people work for a fixed number of hours per week, whereas others are on time plus materials. All of the outsourced functions provide quotations before they are awarded the contract to ensure that they are competitive. These quotations are compared regularly against the competition to check that the organisation is still getting value for money. As there are so many outsourced functions, procedures for briefing the contractors have to be tightly controlled and so formal work orders are issued for every job. Once work has been completed it is checked off in an order book and contractors can then issue invoices.

Even though the various outsourced personnel come from different companies they are encouraged to see themselves as part of the facilities team. Consequently there is a good working relationship between the different outsourced people who work on the site. If contractors notice a problem that is not part of their job, then they will point it out to the people concerned.

In this organisation facilities management covers a wide range of activities, co-ordinated by only three in-house managers who, consequently, are sometimes overloaded. Hence, the facilities manager considered purchasing a facilities management software package to ease the situation. Unfortunately an analysis of the various packages available proved that they were all probably too complex for this particular site and provided a lot of features that would not be used. So the department will have to continue to rely on paper methods, although the department does make use of information technology in other ways. For example, to assist with energy management the organisation has installed a lighting control system. All of the lights are switched off automatically in the evening to save energy, but they can be turned on via the telephone if necessary by cleaners or people working late. Also an internal phone directory is on the network, so that the receptionists are not overloaded.

Meeting current core business needs

Facilities management activities in this organisation are very much user driven. Minor operational problems are dealt with on an informal basis, with users contacting the facilities team directly, who will attend to the problem as quickly as possible. However, the facilities team felt that it was important to actually seek out feedback from their users, rather than waiting for the users to approach them. Consequently more formal procedures have also been established and a facilities meeting is held every two months.

This meeting is attended by two members of the facilities management team and one representative from each department, normally an administration or finance manager. Each departmental representative acts as spokesperson voicing the concerns of people in their department, who will have been consulted previous to the meeting. The representatives are also updated on what has happened as a consequence of the last meeting and any plans for the near future. Recently the issue of staff working late and the resulting security/cost problems have been a major discussion point at these meetings. Therefore, the facilities team has had to investigate how high levels of security can be maintained, whilst allowing staff to leave the building whenever they want to.

Facilities management and external influences

As the headquarters building is located in a new business park, there are certain issues that may affect all of the organisations in the park. Hence, a residents' group has been formed that meets regularly to discuss mutual concerns. The issues tend to relate to physical problems, such as new building work or a lack of car parking and so the facilities team are the most suitable people to attend the meeting.

The meetings are also useful as they allow the facilities team to make contact with other facilities managers. Thus a local network has been set up where facilities managers visit each other's buildings to study different facilities management approaches at first hand.

Strategic facilities management

As stated earlier, facilities management in this organisation is viewed as a purely operational function providing daily services that ensure the smooth running of the headquarters buildings. The organisation believes that the facilities department has no real contribution to make to strategic planning as the property division deals with this. This is probably true as far as the organisation's other buildings go, but the facilities department is not even consulted about decisions that affect the headquarters site. When decisions are made by the core business, the facilities department is often the last to be informed, even though it will have to implement the changes. For example, when the core business decides to move a department to a smaller area within a building, it is up to the facilities department to somehow fit in all of the workstations. This means that the facilities department is forced into a reactive way of working which makes it hard to find the time to discover what the users really want.

Such a lack of communication means that the core business sometimes makes decisions without considering all of the relevant factors. A major example of this occurred when the organisation actually relocated to its present site. The organisation decided to move out of London and build a new headquarters. However, the facilities team was not brought in until the design had been practically finalised. It transpired that no allowance had been made for 'churn' (the physical reconfiguration of offices and workstations) in the design and so future changes would not be easily implemented. No doubt if the facilities department had been involved earlier it would have drawn attention to this fact.

Even though the facilities department is not likely to become involved with strategic planning, there are plans to extend its services. Over the past few years it has gained a lot of experience in managing daily operations. Hence, the team intends to offer its services in a consultancy capacity to other organisations. This suggestion has been accepted in principle at board level and so the department now has to develop the idea and identify potential customers.

Comment
The organisation is unusual in that it contracts out the majority of its facilities management services, however, the arrangement appears to work extremely well in this case. Perhaps the most noticeable effect of this approach is that the facilities systems tend to be much more formal and structured than in the other case study organisations. This is because the contracted staff are not necessarily always on site and so workloads have to be planned carefully to make the best use of people's time.

As the examples above demonstrate, the facilities department has not been involved in strategic decision making in the past. Although strategic planning falls within the realm of the property division, it would actually make sense if the transfer of information was improved between the two departments, because the facilities team actually possess valuable knowledge that is not being utilised at present.

1.3.5 Localised sites example

Case Study 4: Professional group
The group operates from two locations; an old headquarters building in London and a regional office in a new business park located at some distance from the capital. The facilities team consists of a facilities manager based in London, who is concerned with general facilities policies and two assistant facilities managers, one in each building, who are responsible for daily operations.

Background
The focus of this study is a professional organisation, operating from two buildings; an old headquarters building located in London and a regional office in a new business park. The London headquarters houses a conference centre, a retail outlet, a library, a members' club, a restaurant and a number of offices. The regional office is used in the main for administrative purposes and is therefore mostly office space, with additional conference facilities.

Facilities management structure
Facilities management in this organisation covers a wide range of services and hence a separate facilities department is necessary. A core management team comprises a head facilities manager based at the London headquarters and two assistant facilities managers, one at each site. The head facilities manager is concerned with general policies and major issues/problems,

whilst the assistants are responsible for supervising day-to-day operations. The different facilities services that are provided are listed in Table 1.2.

Table 1.2 Different facilities services

Premises	Office services	Central services
❏ Building maintenance	❏ Mailing	❏ Catering
❏ Decoration works	❏ Stationery	❏ Conference
❏ Building sub-contractors	❏ Photocopying	bookings
❏ Telecommunications	❏ Vehicle fleet	❏ Insurance
❏ Security	❏ Printing	❏ Archival filing
❏ Porterage	❏ Courier for regional	
❏ Safety	office	
❏ Cleaning		

These services are carried out by a combination of in-house and contracted personnel. As a general guide, in-house staff undertake activities which are required on a constant basis, such as cleaning and building maintenance. Furthermore the facilities manager also believes it is sensible to use in-house employees for tasks which need to be tightly controlled. This particularly applies to functions which interface with the public, such as reception and the switchboard, as poor service in these areas will reflect badly on the rest of the organisation.

Not all of the above services are needed every day and hence certain functions are contracted out, as there is not enough work to justify permanent members of staff. Plant maintenance, for example, is carried out by a contractor who comes once a week to check that the boilers etc. are functioning correctly. Thus any problems can hopefully be identified before any real damage occurs, however, in the case of an emergency the contractor can be called out at any time. A second group of functions are contracted out due to their specialist nature. Catering falls into this category, as it is subject to particularly stringent health regulations.

Management of facilities management services
One of the main difficulties faced by the facilities department in this particular organisation is how to provide services for two separate locations. Owing to the distances involved, it has been necessary to duplicate some operations for each site, such as cleaning and porterage. Even though these services could be managed from the London office, it has been decided that on-site management allows problems to be addressed more effectively. Therefore, an assistant facilities manager is located at each site, who is responsible for the management of daily facilities activities and who can make simple operational decisions without referring to the head facilities manager. However, in this organisation, complete decentralisation would be an unnecessary expense, as certain activities do not need to be duplicated at both sites. Conference bookings for both locations, for example, are dealt with in London and all facilities budgeting is also centrally controlled.

Communication within the facilities department is also a potential problem area for this organisation, as the facilities team has been split up so that both sites are covered. In a single site situation, members of the facilities team would probably see each other every day and so communicate any developments on an informal basis. In this case it is important to ensure that the assistant facilities manager located in the regional office does not feel isolated from the rest of the facilities organisation. Consequently formalised communication channels have been established which keep the assistant facilities manager in touch with the rest of the facilities team. Thus the head facilities manager visits the regional office once every three weeks to check that things are running smoothly. In the meantime, the assistant facilities managers are encouraged to communicate frequently and sort out any problems between them. Technology also plays a part in maintaining communications, for example, an electronic mailing system is used to inform the regional office of advance conferences bookings. Finally, a daily dedicated courier service runs between the two sites, which can be used as necessary by the facilities department.

Effective communication is also an important consideration for each individual site, as well as between sites. Therefore, two-way radios have been introduced so that certain functions in each building have constant access to the assistant facilities managers. Problems can then be addressed immediately even if the facilities manager is not at his desk.

The facilities manager also believes that a thorough understanding of the way the organisation operates and its culture is essential for the provision of high quality facilities services. Consequently he prefers to appoint new facilities members from within the organisation where possible. Thus the assistant facilities manager in the regional office used to be the head porter. Similarly the London assistant was formerly in the post room, but had a very good knowledge of computers and telecommunications and so he was promoted.

Meeting current core business needs
Much of the London headquarters building is given over to facilities for members and other visitors, including: a conference centre, library, members' club, restaurant and shop. Indeed, at any one time there could be up to 300 visitors in the building. This means that a large percentage of the facilities management effort is directed towards these external users. As there are so many visitors and they are generally in the building for such a limited time, it has been decided that it would not be a worthwhile exercise to actively seek their opinions on facilities issues.

Unfortunately, with the main thrust of the organisation directed at its members, the organisation's employees are forced to take a back seat on most issues, including facilities. If problems occur, then internal users are free to contact the facilities manager, but their wishes are not sought on a regular basis. The head facilities manager would like to conduct internal forums to discuss facilities matters, but feels that this is unlikely to happen in the near future owing to the culture of the organisation.

Facilities management and external influences
One of the main responsibilities undertaken by the head facilities manager in this organisation is to ensure that new legislation relating to facilities issues is adhered to. Consequently when the health and safety directives were recently introduced, the facilities manager had to consider how they were to be implemented. When he tried to discuss the directives and their implications with the senior management he could not engage any response. Unable to act on his own in such an important matter, the facilities manager formally refused to take responsibility for any health and safety issues until the senior managers agreed to discuss the situation. As a result of his action a health and safety committee was established, which has since produced a policy statement that will guide all future decisions.

Strategic facilities management
The facilities management department in this organisation was established to provide daily support services only and consequently the facilities manager is not seen as having a part to play in strategic planning for the core business. This means that the facilities team has to respond as best it can once major decisions have already been made; this is highlighted by the following examples.

Approximately five years ago the organisation had a different regional office, where the lease would not be renewed and so it was necessary to find an alternative location. However, even though it was a facilities related problem, only senior managers were involved in the selection process and they engaged external professionals to investigate the different options. It was not until an actual site for a new building had been chosen that the facilities manager or anyone else in the organisation became involved and by this time it was too late to propose alternatives. During the briefing stage of the building process, the facilities manager did become a member of the steering group which was formed to advise the architect. In reality though any suggestions made by the facilities manager were generally ignored, particularly over larger issues, such as size or location of rooms. The facilities team's objectives, as far as the senior managers were concerned, was not to influence the design of the building, but to purely select, supply and fit out all rooms with appropriate furniture, telecommunications, etc. However, the facilities manager feels that he could have provided useful advice had he been allowed to comment, because of his detailed understanding of how the organisation operated. This applies in particular to room sizes, as it has been established that certain rooms are definitely too small to function properly.

On a more minor scale, the facilities team recently decided that the telecommunications system in part of a building was outdated and so the telephones were upgraded throughout that section. It has since come to light that the decision had already been taken by the senior management to lease out the space, as it was surplus to their requirements. Hence, the facilities team spent money upgrading a system, just to remove it again soon afterwards.

Comment

This organisation's buildings are spread across two locations, hence the major hurdle facing the facilities team was how to provide a cost effective and efficient service across both sites. The team has worked hard over the past few years to meet this challenge and they now have an extremely effective partially decentralised system, which ensures that daily operations run smoothly. By locating an assistant facilities manager at each site, minor problems can be dealt with promptly and so services do not grind to a halt whilst waiting for an answer from the head facilities manager.

A particular point of interest in this organisation is that the head facilities manager has appointed existing staff members as assistant facilities managers. He believes that a thorough understanding of the organisation, its requirements and its culture, are more important than technical knowledge. After all, other people are employed or contracted to carry out the actual work and hence the assistant facilities managers are responsible for overall supervision and co-ordination. However, to complement their existing skills, the assistant facilities managers are also sent on courses to acquire a basic knowledge of the relevant technical details.

The facilities department was established purely to provide operational support and so not surprisingly, strategic facilities management is a minor consideration in this organisation. Even when a major relocation was being planned, the facilities department was very much left in the dark. Consequently the new regional headquarters building probably does not function as well as it might have done had the facilities department been involved at an earlier stage.

1.3.6 Multiple sites example 1

Case Study 5: Private healthcare group
The group has 32 hospitals located around the country. Facilities management exists at four levels: board, corporate, regional and hospital. The facilities director assisted by the corporate level provide guidance on general facilities policies. The latter also oversee new/refurbishment work. The regional level undertakes a co-ordinating role and the hospital level covers daily operations.

Background

The focus of this study is an organisation that provides healthcare services in over thirty private hospitals located around Britain, primarily in cities or larger towns. The organisation also has a separate corporate headquarters and four regional offices. It is therefore a good example of a multiple site organisation.

The organisation comprises 32 hospitals in total, each of which is managed by a general manager. The group is subdivided into four regions, with eight hospitals in each, and a regional general manager has been appointed for each region. At corporate office, there is a chief executive and a board of directors, alongside a team of professional heads of functions covering corporate finance, operational finance, personnel, legal, nursing, para-medical services, marketing and facilities management, together with supporting staff.

The organisation operates within a three-tier general management philosophy, with strategic planning and management at corporate office level, through co-ordinated regional management, to general day-to-day management at hospital level.

Facilities management structure

The fact that this organisation owns over 30 buildings is reflected in the size and complexity of the facilities department. The structure of the facilities department is parallel to the structure of the organisation as a whole, hence the facilities management function is represented at the following four levels throughout the organisation: board, corporate, regional and hospital. This organisation is therefore one of a minority where facilities management is viewed important enough to have achieved representation at board level.

A larger organisation has meant that the facilities department not only has a more complex structure, but that it also includes a greater number of activities. Consequently certain functions are represented that are beyond the scope of most other facilities departments. The organisation, for example, is frequently refurbishing or adding extensions to its hospitals, therefore, an in-house capital project management team forms part of the facilities group located at the corporate office.

The roles and responsibilities of the different levels are as follows:

Board level   The director of facilities has a predominantly strategic role and thus only tends to become involved with the operational side of facilities management if major problems occur. His principal functions can, therefore, be summarised as:

❑   representing the facilities management function to the board of governors and the board of directors;
❑   as one of the directors, he is responsible for advising the board of governors on the general situation of the whole group.

Corporate level   Facilities management at this level is the responsibility of the group facilities manager, assisted by a team of professional and support staff. The principal functions of the corporate facilities group can be summarised as:

❑   setting and policing corporate wide goals, objectives and standards for the facilities management function, in compliance with legal obligations and corporate policy;
❑   servicing the boards of directors and governors with group reports, statistics and policy proposals relating to facilities management;

❑ providing professional support and guidance to operational staff at regional and hospital level.

Regional level The organisation is divided into four regions, each of which has its own dedicated regional facilities manager and assistant facilities manager, located at a regional office. The principal functions of the regional facilities teams relate in the main to the physical structure of the hospitals and can be summarised as:

❑ organising, managing and monitoring performance of directly employed staff, contractors and suppliers engaged on maintenance and project work respectively;
❑ advising and guiding regional general and hospital managers on all issues relating to the planning and use of their physical resources for business purposes;
❑ assisting hospital managers when planning for revenue and minor capital budgets and monitoring performance of facilities against allocated funds.

Hospital level Each of the 32 hospitals has its own facilities manager, who is known as the hotel services manager. As the name suggests, this position is generally concerned with the non-medical services that are provided for the general comfort of patients. Hence, the hotel services manager is responsible for the following activities: catering, domestic services, portering, reception and maintenance. It is up to the hotel services manager to ensure that all of these activities, whether in-house or contracted out, are carried out as required. In essence, therefore, each hospital is similar to the earlier single site examples, in that they tend to focus on operational, rather than strategic facilities management.

Perhaps it is worth pointing out that maintenance has a slightly different relationship with the hotel services manager than the other activities. Each hospital has its own maintenance technician, who is responsible for carrying out a planned preventative maintenance schedule, as well as any necessary breakdown maintenance. Even though the technicians have line responsibility to the hotel services managers, they also keep in close contact with their regional facilities managers. This is because the hotel service managers tend to be from non-construction backgrounds and so will not always be able to adequately address maintenance issues.

Management of facilities management services
The size and complexity of the facilities department means that it is very difficult for each of the different levels to keep track of developments elsewhere within the facilities group. Hence, certain procedures have been established to ensure regular communication across the levels. Conse-quently the four regional facilities managers meet with the group facilities manager on a formal basis every two months to discuss the current

state-of-play in each region. Similarly each regional facilities manager meets regularly with the hotel services managers in that region.

Formal meetings are not the only method employed to monitor facilities developments. In the case of maintenance, for example, a manual has been developed which details a planned preventative maintenance schedule and which must be followed by the maintenance technician at each hospital. Thus, when the regional facilities managers (or assistants) make programmed maintenance visits to individual hospitals, they assume an auditing role and check work against the manual. Such scheduling is necessary and works well as it is impossible for maintenance visits to occur very often. This method also allows the regional facilities managers to focus on maintenance problems, rather than routine operations.

Within the different levels themselves, informal methods of communication are used alongside the more formal methods. Hence, if a regional facilities manager has a problem, he may initially contact a colleague in another region, who may have encountered similar difficulties, rather than approaching the group facilities manager. Such teamwork and lateral communications are encouraged throughout the facilities department and so problems are often sorted out without being passed onto the next level.

Internal benchmarking is another method that is used by the facilities group to improve the services that they provide. The department has access to over 30 hospitals and four different regions, hence there are plenty of opportunities to make comparisons, as the following examples show.

One of the responsibilities of the facilities department is to ensure that the clinical sterilizers are maintained in good working order and so a specialist engineer is employed in each region. The facilities department was unable to fill the post in one region and so it was decided that this role should be contracted-out. This decision was made against the wishes of senior management who wanted to maintain this function in-house, however, when compared against the other regions, the contracting-out option actually proved to be more cost-effective, as the contracted engineer didn't have to waste time doing fill-in jobs. Therefore, benchmarking helped the facilities group to identify an area where cost savings could be made.

Another area that is compared internally are utility costs. The group facilities manager has contracted an external organisation to compare utilities costs on a monthly basis. Hence, consumption of gas, water and electricity are constantly monitored. The results are presented on simple graphs to allow for easy comparison. The graphs are discussed at regular meetings to see if any savings can be made. However, the group facilities manager does not necessarily take the readings at face value and carefully considers the different factors that may affect the results, for example, the size of the hospital, the age and the location. Once this system is firmly established, there are plans to bring it back in-house.

The facilities department is responsible for a large number of buildings and over the years many of the hospitals have undergone substantial refurbishment. Not surprisingly, the department was finding it increasingly difficult to maintain paper records of all the changes. When work was being carried out, the hospital and the corporate office were sometimes working on different plans. Hence an AutoCad system has now been installed and up-to-date plans are being transferred onto it, as will any future changes. Similarly, the department has started to use a database to store details of the plant in all hospitals, which will assist in formulating maintenance schedules.

Meeting current core business needs

When assessing current core business needs, the facilities department has to consider both the requirements of the staff and the patients. Obviously, due to the numbers involved, it would be impossible to consult everybody and so the facilities department has to be selective.

Within the hospitals themselves, the hospital managers are responsible for the smooth running of the hospital. Therefore, the hotel services managers work closely with the hospital managers to ascertain whether appropriate service levels are provided and sort out minor problems. The hospital manager in turn consults with the different departmental heads to see if their requirements are being met and passes this information onto the hotel services manager.

Regional facilities managers are interested in the overall facilities picture at the hospitals, rather than the daily operations. Hence, semi-formal meetings are held quarterly between the hospital managers and the regional facilities managers to review facilities budgets and general service levels. Then once a year very formal meetings are held to set the facilities budget for each hospital. However, regional facilities managers also visit each of their hospitals about once a month to walk round and see for themselves how things are going.

As far as the patients are concerned the facilities department uses more indirect methods to see if their needs are being met and rely on the staff to inform them of any problems that may affect the patients. However, the department also obtains information from a general questionnaire that is sent out to all patients by the marketing division. The 'patient satisfaction survey' asks the patient about different aspects of the performance of its hospitals, including room details and general patient services, such as catering. Quarterly reports summarise the responses and hence problem areas can often be identified and corrected.

A large part of the facilities department's work is related to the refurbishment of the hospitals and five major projects have recently been completed. Consequently the department has decided to carry out an evaluation exercise to see if the users are totally happy with the new facilities and if not, identify where improvements can be made. The aim of the exercise is to hopefully learn from past mistakes and ensure that they are not repeated in the future. Such evaluation techniques are being increasingly used by facilities managers and the subject of 'post-occupancy evaluations' is addressed in detail in Chapter 3.

Facilities management and external influences

Healthcare is a rapidly changing area, with new legislation and approaches appearing all the time. Consequently a principal function of the corporate facilities group is to ensure that the organisation is fully aware of any new developments relating to facilities management. This means ensuring that all of the hospitals are informed of any changes and checking that they go on to comply with them.

As the organisation is a well established name in the field of healthcare, they are often approached by other hospitals for advice. Thus the director of facilities is regularly asked to visit other establishments to discuss different approaches to facilities issues. He also finds it useful to attend conferences etc., so that he is fully aware of new ideas. Similarly other members of the facilities department are sent on courses to ensure that their skills are kept up to date.

Strategic facilities management

The core business of this organisation is the provision of healthcare. However, as far as private healthcare is concerned, medical services are only part of the story. Patients are paying for their treatment and so they expect high quality ancillary services. This means that rooms have to be modern, private, comfortable, etc. and catering has to be of a high standard. Thus the core business has to ensure that its future strategy satisfies increasing customer expectations.

Patient expectations are not the only external pressures that may affect core business strategy. The organisation also has to consider what their competitors are planning to do, as the medical consultants will always want to practise at the best equipped hospital in the area. Consultants are responsible for referring patients to a specific hospital and so the loss of a consultant has vast implications.

A third area affecting core strategy is the speed of change within medicine itself. Improvements in treatment are occurring continually and this means that patients are spending less and less time actually in hospital. Consequently fewer beds are necessary.

All of the above factors have facilities implications and so within this organisation facilities management has become increasingly more important. So much so, that the previous group facilities manager has been promoted to the board as director of facilities. At this level within the hierarchy, the director of facilities is involved fully in corporate decision making and therefore full use is made of his facilities knowledge and experience.

For example, the organisation is currently building a new hospital as a replacement for an existing one located nearby. Originally there were plans to refurbish the old one and just build an extension for new facilities, however, the facilities director suggested that the hospital was perhaps not really worth refurbishing and it might be more cost effective just to build a new one. So feasibility studies were carried out by the facilities department and these proved that the assumptions of the facilities director were correct.

Without his early input, the organisation may have wasted a substantial amount of money.

The director of facilities has also been instrumental in a major reorganisation programme, that has led to the facilities department being in a better position to assist the core business. As a result the structure of the organisation today is somewhat different from how it was in 1988 when the current director of facilities was appointed as the estates manager. At that time the structure of the organisation meant that even relatively simple requests resulted in a complex bureaucratic process. For example, if a hospital manager wished to refurbish a small area of the hospital which included patient rooms and offices, she would have to make contact with, and co-ordinate the input of over ten individuals, namely:

❑   Regional surveyor;
❑   M&E services manager, who would mobilise two separate line managers;
❑   Office service manager, who would utilise three people to cover furniture, equipment and office telephones;
❑   Purchasing manager, who would mobilise staff to cover: nurse call and fire alarm installation, piped medical gas, elevators, equipment, furniture, furnishings, and telecommunications;
❑   Hotel services manager.

Even though the respective managers would manage their own staff members, the hospital manager was still faced with the task of overall co-ordination, for which she was not trained and would also be distracted from her primary role of managing the hospital.

A second problem existed in that capital planning and development was carried out as a separate function altogether, with little or no communication with other corporate functions, and therefore no thought was given to the future management of the facilities which the project managers delivered. A third and final contentious issue was that the different functions reported to three separate directors, thereby placing the ultimate onus of co-ordination on the chief executive.

All of these factors meant that the non-core functions were not assisting the core business to the best of their ability, which meant that operational issues were often dealt with at the expense of strategic planning. Within a short space of time, the newly appointed estates manager had identified the above problems and set about trying to find a solution. His answer was to propose a complete reorganisation of the structure, so that the non-core functions were grouped together under one director to provide a totally integrated service. Over the past few years this idea has been implemented, resulting in a facilities department that now fully supports the core business.

Comment

This organisation operates from over 30 separate sites and hence is substantially larger than the previous case study examples. It is not surprising, therefore, that the facilities department is correspondingly complicated. Communications could be potentially difficult to maintain across the different levels and sites, so a series of well defined communication networks have been established to cope with the complexity.

However, as can be seen from the narrative, facilities operations have not always been so well organised. Indeed it has taken over five years for the organisation to develop its current facilities department and systems. Thus other organisations should not be disheartened when looking at their own facilities departments and should realise that changes or improvements cannot possibly be achieved overnight.

Even though the department is now fully reorganised, the facilities team are determined not to become complacent about the services that they provide and have adopted a policy of continuous improvement. For example, they are already benchmarking internally to see where services and costs could be improved. They are also planning to conduct a series of post-occupancy evaluations to ascertain if users are satisfied with the newly completed hospital refurbishments.

In contrast to some of the previous organisations, facilities management in this case is actually considered to have strategic relevance. This is probably because private hospitals are not only assessed on their healthcare, but also on such features as the standard of patient rooms and catering. Consequently facilities management has become increasingly important. This is reflected in the fact that the organisation now has a Director of Facilities who not only advises on facilities issues, but who is also fully involved in considering strategic options for the organisation as a whole.

1.3.7 Multiple sites example 2

Case Study 6: Historic property group
The group acts as the managing agent for over 350 historic properties, so it can actually be considered as a professional facilities management firm. Many of the properties are open to the public. The group has a three-tier management system: regional, local and site-based. At present most services are provided in-house, but there are plans for privatisation in some areas.

Background
This case study considers an organisation that is responsible for the preservation of many historic properties in this country. The organisation is actually split into two main sections: the conservation group and the historic properties group. In reality the sections operate almost independently and so for the purposes of this study, the historic properties group is regarded as the organisation under focus.

The Historic Properties Group varies substantially from the other case study organisations, in that its core business is the management of historic buildings / sites; so in essence it can be regarded as a professional facilities management firm responsible for over 350 properties around the country. There is a complete cross-section of property types, ranging from grass mounds to castles, and everything in-between. The organisation is primarily funded by a government grant (approximately 90%) and the remainder is mainly raised by opening the properties to the general public.

Facilities management structure

The organisation is divided into five regions, each of which is responsible for the management of the historic properties within its region. The regions are operated on a three tier management system: regional, group and site-based.

❑ Regional – A regional director is responsible for each region and is based at a regional headquarters. He has the support of the three following groups:
– operations who are responsible for day-to-day running of the sites;
– historic who commission building work and maintenance inspections;
– design and works: architects / technical officers who provide technical back-up.
❑ Group – All of the regions are subdivided into smaller areas, each of which is co-ordinated by a group custodian. Broadly speaking, the latter act as local managers, checking that the sites are being run correctly.
❑ Site-based – Custodians are located at many of the sites, some are full-time and others are seasonal. Their primary function is to collect admission charges from visitors, but they also ensure that any problems at the site are reported so that they can be corrected.

In addition, the historic properties group can call on the expertise of two ancillary groups: the corporate services group who provide administrative, legal and financial support systems and advice, and the research and professional services group who, amongst other things, provide an in-house labour force to carry out repairs, building work, etc. as necessary.

Management of facilities management services

Each region is responsible for over 50 sites and consequently formal methods have been developed for ensuring that each site receives the attention it requires and is preserved as appropriate. The sites are divided into two types: fragile and stable. The fragile sites are formally inspected by the design and works team every year to check that they haven't deteriorated and to see if any major work is necessary. The stable sites are inspected in a similar manner every three years. The inspections allow the organisation to feed this information into its rolling four year plan. Thus the organisation has a good idea of how its money will be spent over the next few years.

In addition to these major inspections, many of the larger sites have two individually tailored preventative maintenance programmes. Firstly there is an historic programme which details maintenance relating specifically to the building fabric. Secondly there is a general maintenance programme which ensures that the whole site is suitable for visitors.

As the organisation is spread over the whole country and divided into five regions, a method for achieving effective communications has been a major concern. Consequently formal procedures have been established to ensure that regular communication takes place across the regions. Thus the regional directors meet once a fortnight in London to discuss what is happening throughout the whole of the group. To supplement these meetings, the Regional Directors also undertake site visits in each of the regions, so that they can actually view at first hand what has happened at specific locations.

Meeting users' needs

Unlike the previous organisations, the majority of the users in this case are not part of the organisation, but the general public. In the past the organisation has had a fragmented approach to obtaining feedback from visitors to its properties. Most frequently custodians would talk to visitors informally on site and report any relevant comments to the regional headquarters. Occasional surveys were also conducted by the marketing division. However, now that improvements have been made to a number of sites, the organisation has decided to actively seek feedback and so freepost comment sheets are to be provided, especially at the larger sites. In addition, if visitors have a complaint about a site, a formal complaints procedure has been established, details of which can be found in a new customers' charter.

Facilities management and external influences

Many of the sites that are managed by the group are open to the public, so the organisation is responsible for ensuring that the appropriate safety standards are met. However, it would be virtually impossible for each site to keep track of new health and safety requirements. Thus changes to legislation, etc. are initially researched by the corporate services group who pass on the relevant information to the different regions. The regional offices then check that each site complies, providing assistance as necessary.

As with some of the previous organisations, disaster recovery is now a major concern for the group, particularly in the light of recent fires at historic locations of national importance. These fires have persuaded the organisation that there is a real need to consider how they would deal with similar disasters at their sites. As a result, regional disaster officers have been appointed and a disaster procedures manual has been compiled for each major site. The latter includes prevention measures and the provision of salvage teams.

Strategic facilities management

As stated earlier, this organisation can really be regarded as a professional facilities management group. It comes perhaps as no shock, therefore, that the organisation actually places quite a lot of emphasis on strategic considerations. The organisation has recently produced a corporate planning document, which sets out the organisation's objectives for the next three years. The group's aims as laid out in the document can be basically summarised as below:

❏   to put and keep all of their properties into a condition appropriate to their importance, with regard to the urgency of the work and in accordance with the available resources;
❏   to prepare, review and update a defined basic minimum standard of documentation for all of their properties in order to assess their importance and condition;
❏   to make their properties accessible to the public, providing interpretation and facilities to make the visits enjoyable and informative in a way that reflects their relative importance as part of the national and international heritage;
❏   to play a leading role in the wider world, making use of their properties to demonstrate good practice and management, and to promote among others a commitment to conservation.

Now that the organisation has decided what it wants to achieve, the above aims have to be translated into action. Even a quick glance at the list suggests that this will not be an easy task, not only due to the number of factors involved, but also because there are direct conflicts of interest. The organisation wishes to make their properties more accessible to the public through the provision of improved facilities, but an increase in visitor numbers could well have a detrimental effect on the building fabric. However, visitors are a major source of revenue and thus should be encouraged so that the organisation has more money to spend on preservation. The organisation, therefore, has to try to achieve a balance so that all of the aims can be realised as far as is feasible.

Overcoming these internal conflicts is a daunting task in itself, however, the organisation understands that external forces will also have an influence on the way that they approach the various aims. For example, when they are trying to decide which properties have the greatest development potential, they have to consider what their competitors are doing, as well as deciding which sites are historically the most interesting or the easiest to build upon. They have to decide whether it is worth developing a site of great historical interest located miles away from any other attractions, when a less important property may benefit from passing trade to a newly improved competitor's site. The situation is further complicated by the fact that the organisation is not just competing for visitors with other heritage groups, but also with the rest of the ever increasing leisure industry.

Thus the organisation is being forced to take a much more commercial attitude than ever before to ensure that they attract enough visitors to finance necessary maintenance and building work. To address this the organisation is planning to conduct a series of advertising campaigns in order to increase public awareness of its properties.

In addition, the historic properties group is already involved with other strategic initiatives in conjunction with the other groups within the larger organisation. For example, it has been agreed that the direct labour force currently employed in-house which carries out building and maintenance work is to be privatised within the next three years. It is anticipated that this move will make the labour force more efficient as they will actually have to compete for the work that they now get automatically.

Comment

This organisation is responsible for the management of a considerable number of properties and hence in many ways it has quite well developed systems, both operational and strategic, compared to the previous organisations. However, the organisation is not happy to stand still and is continually striving to improve its services, for example, by actively seeking feedback from visitors.

This particular case highlights the fact that strategic facilities management is often a complicated balancing act. On one side the facilities team have to consider what internal improvements are desired by the core business and users, whereas external forces may well be pushing the organisation in another direction. Thus a strategy has to be worked out which considers all of the different factors.

On a final point it is interesting to note the fourth aim listed above. This shows that certain organisations are beginning to realise that perhaps they have a duty to the world at large and that where possible they should share their knowledge, so that others may follow their lead.

1.4 Facilities Management Systems

1.4.1 Overview

This section begins by summarising the findings of the case studies and highlights the potential problem areas within facilities management systems. The section goes on to consider suggestions for good practice within facilities management. Finally a generic model is presented which illustrates how an ideal facilities management department would operate if designed from scratch. The latter emphasises the range of continuing interactions that should be maintained if a facilities department is to fully support its core business.

1.4.2 Case study findings

The case studies presented in section 1.3 provide an indication of the varied nature of facilities management. Even though only six organisations are considered, facilities management is viewed very differently by each one. In some of the organisations, for example, facilities management is expressed primarily as a maintenance function, whereas in others the scope is very much wider, including services such as catering or security. Another area where the organisations differ is whether services are provided in-house or contracted out.

Such differences are not surprising and are to be expected, as facilities departments are necessarily tailored to meet the individual needs of their particular organisation. In addition, it is a new discipline and as such is still trying to find an agreed identity.

The case studies, however, do draw attention to a major issue which is neglected by many organisations, namely the strategic relevance of facilities management. In several of the organisations, facilities management is considered to be a purely operational function. Hence, the facilities departments exist to provide a day-to-day service, not to consider how facilities could benefit the core business in the long term. In these organisations, senior management fail to comprehend that their facilities personnel possess valuable knowledge that could be utilised when making major corporate decisions.

In two of the cases, for example, the organisations had recently relocated. In each case the facilities department was not involved in the decision-making process and was only brought in to advise after sites had been purchased and new buildings designed. Hence, certain important factors, such as churn, were not taken into consideration and problems have occurred as a result.

In contrast, some of the organisations had come to realise that facilities had an important role to play in strategic planning. The private healthcare group (Case Study 5), for example, had recognised that they were not only judged on their medical care, but also on the physical state of their hospitals and ancillary services, such as catering, both of which fell under the facilities umbrella. Therefore, in order to remain competitive, an appropriate facilities strategy was essential. Indeed, facilities issues have become such a major concern in this organisation, that the facilities manager has been appointed to the board, so that he is involved fully in strategic decision making.

It should not be assumed, however, that only larger organisations can benefit from strategic facilities management. It can also play an important role in smaller organisations, as was demonstrated by the independent school (Case Study 2). When one of their buildings suddenly became vacant, the facilities manager took the opportunity to devise a comprehensive facilities strategy. This in turn led to an improved layout for the whole school, incorporating a number of new well-equipped facilities. Hence, the school has gained a certain amount of competitive advantage as it can now offer additional subject areas.

The organisations that do not consider facilities management to have a strategic role are therefore neglecting a source of information that is just waiting to be utilised. However, it is not only at the strategic level that opportunities for improvement are being wasted, but also at the operational level. Communication actually within facilities departments was normally effective and the different functional units generally worked together to provide an integrated service. On the other hand, communication outside of the department, i.e. with the rest of the organisation was often ineffective, as the facilities department waited to receive instructions rather than actively asking their users what they required.

The preceding analysis indicates that there is often room for improvement within the facilities management field and so the following sections make suggestions on how these could be achieved. Even though the case studies highlight problems, they also provide many examples of well designed facilities management systems and so the proposals can be regarded as a synthesis of best practice as demonstrated by the case study organisations. It should be remembered, however, that all organisations are different and not all of the proposals will be applicable to every organisation.

1.4.3 Facilities management structure

The facility management models and the case studies show that there are various ways to organise the facilities department; basically there is no one method that will guarantee success. Bearing that in mind, the following points should be taken into consideration when organising a facilities department.

The size of the organisation is the starting point for deciding how any facilities department is to be structured. Different sized organisations will require different staffing levels. If an organisation is quite small and located in just one building, for example, there is probably no need for a full-time facilities manager, as the amount of facilities work undertaken will be minimal. At the other end of the scale, a large organisation may need a correspondingly large facilities department.

Location is also important. If a facility department is dealing with multiple sites it will undoubtedly require a different approach to one operating on a single site. With a multiple site organisation, the facilities manager will have to decide whether services are to be provided on a centralised or decentralised basis. It is likely that a certain amount of autonomy must be granted to each site to make everyday facility decisions or else services could grind to a halt. For example, in the case of the professional group (Case Study 4), an assistant facilities manager is located at each site to deal with day-to-day operations, leaving the head facilities manager free to address major problems.

Another major consideration for the facilities manager is what services should be provided by the facilities department. Again there is not a definitive guide as to what should be included. The case study organisations, for example, vary considerably in their choice of functions, some concentrate primarily on maintenance, whilst others include general office services. As a rough guide, any facilities department is likely to perform some of the activities listed in Table 1.[2] However, facilities managers should not just select items from the list at random, but provide only those services that are needed by their particular organisation. Once established, facilities departments do not have to limit themselves to their original activities and so the list can be extended as necessary.

A trend in many organisations seems to be that the *conception* of what should come within the audit of facilities management is changing. So, although, for example, an organisation may have traditionally used an architect to do major refurbishments as something separate from a maintenance orientated role for the facilities department, it may decide to put all of these activities under the facilities banner. The architect may well still do the major refurbishments, but his point of contact will be the facilities manager and the building related issues of the organisation will be more closely integrated.

Table 1.3   Typical facilities management activities

Facility planning	Building operations and maintenance
❑ Strategic space planning ❑ Set corporate planning standards and guidelines ❑ Identify user needs ❑ Furniture layouts ❑ Monitor space use ❑ Select and control use of furniture ❑ Define performance measures ❑ Computer-aided facility management (CAFM)	❑ Run and maintain plant ❑ Maintain building fabric ❑ Manage and undertake adaptation ❑ Energy management ❑ Security ❑ Voice and data communication ❑ Control operating budget ❑ Monitor performance ❑ Supervise cleaning and decoration
Real estate and building construction	**General/office services**
❑ New building design and construction management ❑ Acquisition and disposal of sites and buildings ❑ Negotiation and management of leases ❑ Advice on property investment ❑ Control of capital budgets	❑ Provide and manage support services ❑ Office purchasing (stationery and equipment) ❑ Non-building contract services (catering, travel, etc.) ❑ Reprographic services ❑ Housekeeping standards

A further decision to be made relating to the choice of services, is whether they are to be provided in-house or contracted-out. The latter has gained in popularity recently, but as the case studies demonstrate there are no hard and fast rules concerning what should be kept in-house and what should be contracted out. Some organisations favour a totally in-house option, while others literally contract every service possible and then there are those that will use a combination of both. Due to the number of possibilities and issues involved, contracting-out is a major subject area in itself and therefore is discussed in detail in Chapter 4.

The background of personnel may be another influential factor when deciding how to staff a facilities department. As facilities management is such a new profession, there are very few people as yet who possess qualifications in this specific field. Most facility managers, therefore, will have previously trained or worked in other areas; sometimes in related professions like surveying, but often in totally different areas like human resources. A lack of technical skills is not necessarily a problem, as the facility manager's role is to co-ordinate work, not implement it. Indeed several of the case study organisations had chosen to appoint existing staff as facilities managers. The reasons put forward to support these decisions included: they had proven track records as managers and they were already familiar with the operations and culture of the organisation. These organisations complemented these existing skills by sending their facilities managers on courses to acquire the necessary basic technical knowledge. Another approach used by some of the organisations, where there were assistant or regional facilities managers, was to employ people from different disciplines who could support each other.

1.4.4 Management of facilities management services

A facilities manager can be responsible for the provision of many varied services, as Table 1.3 shows. A common mistake made by many facilities managers is to think that they have to be involved at every stage of the delivery process and know every last detail about what is happening, but it should be remembered, that it is a facilities manager's role to co-ordinate, or as the name implies manage these services. Only when facilities managers learn to manage effectively and efficiently, will they be able to turn their attention towards strategic issues, which is where facilities management may really be of use to its core business. So how can facilities managers make time to consider strategic considerations?

Information overload is a major problem for many facilities managers, who find that they spend all their time attending to basic operational problems. Hence, the facilities manager should empower other members of his team to make decisions, encouraging problems to be addressed at lower levels in the hierarchy. Depending on the nature of the problem, this could mean either the functional units or assistant facilities managers. For example, in the case of the school, (Case Study 2) the different functional units worked together initially to sort out problems and only approached the facilities manager (bursar) with major difficulties. In organisations with various sites, such decentralised decision making will be essential if operations are to be maintained.

A further way to ease information overload is to ensure that all of the facilities team, both in-house and contractors, know exactly what is expected of them. Thus it is often worth establishing procedures to address this issue. In larger organisations this will probably mean making use of formal work programmes, service level agreements, maintenance schedules, etc. as briefing tools. Regular meetings to discuss workloads and performance may also be useful. It should be remembered though that informal methods can be utilised as well and may be just as effective, particularly in small firms. In the school (Case Study 2), for example, the bursar held formal weekly meetings to discuss workloads, but he also checked on progress while he walked around the school attending to other duties. Consequently problems could be sorted out on the spot, rather than waiting for the next meeting.

Investment in information technology may be another way to make information processing easier. This is becoming a popular option and there is an ever increasing number of specialist facilities management software packages appearing on the market. These packages offer a variety of different features and so the facilities manager should evaluate possible systems to ensure that they meet an organisation's particular needs. In some cases, the facilities manager may find that IT solutions are just not appropriate, as in the case of the corporate headquarters (Case Study 3), when the facilities manager found that all of the systems he reviewed were far too complex for his requirements. In order to help the facilities manager make an appropriate decision regarding this subject, the issues involved are covered in detail in Chapter 5.

Even though facilities managers have easy access to a variety of information sources, opportunities to utilise or manipulate information are frequently wasted. Facilities managers are often responsible for a number of buildings and therefore they should perhaps consider making comparisons across buildings to identify where improvements or savings could be made. Such internal benchmarking can be used in a variety of ways. Many facilities managers, for example, will have data relating to energy consumption of their buildings. These figures could be compared to see if certain buildings were performing better, reasons for this could be established and perhaps applied elsewhere. In a similar vein, the hospital (Case Study 5) used internal benchmarking to see if it was more cost-effective to employ in-house staff or contractors to perform a specific function.

1.4.5 Meeting current core business needs

Even though facilities management exists to support the core business, it is often this relationship that runs into difficulties. As it is a support service, many facilities managers have taken on a reactive role, waiting for instructions before they perform any action. This often means that dialogue will only occur when problems arise. The result is that the facilities manager has to remedy the situation quickly, rather than assessing what would be the best long term solution. It would be far better in some cases if the facilities manager had time to discuss the various implications. Such a lack of consultation is likely to result in a facilities management service that does not necessarily support the core business to the best of its capabilities.

A typical example of this lack of communication would be an office move. Ideally in this situation the facilities team would consult with the users to find out how each person worked and who they needed to be located next to. However, facilities groups are rarely given enough time to do this and so the users are often moved into an impersonal office space that does not support their particular working patterns. Consequently the whole department is likely to be demoralised and productivity may be reduced.

One of the ways to improve facilities services therefore is to become more proactive, i.e. actively seek out problems and requirements before they become critical. In several of the case study organisations, this meant arranging regular meetings to discuss the services provided by the facilities management group. In Case Study 3, for example, formal meetings are held every two months which are attended by the facilities team and representatives from each department, who will have been briefed prior to the meeting.

In some organisations, staff are not the only people who will be on the receiving end of facilities services. In the private healthcare group (Case Study 5), for example, facilities management efforts are directed towards making a patient's stay as pleasant as possible. In a situation where the users are not part of the organisation, it is not always possible or sensible to try to ascertain what they think of facilities management services. Therefore, facilities managers should try to target people that will provide them with useful information. In the case of the hospitals, it can be argued that it makes more sense to discuss the provision of services with people who are there full time and who can speak on behalf of the patients, namely the nurses and consultants.

Even though meetings are a useful way of gauging satisfaction with facilities services, there is generally not time to discuss things in great detail and only certain people's views will be represented. Facilities managers should therefore consider developing an audit system that seeks to improve services through feedback.

A variety of techniques have been developed to allow facilities managers to do this and can be grouped together under the title of post-occupancy evaluation (POE). At its most basic level, POE is a formal assessment of a building by its occupants after it has been completed or occupied, to identify areas that do not meet users' requirements. However, despite its title POE is also useful when planning new facilities or altering existing ones, as data generated during an evaluation can be used in the briefing process for a new project. Due to its flexibility, POE is a tool that will be useful at various times for many facilities managers and hence is covered in detail in Chapter 3.

1.4.6 Facilities management and external influences

Facilities management is a very wide field and consequently a continually changing one. New legislation and new techniques are appearing all the time and it would be virtually impossible for one person to keep track of all the different changes. Therefore, the facilities manager needs to employ certain methods to make this information processing task easier.

Firstly, the facilities manager should utilise the expertise which already exists within the department. The facilities manager's role is that of co-ordinator, therefore, each of the functional units should ideally ensure that they are fully aware of developments within their own area of expertise and report any significant changes to the facilities manager. This should apply to both in-house personnel and contractors. The facilities manager will often have to take positive action to enable the functional units to acquire this knowledge. For example, one of the case study organisations sends its maintenance technicians on regular courses to guarantee that they are fully aware of the latest techniques and legislation.

Secondly, another way for the facilities manager to keep abreast of changes is to make use of existing external contacts. Facilities managers have to deal constantly with many different specialists as part of their work, such as insurance firms, fire officers, building control, etc. Therefore, it makes sense to maintain good communications with these people so that they can advise on new developments in their areas. In the case of the school (Case Study 2), for example, the facilities manager has established a strong working relationship with the local fire service, who carry out frequent fire inspections to check that current standards are met and also advise on potential changes. In this way the school can plan refurbishment work with the new changes in mind.

Thirdly, facilities managers may also find it helpful to make contact with other local businesses and exchange ideas. One of the case study organisations (Case Study 3), for example, is located in a business park and so the facilities manager attends residents' meetings to discuss mutual concerns. As a result of these meetings, the facilities managers have established a local benchmarking group, whereby they visit each other's buildings to study at first hand how different organisations operate. With benchmarking the number of possibilities for gaining information is almost limitless and depends purely on the nature of the relationship between the participants. Benchmarking could be used to compare processes, services, performance of plant, etc.

Finally, the facilities manager can take advantage of the growing number of specialist information sources dedicated to facilities management. This includes:

❑ Professional associations – such as BIFM (British Institute of Facilities Management)
❑ Books
❑ Periodicals

❑   Conferences
❑   Short courses
❑   Postgraduate degree courses
❑   Collaborative research projects (joint academic and industry).

1.5 Generic Model

Facilities management involves many interactions. One of the main objectives of investigating a diverse set of case studies was to clarify these interactions at a general level.

The generic model shown in Figure 1.1 illustrates the range of continuing interactions which are involved in facilities management. The generic model is based on a combination of systems theory and information processing perspectives [3-5]. It shows how an ideal facilities department would interact with the core business and the external environment. The model differentiates between strategic and operational facilities management, highlighting the need to consider the future situation, as well as the current one. In each of the following examples, the term facilities manager is referred to, however as the case studies demonstrated, it is unlikely that any one person could be responsible for all of these areas and a facilities team is more likely, quite possibly with different people responsible for the strategic and operational areas.

The different interactions are as follows, with the numbers cross-referencing to Figure 1.1.

Operational facilities management

(1)   Interaction within the facilities department itself, between the facilities manager and the different functional units. The latter are the actual operational units of the facilities department and are likely to correspond to the list of functions mentioned earlier, i.e. maintenance, interior planning, architecture and engineering services, etc. It should be noted that the functional units can either be in-house or contracted-out. With reference to this particular relationship, the facilities manager is acting in the role of co-ordinator, rather than implementer.

The functional units are expected to carry out their duties as directed, only referring major exceptions back to the facilities manager. In this way, the latter can concentrate on the other interactions. Each of the functional units should be fully aware of current techniques and legislation relevant to their specific area. They should also scan for possible future changes and inform the facilities manager as necessary.

(2)   The facilities manager interacts on a regular basis with the core business to identify current facilities requirements. This could be achieved on a formal or informal basis, depending on the organisation. Audits or post-occupancy evaluations should also be conducted to ensure that these needs are actually being met and to identify areas that could be improved.

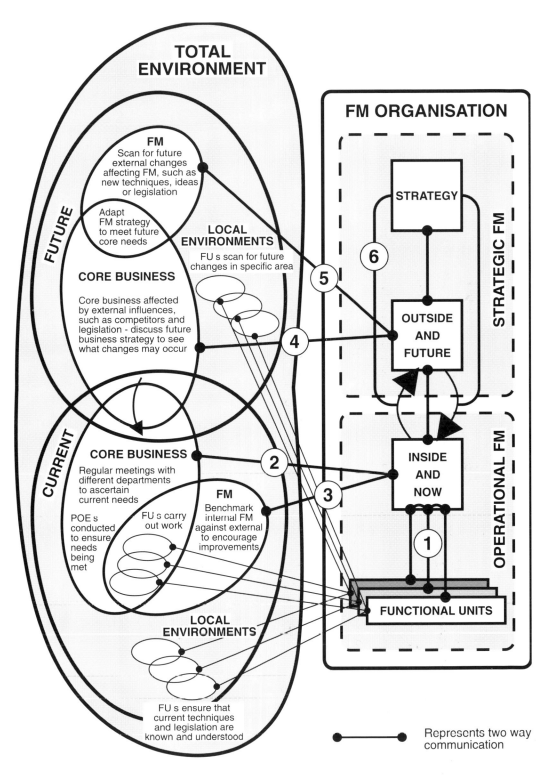

Figure 1.1   Generic model for facilities management systems.

(3)   The facilities manager benchmarks existing internal facilities services against other facilities management organisations, so that possible areas for improvement can again be identified.

Strategic facilities management

(4)   The facilities manager interacts with the core to ascertain what future changes may occur to the business, as a response to external influences, such as competitors' plans.
(5)   The facilities manager will also scan for possible developments within the facilities management arena.
(6)   Strategy is the policy framework, which provides the context for decision making within the facilities department. Interaction occurs between strategic and operational facilities management, the aim being to synergistically balance current operations with the needs of the future.

It should be noted that the generic model should be used as a framework only as to what could ideally be done. In reality, how the issues are handled will vary for each organisation, as will the emphasis given to particular activities. What matters is that the facilities management organisation handles each of the six interactions *appropriately* in the context of their particular circumstances.

Many facilities organisations are firing on two or three cylinders not six. This means less power with the dormant interactions not contributing, or in fact acting as a drag on the active interactions.

For the facilities function to achieve its full potential all six interactions must be dealt with appropriately. For most organisations this will mean some scope for improvement. The next section considers how organisations can move from their current position towards this ideal.

1.6 References

1.   Cotts, D. (1990) Organising the department. *Conference Papers of Facilities Management International,* Glasgow.
2.   Thomson, T. (1990) The essence of facilities management. *Facilities,* **8** (8).
3.   Beer, S. (1985) *Diagnosing the System for Organizations.* John Wiley, Chichester.
4.   Kast, F. and Rosenzweig, J. (1985) *Organization and Management: A Systems and Contingency Approach.* McGraw-Hill, New York.
5.   Galbraith, J. (1973) *Designing Complex Organizations.* Addison-Wesley, Massachusetts.

Chapter 2
Improving Facilities Management Performance

2.1 Introduction

2.1.1 Context

The previous chapter presented a number of case studies and discussed the various systems that would be included in the 'ideal' facilities organisation. This chapter goes one step further and suggests ways in which performance can be enhanced.

In practice, few organisations have the opportunity to design a facilities organisation with a 'blank sheet of paper'. For most organisations there will be existing activities, probably fragmented, possibly with gaps in the provision and maybe with overlaps and some confusion. It is from this base that those seeking change must move.

Obviously, it would be theoretically possible to scrap the current facilities provision and start again, but this is not very realistic. Most organisations will seek to *evolve* a better provision from their existing base. Thus the question is how can an organisation consistently and continuously improve its facilities provision? Or where should it start and how can it keep going? This section seeks to address these questions.

2.1.2 Overview

It is quite easy to improve something specific, say to negotiate better terms on a contracted-out service for grounds maintenance. What is notoriously difficult is, consistently and in an integrated way, to achieve an ever better level of service over the long term. What is needed for this is to simultaneously take action on a number of fronts. The facilities management function must have information on its performance on the full range of interactions; it needs to develop a broad strategic thrust to align individual actions with the core business strategy and with each other; it needs to develop the capabilities of staff so that they actively overcome problems and spot opportunities for doing things in better ways.

The objective, therefore, is to know what needs to be done, to know how to mesh individual actions to greatest effect and to have people involved who, once they know what is needed, are capable of, and motivated to produce, innovative solutions.

Although ultimately all of the above factors are needed for optimum performance it is more realistic to think in terms of a sequential development moving from a sound base of integrated feedback data to a clear strategic view with the capability of staff being enhanced by involvement in these activities and then through targeted efforts over the long term.

2.1.3 Summary of the different sections

- ❏ Section 2.1 – Introduction.
- ❏ Section 2.2 – A brief review of the nature of professional services is provided together with the implications for facilities management.
- ❏ Section 2.3 – The use of multiple feedback mechanisms is illustrated as the primary means of first stimulating improvements and then sustaining the momentum created. An approach termed 'supple systems' is described.
- ❏ Section 2.4 – The important area of strategic management is considered and advice given on how to create a longer term orientation.
- ❏ Section 2.5 – People are linked to the above plans and information in this section. The necessity of developing 'learning individuals' to support an improving organisation is illustrated.
- ❏ Section 2.6 – Summarises the previous sections and stresses the interactive nature of the various issues.

2.2 Client Perception of Facilities Management Services

2.2.1 Context

By definition those providing the facilities function are rendering a *service* to the core business. Given the objective of continuously enhancing facilities performance it is important to fully appreciate the nature of services. The following section is designed to put the familiar aspects of facilities provision in a broader context. This context includes the perceptions of key *clients* of the facilities provision.

2.2.2 The nature of professional service quality

Intangibility of services

Facilities management is geared towards providing a service and hence its contribution to an organisation may be difficult to identify in concrete terms; there is no end product that can be held up and shown to the customer. The implications of this intangibility can be far reaching, especially in terms of the client's assessment of the facilities department's performance. The assessment of facilities services is likely to revolve around the client's *perception* of the service received compared with the client's *expectation* of the service.[1] Thus the facilities group can make efforts in two distinctly different areas – namely, managing the client's initial expectation and managing the client's perception of the service rendered, as shown in Figure 2.1.

Figure 2.1   Expectation perception gap.

It can be seen that *service quality* figures prominently in the above way of looking at performance from the client's point of view. Insights from the field of quality management will therefore be drawn upon at various points in this chapter.

Expectation

The client's expectation of any service will be conditioned to a great extent by past experience, but also by the initial messages concerning the service. Thus, the facilities manager should be careful not to overstate what the facilities department is capable of delivering. If this occurs, it is obvious that the client is unlikely to be satisfied with the service provided. However, in a similar vein, it is important to portray a positive, rather than negative image.

For example, if an already overworked facilities department was approached about a possible office reorganisation, they should not just dismiss the proposal out of hand. Instead, after checking that the work was not urgent, they could take the initiative by saying that they would like the time to prepare reasoned proposals and then suggest a suitable date to discuss their ideas. In this way the message is conveyed that an in-depth analysis will be provided. It also demonstrates that the facilities department actively controls its time, and when a meeting is held, and an impressive presentation made, it will also confirm that the facilities group produces high-quality work, on time. This can be contrasted with an attempt to react immediately, in which case the facilities department would not provide itself with sufficient time to prepare a sensible solution.

Perception

The second area where effort can be directed is at the client's perception of the service rendered. It is important to stress that there is never any objective measurement of a professional service; it will always depend on individual assessments, which in turn will be based on multiple impressions from a variety of sources. It is, perhaps, easiest to highlight the problem by looking at one extreme situation: the job where everything goes right.

In such a case, the objective quality of the service provided is clearly high; however, it is quite possible that the client will be unaware of the facilities department's efforts simply because nothing has gone wrong. Doubtless the facilities group will have foreseen potential difficulties and taken action early on so that matters do not get out of control. Quite simply they have avoided problems and, as a result, their work may appear deceptively simple to the rest of the organisation.

A positive reaction to this is for the facilities department to keep appropriate people informed of potential problems and the steps being taken so that it is clear that the input of the facilities group is positive, proactive and is working. This approach involves taking the client through the job with you, rather than just handing over the final product. However, this suggestion should not be taken to an extreme and it would probably be inadvisable to provide the client with details of every decision, but the general suggestion of *taking the client with you* is very sound.

Technical and functional quality

Figure 2.2 builds upon Figure 2.1, but includes information on how the judgement between expectation and perception is conditioned. Two main categories of factors are shown, which together form the corporate image of the facilities department, which in turn provides the main input to the client's assessment of the service provided. The two main areas are concerned with *technical quality* and *functional quality*. The importance of the individual factors will vary for different organisations, however, any assessment is likely to be a rich mix of both types of factors.

Technical quality is concerned with *what* is done and includes how well the problems were solved and the systems and techniques used. This is the area that facilities managers would normally be mainly concerned with.

However, facilities managers may be less inclined to consider the other factors, namely functional quality. The functional factors revolve around *how* the service was rendered. This includes items such as the appearance of staff, their attitude towards clients and how accessible and responsive the facilities department was to the client.

There is a growing body of research which indicates that when clients judge the quality of a service, they give unexpectedly high weightings to the functional factors as well as the technical factors. It is, therefore, important for the facilities department to think through how they deal with the core business as an important, and quite separate, issue from what they do to solve the technical problems that they are faced with. (Chapter 6 illustrates how the facilities department can successfully manage people through change.)

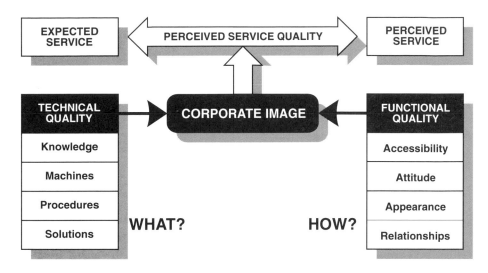

Figure 2.2　Technical and functional quality

Summary

It has been suggested that it is of critical importance to take the client with you in the delivery of the facilities function. This is important in really finding out what is required and implicit in giving consideration to how the service is rendered.

It can be seen that a key variable to be measured is the client's perception of facilities service quality. This is not to suggest that a purely reactive approach should be taken. Informing and explaining to clients the implications of various alternatives, often revealing conflicts between short-term and long-term solutions, is vitally important. It is, however, *not* advisable to say 'the client does not understand what they need, we will sort it out for – or possibly despite – them.'

We have heard this sentiment on many occasions and the following sections endeavour to demonstrate how a client orientation can be introduced, so that the technical skills present can be developed and applied to greatest effect.

2.3 Stimulating and Sustaining Improvements

2.3.1 General approach

The previous section highlights the fact that the assessment of facilities management services is likely to be highly subjective and consequently each client could well apply different criteria. From this it naturally follows that facilities management departments must interact with their clients if they wish to improve their services. Many facilities managers may argue that they already interact constantly with their clients – if they didn't they would not have any work to do. However, as the case studies in the previous chapter demonstrated, the purpose of this interaction is often purely to obtain instructions for the next task and as such is unlikely to lead to improved client services.

The key to achieving improved services is to introduce feedback mechanisms so that the facilities department actually learns from occasions where it could have done better or from opportunities/ideas from other sources. The range of possible sources of feedback/stimuli is shown on the generic model (Figure 1.1) and comprises:

❑ interaction within the department between the facilities manager and the functional units;
❑ interaction between the facilities department and the core business;
❑ benchmarking of internal facilities services against other facilities organisations ;
❑ interaction with the core to ascertain what future changes may occur to the business;
❑ scanning for possible developments within the facilities arena;
❑ interaction between strategic and operational facilities management to achieve a balance between current operations and future needs.

In simple terms, the facilities department collects feedback externally, as well as internally, then analyses the information and integrates it to achieve improved service levels. It should be stressed that the process is iterative and thus encourages continuous improvement. The concept is shown in diagrammatic form in Figure 2.3 which gives the International Organization for Standardization's Quality Management Loop for Services drawn from ISO 9004-2.[2] The feedback mechanisms occupy the lower half of the diagram.

Linking this diagram with the above listing of potential sources of feedback and acknowledging that it would not be sensible, or possible, to wait until the end of the provision of a service before getting some feedback, a richer picture emerges within the same general framework.

Based on this and aiming for systems which are client-responsive and facilitate a continuing cycle of improvements, an approach has been developed, through debate and observation, which endeavours to meet these criteria. The approach has been styled *supple systems* and is discussed next.

2.3.2 Supple systems

The key features of supple systems are given in Table 2.1.[3] The following paragraphs consider each aspect in some more detail. However, in summary,

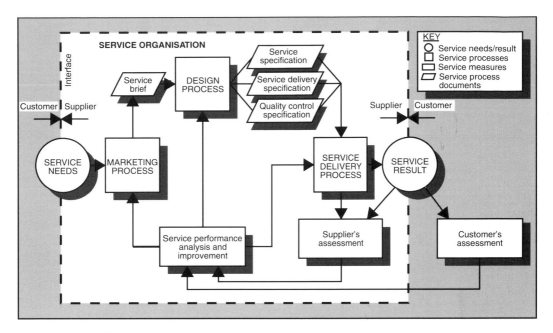

Figure 2.3   Service Quality Loop.

the approach advocates that a strong, but flexible *audit* system is developed which ensures that improvements in the quality of the service are being achieved. The audit system identifies sources of feedback, assesses if action is required, and at what level, prioritises between alternatives, allocates responsibility, checks later that action was taken, tries to objectively assess the impact of the actions and finally feeds these findings back to those involved.

Client orientated

The supple systems approach is in line with the ISO 9004-2 method (Figure 2.3), in that emphasis is placed on the importance of interaction with the client. Thus, it can be seen that the above approach argues that feedback mechanisms should be introduced (or improved), so that existing systems can be tested to see if they really are meeting client requirements. It is important to remember that the quality of services will be assessed from a number of different perspectives, as discussed in section 2.2, and consequently the facilities department should collect both hard and soft data. In this way true client orientation can be achieved and then improvements can be made from a basis of knowledge in such a way that maximum impact is achieved from the effort and energy available. Chapter 3 gives detailed advice on the crucial issue of measuring users' needs and perceptions. By emphasising feedback *first* the danger of fossilising defective aspects of systems is avoided.

Table 2.1   Key features of supple systems

Feature	Comment
Client orientated	Above all the systems are tested against client requirements by actively seeking feedback through both hard and soft data.
Minimalist/holistic	'As much as you must, as little as you may', that is, not having systems for their own sake, but rather targeting high risk/gain areas. Better to have made some progress on all important fronts than to have a patchy provision.
Loose-jointed	The systems operate at an audit level: clarifying objectives, checking performance and integrating efforts. At an operational level different styles and approaches can be accommodated, especially when they have proved themselves over time.
Evolutionary	Allow incremental and continuing progress to be made from whatever base.
Symbiotic with social systems	Build on the norms and culture of the organisation, for instance allowing self-control or group pressure to operate where appropriate.

Minimalistic/holistic

'As much as you must, as little as you may' is a statement that should be applied to quality management systems, especially formal ones and particularly when they involve the creation of paperwork. Given that resources are bound to be limited, it is important to consider how best to use the time and effort available. The well known 'Pareto effect' or '80/20 rule' suggests that action in any one area will tend to be subject to diminishing returns, see Figure 2.4.

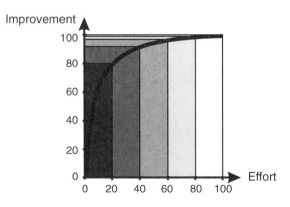

Figure 2.4   The 80/20 Rule.

In practice this means that it is likely to be more effective to take some action on *all* major fronts rather than put all of the available effort in one direction. The generic model at the end of Chapter 1 (Figure 1.1) indicates the range of interactions. The idea being stressed here is that it is better to make some improvements on all dimensions rather than, say, putting all the available effort into creating brilliant contracts for contracted-out services, but being unsure of the contribution made to the core business strategy or the level of satisfaction of users with the facilities management provision, etc. This general approach also applies to the suggested sequencing of activities given in section 2.1.2. Perfection should not be sought in one area before addressing the next.

In the context of quality management, this perspective casts doubt on the likely effectiveness of an over-emphasis on the BS EN ISO 9000 (BS 5750) approach. In this, importance is placed on the production of a 'quality manual' that provides a comprehensive description of the quality system as a permanent reference. Hence, organisational effort is concentrated on recording the systems so that they can be included in the manual, rather than considering where improvements could be made.

Loose-jointed

One of the key aspects distinguishing the supple systems approach is the emphasis on an audit level of activity. This is in contrast with the usual quality management approach which, as mentioned above, stresses recording all existing systems. The supple system method advocates that the existing systems can be left largely as they are, except when the feedback gained identifies a need for action. The audit system is designed to ensure that problem areas are spotted, the root cause identified, effective action taken and the lessons learnt encoded in the formal system if appropriate. Consistency of effort towards satisfying core business needs *is* essential. Consistency at all levels in how this is done is not essential. This facilitates an organisation which can respond to individual needs using individual skills. Most importantly it means time is not wasted scrapping and redesigning the things that are already done well. Thus effort is concentrated where it is needed.

Evolutionary

Where traditional quality management systems aim to produce consistency, that is manage the steady state, supple systems stress the management of the dynamic aspects of the firm. A continuous thrust of improvement is emphasised. As such, it is an approach that any facilities management organisation can take, from whatever baseline, keeping what already works well and flexibly addressing any problem areas identified. The essence of this is given in Figure 2.5.[4]

This suggested approach means that firms can be more certain that their performance is improving, without the heavy load of formally demonstrating that their existing systems (not performance) are all in order up to a minimum level at a given point in time. Thus over time the supple systems approach will lead to high performance, not just an adequate level, but potentially well beyond. At the same time formal systems will have been created, but only where appropriate, generated by the feedback/ improvement cycle given in Figure 2.5. This does not mean the paper systems will grow endlessly. Where the feedback shows formal procedures are causing problems, they will be discontinued.

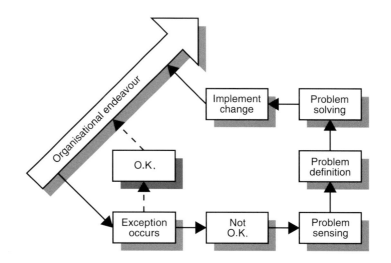

Figure 2.5   The process of planned change.

Thus, it will be possible to proceduralise steady state activities for efficiency and reliability whilst still retaining a capability to identify key situations where change is demanded in order to ensure effectiveness and responsiveness. In short the organisation will become adept at 'switching cognitive gears', as illustrated in Figure 2.6.[5]

In this figure 'automatic mode' equates to proceduralised activities and 'conscious mode' to active problem solving. It is stressed that the real problem is knowing *when* to switch from one to the other. The feedback mechanisms are a key way of increasing awareness of when to move from automatic to conscious mode. Further advice on this is given in Chapter 7 in Table 7.2, where the criteria are set out which identify key dimensions of problems that need in-depth analysis. Moving from conscious to automatic mode, that is taking a specific solution and deciding to generalise from it using policies and procedures can also be problematic. This is a key way in which experience from one part of the facilities organisation can be communicated to other parts. Solutions depend principally on judgement and awareness of the issue. Hard (paper) and soft (say, seminars) approaches should both be used.

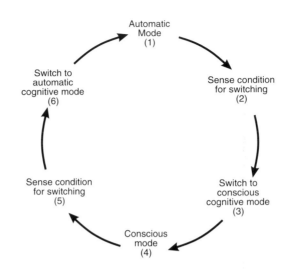

Figure 2.6 Switching cognitive gears.

Symbiotic with social systems

There is often a strong culture which itself can encourage the achievement of high quality work. This can be an ethos of professionalism derived from pride in the discipline of facilities management. It can be something that has developed over time within the given firm, possibly generated by the example of key leaders in the firm. Whatever the foundation of the organisation's culture, every organisation is likely to have a distinctive set of norms. Generally it seems reasonable to suggest, the culture will have developed as a response to the particular nature of the organisation's workload as it interacts dynamically with the specific people making up the organisation's staff. The culture will not be an accident, it may even be appropriate to the circumstances!

Proposals for change should therefore take this existing aspect of a given organisation into account. More particularly the development of supple management systems should aim, where possible, to work with the social systems in the firm so that the maximum synergistic effect $(2 + 2 = 5)$ can be achieved. This requires a systemic perspective which recognises that the formal and informal parts of the organisation may in some circumstances be considered as alternatives. This notion is illustrated in Figure 2.7.[6] It can be seen that many of the alternatives are factors typically found in professional organisations. By acknowledging these factors the need for heavy formal systems can be kept to a minimum. This can be especially important in a small facilities department where informal mechanisms rightly predominate.

Summary

Overall supple systems are proposed as an approach which can provide positive benefit to facilities departments by allowing any department however small to do something, start somewhere, in what will become a continuous development in the capability to identify and satisfy client requirements. As time goes on a robust, but flexible framework of systems and processes will be created. At the same time staff should develop an understanding of their clients and of the key interrelationships within the organisation, leading to a successful service-orientated culture pervading the department and ensuring the effective and efficient delivery of facilities services.

For all but the smallest department a *senior* group meeting as a committee on a regular cycle can help ensure continued implementation over the longer term. It becomes a focus for collecting feedback and then prioritising effort.

As mentioned at the start of this chapter the improvements that the supple systems approach can generate can be enhanced if linked to a strategy for facilities provision. This provides an overall thrust for the individual actions and especially for the prioritising of actions.

This relationship between an overall thrust and individual initiatives is well illustrated in Figure 2.8.[7] This figure stresses that the intended strategy is an overall direction, which may be discarded in part on the light of events (unrealised), which may be diverted somewhat by individual initiatives (emergent), but *still defines the overall direction*. The next section turns to strategy formulation in this context.

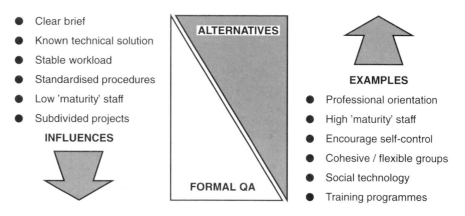

Figure 2.7   Factors supporting formal QA/alternatives.

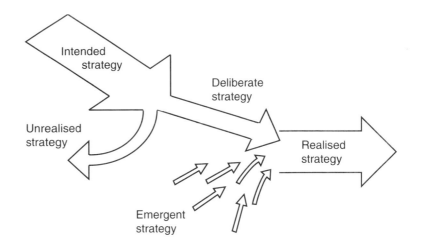

Figure 2.8   From intended to realised strategy.

2.4 Strategic Facilities Management

2.4.1 Possible relationships between facilities management and strategic planning

It is critical that facilities management and corporate strategic management mesh. It has been suggested that there are four possible relationships that could exist between facilities management and corporate strategic planning.[8]

❑   *Administrative linkage*, in which facilities management provides day-to-day operating support, but is itself relatively unimportant in the planning process.
❑   *One-way linkage*, in which facilities management largely reacts to corporate strategic initiatives. This is the most typical relationship and the one that many facility managers would like to consign to the dustbin!
❑   *Two-way linkage*, in which there is a reciprocal and interdependent relationship between facilities management and the corporate strategic planning process. Here facilities management is viewed as credible and important. It is proactive and fully involved in helping guide the development of strategic plans. For example, the facilities manager would be asked to evaluate potential acquisitions and help plan their integration into existing facilities.
❑   *Integrative linkage*, the highest level of integration in which there is a dynamic, ongoing dialogue, both formal and informal, between the facilities management planners and corporate planners. At this level the facilities manager would be involved in all strategic business decisions, even those that do not directly concern the facility function.

The case studies in Chapter 1 would appear to back up the view that the second option is probably the most common at present. The benefits of involving the facilities manager in strategic decision making have also been highlighted on a number of occasions throughout Chapter 1. So why are so many organisations neglecting a major source of expert knowledge that could easily be utilised? A number of possibilities are discussed below.

2.4.2 Factors preventing inclusion of facilities management in strategic planning

Management structure of organisation

As the case studies show, facilities managers are rarely high up within organisational hierarchies. They tend to be located at the second or third management level, hence many facilities managers find it difficult to influence corporate decision making in any way. In only very few companies are facilities managers on the board and thus in a good position to fight for the inclusion of facilities issues in the strategic plan. Even when facility managers are at quite a high level, this does not necessarily indicate that they will have equal power or influence as other staff at the same level. This may be because as a non-core service facilities management is often viewed as expendable.

Organisation's understanding of facilities management/property

Owing to the fact that facilities management as a profession is still relatively new, there is a certain amount of mistrust and misunderstanding of what it is about. Support of senior management is therefore an essential factor that can contribute to the influence that facilities management can have. Thus when facilities issues are properly understood by senior management, it is likely that facilities managers may become more involved in strategic planning. At present, upper level managers often take a short-term view of property issues, for instance, maintenance budgets may be one of the first to be cut in times of hardship. These executives fail to see that small savings in the short term may lead to greater expenditure later.

Senior executives may also feel that organisations are continually changing and thus it doesn't make sense to plan too far into the future, however, because of the lead times involved, property decisions often do have to be taken quite a while before the situation becomes critical. For example, if an organisation decides to manufacture a new product, as happened in one of the case studies (Case Study 1), new premises may be required. Hence, the organisation should consider their options sooner rather than later, otherwise they may end up having to refurbish an existing building when it would have been better to have a new one designed specifically for the new product.

Facilities managers' understanding of organisation's objectives

In a similar vein, facilities managers do not always have a clear understanding of the core business and hence they are left out in the cold when important decisions are made. It is therefore essential that facilities managers take the time to learn what the core business is really about. Without this understanding, it is impossible for facilities departments to be more proactive. If facilities managers are unable to take the initiative for themselves, senior managers may conclude that they are happy to remain in a reactive mode. Thus facilities managers should recognise the need to provide high-quality, proactive and cost effective services to maintain credibility with their client base.

Staffing/structure of facilities management department

As would be expected many facilities professionals are from a construction background, such as architecture, surveying, electrical/mechanical engineering. Consequently many have had very little training in general management and often find it easier to focus on the technical aspects of facilities management, rather than the people aspect. Hence, a facilities manager who does not appear to manage his own department very well, will probably not be viewed favourably by the core business.

The structure of the facilities department in relation to the rest of the organisation is also a critical factor. Many facilities departments have not really been planned and have therefore developed in a haphazard fashion. Consequently not all building related functions are grouped together under facilities management and so strategic building decisions may be the responsibility of a separate department. For example, in one of the case studies (Case Study 3), the property division is responsible for strategic issues, whilst the facilities department is purely operational. In contrast, some organisations have found that it makes sense to merge their different property sections, so that all building related decisions and information is grouped together, as in the case of the hospital group (Case Study 5).

2.4.3 Facilities strategy

In simple terms, the aim of strategic facilities management should be to achieve a strategic fit between core business needs and the provision of facilities management, however, the above factors, backed up by the case studies, illustrate that in reality there may be a huge chasm of misunderstanding between the two groups and thus many facilities departments are forced to remain in a reactive operational mode. Obviously such problems cannot be conquered overnight and changes are unlikely to happen unless the facilities team can demonstrate how a facilities strategy, designed to support the core business strategy, could benefit the organisation. It may be that the facilities team will have to formulate a strategy, discussing the implications at various stages with key members of staff within the core business, in order to gain their support. Then hopefully the facilities team will be in a position to approach senior management and demonstrate why the facilities strategy should be considered alongside the core business strategy. It can be seen that this can be a natural progression from the relationships and information sources developed through the supple systems approach already described in section 2.3 of this chapter.

So how should a facilities department go about producing a facilities strategy? Obviously organisations vary substantially and so will their strategies, but the facilities manager may find it helpful to follow the process illustrated in Figure 2.9.[9]

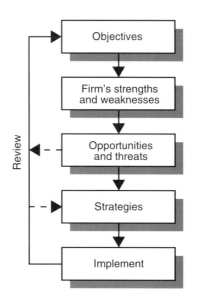

Figure 2.9   Strategic planning process.

Objectives

The first stage of any strategic planning process is to determine the objectives of the organisation. In the case of a facilities strategy this will mean interacting with the core business to see what its objectives are and what changes are likely to occur over the next few years. As stated earlier, many facilities departments do not really understand what the core business is about and so this stage may take a while. Only when the facilities group understands what the organisation's objectives are, will they be able to identify how they as a group will need to change to meet the challenge ahead. In doing this, a 5–10 year perspective should be taken to draw consideration beyond a purely financial view.

SWOT analysis

Having identified what the organisation intends to do, the next stage is focused on the facilities department itself and involves analysing the group's *internal* strengths and weaknesses and then the *external* opportunities and threats that it may encounter in the future. 'External' in this context would include the core business. This element of the process is becoming increasingly well known and is commonly referred to as a SWOT (**S**trengths, **W**eaknesses, **O**pportunities, **T**hreats) analysis. The aim is to produce a relatively short list of the major factors that the department ought to take into account when arriving at its strategies. For internal facilities departments market testing is often seen as a threat. For consultants it is a great opportunity.

The reader may find it useful to consider the points in Table 2.2 when compiling a list of major factors.

Table 2.2   SWOT analysis

Internal strengths/weaknesses	External opportunities/threats
People	Political (legal)
Economics (finances)	Economics
Structure	Social
Technology	Technical

Typically a long list of all possible factors is created first, often involving a wide range of people. This is distilled down to the, say, five major influences in each of the four areas, strengths, weaknesses , opportunities and threats. This small group of factors is the basis from which the creative phase of strategy formulation can be started.

Strategies

The facilities group should now know what it is trying to achieve; what sort of shape the department is currently in and what external forces pose threats or provide key opportunities to the department in the longer term. The next stage is to identify what changes will need to be made within the department, taking all of the above factors into consideration, so that the organisation's objectives can be realised. A good way of doing this is for the facilities group to imagine an ideal world scenario which sets out what the facilities department should be like in the future and then compare this with the current situation.

When the facilities group is assessing what changes will need to be made, there are a number of areas that they should take into consideration.

❑ *Buildings/space* – is the existing building stock compatible with the proposed changes? If not, would it be better to construct a new building, refurbish an existing one or move elsewhere? The facilities group may find it useful at this stage to conduct a property audit, such as that conducted by the school (Case Study 2), to ascertain what the current property situation is and compare this with the required future property to determine where action will be necessary. This comparison should consider not only the amount of property, but also its location, size, appropriateness for use, state of repair, maintenance and running costs, tenure and lease terms, and general quality. From this analysis, a strategic plan for the development of the property can then be established.

❑ *Deployment/structure* – this relates to the choice of the functional units. Are new services likely to be required within the department in the future in order to meet changing needs? For example, is it likely that the organisation will need to carry out a lot of building work? If so, the organisation may wish to expand its facilities services to include an in-house project management team, so that the organisation has more control and is better informed about new building work. In a similar vein, would the organisation benefit if certain existing services were merged with the facilities department to provide a more integrated service, such as occurred in the case of the hospital group (Case Study 5).

❑ *Resources/staff, technology, finance* – what changes will be required in the way of resources? Are existing facilities staff capable of meeting the challenges ahead? If not, should they be retrained or would it be better to take on new employees? Will the organisation's/facilities department's existing information technology be able to cope with the changes or will new computers, etc. be necessary? Finally, the financial implications of all the above changes will have to be considered.

❑ *Contracting-out* – in principle what balance does the organisation want to strike between in-house and contracted FM services? Chapter 4 examines this issue in detail.

Once the strategies for each of these individual areas have been worked out, it is important to check that they are mutually supportive and the facilities team will have to combine the various points to ensure that the greatest collective impact is achieved.

Implementation

By this stage the facilities team should have a workable facilities strategy, that has been developed with the co-operation of key staff from the core business. Consequently, the facilities team should now be in position to approach senior management with their ideas. It is probably highly unlikely that senior management will agree in the first instance to every proposal and so the facilities manager should not be disheartened if he is not welcomed with open arms. As stated earlier, it may take years before facilities strategies are viewed as an integral part of the organisation's strategic planning process. However, if the facilities team have a fully researched and co-ordinated strategy, senior management will hopefully be persuaded to allow some of the suggestions to be put into practice.

Consequently the facilities team will now be at the implementation stage. Thus it will be necessary to identify individuals within the department who will be responsible for pursuing matters on a day-to-day level. A mechanism that can assist in this respect is to request that those identified for a given area provide a brief review of that area and also provide specific targets for the next year, plus an outline of future actions. In this way the strategies become owned at operational level and thus the department should make definite progress towards achieving the required changes.

Review

The setting of specific individual targets means that a control mechanism is now in place that allows the targets to be periodically and systematically reviewed. Thus the next stage is to establish a monitoring system to track whether the targets are being achieved and whether this is being done in the most effective and efficient manner. It is important to remember, however, that the targets are being pursued for the benefit of the whole organisation and so the facilities group must ensure that their activities remain relevant to what is occurring in the core business. If necessary, the department may have to reassess the situation and revise their targets, or even rework their strategy entirely.

Summary

The above discussion should give the facilities manager some idea of how to address the subject of strategic facilities management. The reader should try to remember that senior management may not be very receptive at first to the idea of developing a facilities strategy alongside the core business strategy, but it is worth persevering as the potential benefits to the organisation could well be substantial, as the case studies demonstrated.

The other key benefit is the integrating focus it can create for the initiatives generated within the facilities management department. The outcome of these initiatives will of course depend on the *individuals* involved and the next section considers this specific aspect in more detail.

2.5 Learning Organisations

2.5.1 Context

The ultimate objective of any organisation (or department) must surely be to achieve self-managing workers who are motivated to achieve high quality, capable of achieving high quality and able to exhibit self control. To the extent that this can be achieved there will be little need for systems, nor for leaders in the traditional sense. A current school of thought has suggested that such objectives can be attained by creating 'learning organisations'. This section will discuss how learning organisation principles could be utilised by facilities managers.

In order to become a learning organisation the majority of organisations would require a radical change in the way people behave and consequently, the transition is bound to take several years. However, once an organisation has encompassed truly sustainable organisational learning principles, they will undoubtedly have achieved a substantial competitive advantage. Bearing this in mind, it is obvious that organisational learning is a complex subject and as such cannot possibly be summarised successfully in a couple of pages. The following discussion is meant only as an introduction to the subject and readers should consult the references and appendix to this chapter for further information.

2.5.2 *Individual learning*

'Organisations learn only through individuals who learn. Individual learning does not guarantee organisational learning. But without it no organisational learning occurs.'[10]

Thus the first step on the way to becoming a learning organisation is to encourage individual learning. The key to individual learning is to expand our awareness and understanding by questioning and challenging our actions and assumptions.

There are two goals in any learning process. One is to learn the specifics of a particular subject and the other is to learn about one's strengths and weaknesses as a learner. However, people are very different and learning styles are similarly unique. Thus people should try to work out the learning method that best suits them. Just to give an indication of the possibilities, they could adopt one of the following methods: action learning, on-site and off-site courses, self development programmes, distance learning systems, coaching and counselling, job rotation, secondments and exchange programmes.

Even though people may express the desire to learn, they may often be hampered by their 'mental models.'[10] Mental models are deeply ingrained assumptions/generalisations that influence how we understand the world and how we take action. Consequently when people make decisions they not only consider all the facts, but also unconsciously refer to their mental models. Individual learning requires that we try to uncover our mental models, so that we can see how they affect our actions and prevent us from learning.

The *left-hand column* is a technique that allows people to 'see' how their mental models operate in particular situations. The left-hand column exercise helps managers to identify how their mental models play an active, but often unhelpful part in their management practices. It shows how managers will often manipulate a situation to avoid dealing with difficulties head-on and thus problems will not be solved. After carrying out the exercise, facilities managers should begin to see why they should deal with their assumptions more forthrightly in the future.

To carry out the left-hand column exercise, the manager first selects a specific situation where he is interacting with another person or people in a way that he feels is not working. Then on the right-hand side of a sheet of paper, the manager writes exactly what is said. While on the left-hand side, the manager writes what he is actually thinking, but not saying. The following example outlines a typical problem conversation.[10]

Imagine an exchange with a colleague, Bill, after a big presentation to your boss on a project that you are doing together. You had to miss the presentation, but have heard that it was poorly received.

What you're thinking	What is said
Everyone says the presentation went very badly.	**You:** How did the presentation go?
Does he really not know how bad it was? Or is he just not willing to face up to it?	**Bill:** Well, I don't know. It's really too early to tell. Besides we're breaking new *ground here.*
	You: Well, what do you think we should do? I believe that the issues
you were raising are important.	
He really is afraid to see the truth. If only he had more confidence, he could probably learn from a situation like this. I can't believe that he doesn't realise how disastrous that presentation was to our moving ahead.	**Bill:** I'm not so sure. Let's just wait and see what happens.
I've got to find a way to light a fire under him!	**You:** You may be right, but I think we may need to do more than just wait.

The most important lesson to be drawn from the above example, is how people undermine their opportunities for learning when faced with a difficult situation. Rather than dealing with the problem head on, the two people talk around the subject. Consequently the problem is not resolved and there is no clear way forward. There is no one 'right' way of dealing with difficult situations such as this. However, the left-hand column enables managers to see that their actions may actually be making a situation even worse. The next stage is to try to work out how the situation could be improved, so that managers and their staff can both learn from the experience.

One method of doing this is known as 'balancing inquiry and advocacy'.[11] The use of pure advocacy encourages people to argue, putting their opinion ever more strongly just to win the argument, without really considering other peoples' viewpoints. Similarly, pure inquiry is also limited, just asking lots of questions can be a way of avoiding learning, as people may do so to evade having to put their own opinion forward. It therefore makes sense to combine advocacy and inquiry, so that everyone makes their thinking explicit and subject to public examination. In this way people can begin to question their own mental models through discussion with others and discover that there are alternative, perhaps better, options.

The above discussion highlights the fact that individual learning involves taking risks. If managers want to learn from situations, they must be prepared to put their own views on the line and be prepared to admit that they were wrong. In a similar vein, managers must allow staff to make their own mistakes (within safe limits), so that they can also learn from them.[12] However, many individuals may feel that mistakes will result in punishment of some form and so the facilities manager should take steps to ensure that staff are fully aware that this is not the case. In essence, facilities managers should recognise the need to foster environments which encourages individual learning, making clear the sort of behaviour that they would like to see, such as that listed in Table 2.3.[13]

Table 2.3   Wanted and unwanted behaviours in a learning organisation

Wanted behaviour	Unwanted behaviour
Asking questions	Acquiescing
Suggesting ideas	Rubbishing ideas
Exploring alternatives	Going for expedients, quick fixes
Taking risks/experimenting	Being cautious
Being open about the way it is	Telling people what they want to hear/ filtering bad news
Converting mistakes into learning	Repeating the same mistakes
Reflecting and reviewing	Rushing around keeping active
Talking about learning	Talking anecdotes (i.e. what happened, not what was learned)
Taking responsibility for own learning and development	Waiting for other people to do it
Admitting inadequacies and mistakes	Justifying actions/blaming other people or events

2.5.3 Team learning

'Individuals learn all the time and yet there is no organisational learning. But if teams learn, they become a microcosm for learning throughout the organisation. Skills developed can propagate to other individuals and to other teams. The team's accomplishments can set the tone and establish a standard for learning together throughout the organisation.'[10]

As far as team learning is concerned, the goals remain the same as individual learning. Namely learning about the specifics of a subject and learning about one's strengths and weaknesses as a team learner. With regard to the learning process, the learning cycle may actually work better in the case of a team, than with an individual. This is because individuals cannot realistically be expected to be equally skilled in each stage of the process and as a consequence may well take short cuts. Whereas a team containing individuals who are good at different stages of the process will have the potential to learn well. However, unless the individuals are actually able to work well together, their individual skills will be wasted.

Learning to work together as a team can be quite difficult. This is because the needs of the individual, as well as those of the team, will come into play. Belbin's research[14] into team learning has discovered that successful teams are composed of members offering a wide range of team roles and a spread of mental abilities. Surprisingly, teams composed wholly of individuals with high mental abilities did not perform very well, as the members tried to compete with each other. Table 2.4 lists the major team roles that are required for an effective team.

It should be noted that different roles need not each represent an individual; one person can perform more than one role. In reality, of course, teams are not always composed of people with these complementary skills. Consequently, if teams find they do not have the ideal distribution of talents, they may find it useful to identify where gaps exist and assign specific team members to cover the missing roles.

Table 2.4   Belbin's team roles

---

(1) *Chairman* ensures that the best use is made of each member's potential. Is self-disciplined, dominant but not domineering.

(2) *Shapers* look for patterns and try to shape the team's efforts in this direction. They are out-going, impulsive and impatient. They make the team feel uncomfortable, but they make things happen.

(3) *Innovators* are the source of original ideas. They are imaginative and uninhibited. They are bad at accepting criticism and may need careful handling to provide that vital spark.

(4) *Evaluators* are more measured and dispassionate. They like time to analyse and mull things over.

(5) *Organisers* turn strategies into manageable tasks which people can get on with. They are disciplined, methodical and sometimes inflexible.

(6) *Entrepreneurs* go outside the group and bring back information and ideas. They make friends easily and have a mass of contacts. They prevent the team from stagnating.

(7) *Team workers* promote unity and harmony within a group. They are more aware of people's needs than other members. They are the most active internal communicators and cement of the team.

(8) *Finishers* are compulsive 'meeters' of deadlines. They worry about what can go wrong and maintain a permanent sense of urgency which they communicate to others.

(9) *Specialists* do not have a recognised team role, but will often be a necessary part of a team as they possess unsurpassed technical knowledge and experience.

As well as being better able to accomplish tasks jointly there are, of course, many opportunities for the individual to learn from working in a team. Creating different groupings for different assignments is thus a way by which individual learning can be spread more widely within the organisation. To show how some of these factors combine in a practical situation, a brief case study is presented next.

Case study of an organisation learning to learn

The organisation is well known for being at the forefront of facilities management developments. The problems it encounters are a reflection of its willingness, indeed desire, to achieve constant improvements. Their theory-in-use is 'you do not have to be sick to get better'.

The provision of facilities management services was carefully studied by various people within the facilities group and it was concluded that cultural change was required to achieve the next level of service quality desired. Various barriers to this change were identified which resulted from the organisational context and past experiences of the people involved. These are summarised in Table 2.5.

Table 2.5   Barriers to cultural change

Factor	Description
Cultural	The 'fixer' is encouraged by the organisation. Facilities management organisations have grown from the caretaker and servant of the firm. Recognition by senior management in the FM organisation, as well as the core business, was given for reactive solutions to problems. Retribution would be given if you questioned the way things were done. Subordinates were out of line if they suggested that there was a better way of doing something to their senior management.
Hierarchy	Structures of organisations provide levels of power within departments and across departments, e.g. juniors must not speak to seniors in other departments. This is compounded by the view that internal service departments have been expected to provide 'services' to the management of the core business. Individuals at all levels in the FM and core organisation have built their power base on this formality of communication.
Processes	Processes have evolved over time, built up from convenience, compromise, rituals, past experiences, existing departmental structures and established responsibilities. They are tried and tested, they are seen to work, and thus are best left alone.

Despite these barriers, the facilities department decided that change was necessary. Hence during 1991–1992 a TQM programme was implemented based on previous experience and focusing on: management commitment, focus on teams, continuous improvement activity, training, empowerment, use of quality tools, recognition of performance and customer orientation. A successful workshop was held at the start of the process and a lot of enthusiasm was generated. A range of process improvement teams were created which identified and documented 91 processes and 487 process improvement actions.

Unfortunately, the volume of work involved resulted in widespread demotivation and so the activities were synthesised around seven key processes. Some good progress was made, but the overall effect was patchy. It was concluded that the use of the TQM tools described was *not* producing sustainable change based on improved teamwork and responsiveness to customers.

Consequently from March 1993 the emphasis shifted to interventions designed to produce a learning organisation. This was and is to be based on effective 'learning individuals'. Thus the organisation is endeavouring to build on its TQM experience, but is emphasising a cultural change which revolves around individuals at all levels becoming adept at more systemic thinking than is usual. In this way individuals will be addressing issues, inventing solutions with a much richer palette – looking well beyond the confines of their local situation. The objective is to push back people's 'learning horizons'. At a low, but important level, an example was the tea boy, *himself*, suggesting that he took the mail round.

Another key development is shifting the emphasis from facilities managers as fixers to facilities managers and their staff as thinkers and planners. For example, they will now not accept a brief from a client which simply says 'I want to be able to retrieve any file within one hour.' Instead they ask 'why do you need that level of service? Do you realise how expensive it will be ?' etc. This has caused some initial friction, but as benefits flow from a more careful analysis based on the client's real needs, the facilities staff are becoming more confident in this role of analyst, and the clients are beginning to value it as a valuable part of the service on offer.

As stated earlier, individual learning is necessary, but not sufficient to create a learning organisation. The next building block is the operational team. Consequently in the facilities department, teams are now being assessed against Kolb's learning cycle[15] (Figure 2.10) with the objective of making sure the full range of problem-solving orientations are present. They are also studying how the connections between the quadrants can be made to operate effectively, so that the learning cycle can genuinely spin from internal sensing of an issue, to careful observation (watching), to thinking and then action (doing). This is being linked to consideration of Belbin's team roles.

It is known that to be creative an organisation must be tolerant of errors. This problem has been recognised within the facilities department and so, within safe limits, the facilities manager consciously lets teams make what he perceives as mistakes. Very often he is right, but the growth in learning capability of the team justifies it. Sometimes the team is triumphantly right and their motivation soars.

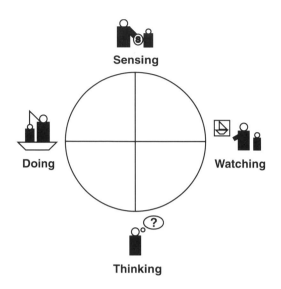

Figure 2.10   Kolb's learning cycle.

One of the key lessons from this case is that an extra dimension is added to the facilities manager's decision making. He may decide to do things in a particular way not for operational reasons, but because it will assist the longer term learning *capabilities* of his organisation. Another key lesson is the need to try things, experiment, on a small scale at first, but an investment without a risk rarely produces a high return.

2.6 Summary and Interactions

This chapter has focused on ways of improving facilities management performance.

The thrust of the argument is that an environment must be created in which people know what needs to be done to support the core business better. This is achieved through *information*, feedback within supple systems, and *direction*, provided by a strategy linked to corporate aspirations. Underpinning these mechanisms are actions to create learning individuals and groups within an organisational context which encourages them to *innovate*.

It should now be apparent that the full effect is dependent on all three aspects working in unison, however, it has been argued that in general the feedback information is the first place to start as this will inform strategy formulation and begin to create a better informed customer orientation amongst staff. If, for a given organisation, say, a strategy already exists then this can be the springboard for the other areas instead. The particular order is not critical.

The view presented here can be summarised as shown in Figure 2.11. The improved level of performance is the product of innovations, at all levels of the facilities management organisation, each orientated towards clearly stated strategic goals by integrative supple systems. The end result of this enhanced dynamism is the creation of a continuously learning and innovating facilities management function that meaningfully contributes to organisational strategy formulation.

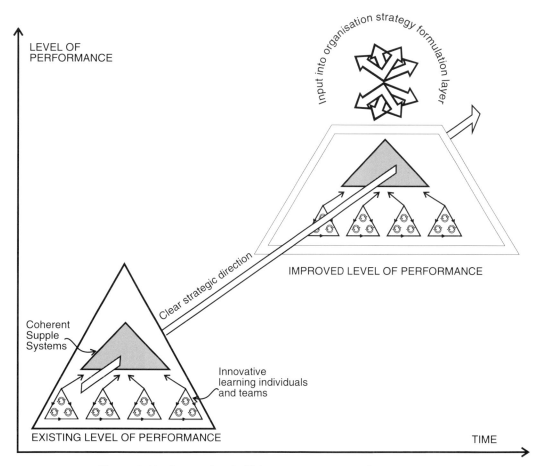

Figure 2.11   Improving facilities management performance.

To successfully address all three areas will take an organisation several years, but the prize is continuous improvement in line with the needs of the core business. With this come satisfied clients and, therefore, success and security for the facilities team.

2.7   References

1. Gronroos, C. (1984) *Strategic Management and Marketing in the Service Sector.* Chartwell-Bratt, Bromley.
2. ISO (1991) *ISO 9004–2: Quality Management and Quality System Elements – part 2: Guidelines for Services.* International Organization for Standardization, via British Standards Institution, London, as Part 8 of BS 5770.

3. Barrett, P. (1994) *Supply Systems for Quality Management*. RICS Research Paper Series, RICS, London.
4. Kast, F. & Rosenzweig, J. (1985) *Organization and Management: A Systems and Contingency Approach*. McGraw-Hill, New York.
5. Louis, M. & Sutton, R. (1991) Switching cognitive gears: from habits of mind to active thinking. *Human Relations*, **44** (1) 55–76.
6. Barrett, P. (1989) Quality assurance in the professional firm. *Quality for Building Users Throughout the World,* 3 volumes, CIB, I, 181–190.
7. Mintzberg, H. & Waters, J. (1985) Of strategies deliberate and emergent. *Strategic Management Journal*, **6**, 257–72.
8. Adapted from: Becker, F. (1990) *The Total Workplace – Facilities Management and the Elastic Organisation*. Van Nostrand Reinhold, New York, p.81.
9. Argenti, J. (1980) *Practical Corporate Planning*. Allen and Unwin, London.
10. Senge, P. (1990) *The Fifth Discipline: The Art and Practice of the Learning Organization.* Doubleday, USA.
11. Argyris, C. (1982) *Reasoning, Learning and Action: Individual and Organizational*. Jossey-Bass, San Francisco.
12. Byham, W. (1988) *Zapp – The Lightning of Empowerment*. Century Business, London.
13. Honey, P. (1991) The learning organisation simplified. *Training and Development*, July, 30–33
14. Belbin, R. (1981) *Management Teams: Why They Succeed or Fail*. Heinemann, London.
15. Kolb, D. (1976) *The Learning Style Inventory Technical Manual*. MacBer, Boston.
16. Jashapara, A. (1993) Competitive learning organisations: A way forward in the European construction industry. In: Proceedings of *CIB W-65 Symposium 93: Organisation and Management of Construction – The Way Forward,* Trinidad, September 1993.
17. Revans, R. (1982) The enterprise as a learning system. In: *The Origins and Growth of Action,* Chartwell-Bratt, Bromley.
18. Mumford, A. (1991) Learning in action. *Personnel Management*, July , 34–7.
19. Pedler, M., Burgoyne, J. & Boydell, T. (1991) *The Learning Company*. McGraw-Hill, New York.
20. Easterby-Smith, M. (1990) Creating a learning organisation. *Personnel Review*, **19** (5), 24–8.
21. Nonaka, I (1991) The knowledge creating company. *Harvard Business Review,* November/December.
22. Attwood, M. & Beer, N. (1990) Towards a working definition of a learning organisation. In: *Self-Development in Organisations,* (eds M. Pedler, J. Burgoyne, T. Boydell, G. Welshman). McGraw-Hill, New York.

Appendix A: Current Models of Learning Organisations

The following table is adapted from Jashapara's literature review on learning organisations[16] and summarises various current approaches to organisational learning.

(1) Learning organisation as five disciplines	
Senge[10]	*Personal mastery* is seen as developing our capacity to clarify what is important to us in terms of our personal vision and purpose.
	Team learning is seen as developing our capacity for conversation and balancing dialogue and discussion. There can be a tendency in many decision making processes towards discussion where different views are presented and defended. Senge promotes the greater use of dialogue where different views can be presented as a means towards discovering a new view.
	Systems thinking is seen as developing our capacity for putting the pieces together and seeing wholes rather than disparate parts.
	Mental models is seen as our capacity to reflect on our internal pictures. This discipline involves balancing our skills of inquiry and advocacy as well as understanding how our mental models influence our actions.
	Shared vision is seen as building a sense of commitment in a group based on what they would really like to create. Senge believes that leaders will play a critical role in developing learning organisations especially through building a shared vision which is rooted in personal visions.
(2) Learning organisation as action learning	
Revans[17]	Revans explores the notion of the enterprise as a learning system. He suggests that such organisations encourage people to regularly study and reorganise their systems of work through learning and the quality of learning is determined by the morale of the organisation. He uses the following equation:
	Organisational learning $L = P + Q$, where P = programmed learning (highly specialist) and Q = questioned learning (asking discriminating questions).
	Such organisations provide 'action learning groups' where managers can learn to take effective action by closely studying and questioning their everyday work. This is in contrast to traditional methods where managers would perform an analysis and make recommendations, but not necessarily take action.
Mumford[18]	Mumford proposes four 'Is' to achieve effective forms of action learning: *interaction* with major organisational players, *integration* of appropriate skills and knowledge, *implementation* for which managers are personally accountable and *iteration* which views learning as a process. There can be high opportunity costs to action learning and the process is time consuming. An environment needs to develop to create special assignments for action learning which may include exchanges, sabbaticals, counselling and coaching skills.

(3)   Learning organisation as encouraging wanted behaviours

| Honey[13] | Honey's method for creating learning organisations revolves around establishing a number of learning behaviours which need to be encouraged in an organisation and working out suitable triggers and reinforcers for the wanted behaviours. The establishment of the relevant learning behaviours is likely to be critical for sustaining competitive advantage. (Table 2.3 shows possible wanted and unwanted behaviours.) |

(4)   Learning organisation as continuous transformation

Pedler *et al*[19]	*Strategy* includes a learning approach to strategy with small scale developments and feedback loops to enable continuous improvement and participative policy making.
	Looking in includes using IT to help individuals understand what is going on and using formative accounting and control to assist learning and delighting internal customers. In addition, this area includes developing an environment of collaboration between internal departments and exploring basic assumptions and values of the reward system.
	Structures implies the need for roles and careers to be flexibly orientated to allow for experimentation, growth and adaptation.
	Looking out includes regularly scanning and reviewing external environment and developing joint learning with competitors and other stakeholders for 'win:win' learning.
	Learning opportunities includes a climate of continuous improvement where mistakes are allowed and encouraged together with self development opportunities for all.

(5)   Learning organisation through experimentation

| Easterby-Smith[20] | Easterby-Smith suggests organisations promote experimentation in various ways: in people to generate creativity and innovation, in structures to introduce flexibility, in reward systems so as not to disadvantage individuals who take risks and in information systems to focus more on unusual variations and to engender an attitude of looking forward rather than living in the past. |

(6)	Learning organisation as a knowledge creating company
Nonaka[21]	Nonaka believes that the lasting source of competitive advantage is knowledge where successful companies continuously create new knowledge, disseminate it widely and embody it in their products. He makes a distinction between tacit and explicit knowledge. Explicit knowledge is systematic and formal and can be easily communicated, whereas tacit knowledge is highly personal 'know-how' and consists of our mental models. It is tacit knowledge which is more illusive and contains our subjective insights, intuitions and hunches. Nonaka sees the continual challenge of knowledge creating companies as re-examining what they take for granted. In such organisations, employees are likely to share overlapping information to encourage frequent dialogue and communication. In addition, employees are more likely to be engaged in strategic rotation so that they can understand the business from a wide range of perspectives and have free access to company information. The principle of 'internal competition' is promoted, where numerous groups develop different approaches to the same project and argue over their merits and shortcomings.
(7)	**Learning organisation models developed through practice**
Attwood and Beer[22]	In their work on learning organisations, Attwood and Beer suggest a role for management to provide continuous and relevant learning at all levels with the aim of improving organisational effectiveness through individual development. They propose a role for organisational development/personnel staff to offer expertise on a wide range of learning strategies. Such organisations have shared responsibility of staff for the learning process with continuous and regular feedback. For the organisation's survival, the rate of learning is seen as equal or greater than the change in the environment. These organisations require liberating structures, organisational sub-climates of learning and a culture of responsible freedom.

Part 2

Key Facilities Management Issues

Chapter 3
User Needs Evaluation

3.1 Introduction

3.1.1 Aims

This chapter is concerned with the relationship between buildings and their users. The chapter aims to demonstrate how building evaluations can be used to improve an organisation's performance and why users are integral to this process. It is intended that this chapter will provide facilities managers with the necessary information to enable them to conduct their own building evaluations.

3.1.2 Context

At present many organisations implement a linear building process, as shown in Figure 3.1.[1] Organisations will identify their need to build and will then work through the process from the planning stage to the occupancy stage. This same process will be repeated for every new building project that an organisation may undertake. Even though this is the typical method, it is not necessarily the best one. This chapter argues that organisations should instead implement a new building method, as shown in Figure 3.2.

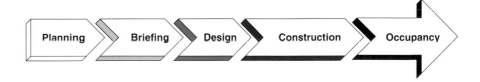

Figure 3.1 Traditional building process.

The new method is cyclical rather than linear. Even though five stages are the same there is one important addition: the stage of evaluation. The latter is added as organisations are not making use of a valuable resource that they already have at their fingertips, namely their staff. Very few organisations ask their staff whether a building meets their requirements, even though the people that understand a building best are the people that use it everyday. The cyclical method encourages organisations to learn from their staff whether a building is performing as well as it should. This information can be used in various ways: it can be fed forward into the design of a new building or it can be fed back to improve an existing building.

> 'Evaluation is the missing link in the design process. Evaluation, programming (briefing), and design are three linked activities drawing information from a systematic look at how people use existing environments. Analysing environments leads to programming (briefing).'[2]

This statement makes it clear that evaluation and briefing are closely linked, hence these two subjects are the main concern of this chapter.

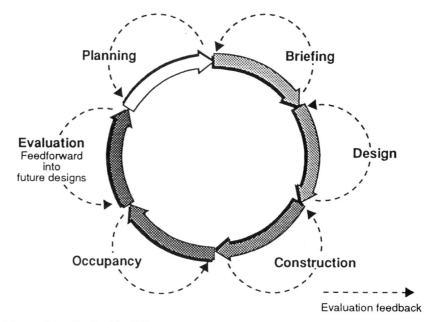

Figure 3.2   Cyclical building process.

3.1.3 Summary of the different sections

- ❑ Section 3.1 – Introduction
- ❑ Section 3.2 – This introduces the subject of building evaluation and discusses how organisations can benefit by implementing appraisals on a regular basis. The importance of user knowledge is also demonstrated.
- ❑ Section 3.3 – This is dedicated to briefing. Common problems associated with briefing are discussed, so that facilities managers can avoid making basic mistakes. The section goes on to look at how the briefing process is managed and what sort of information is needed for a good brief.
- ❑ Section 3.4 – This presents three different post-occupancy evaluation techniques which could easily be used by facilities managers.
- ❑ Section 3.5 – This considers various data collection methods that can be used during briefing and post-occupancy evaluations. Techniques for data analysis and presentation are also discussed briefly.

Case Study: Background information

The case study material is derived from the study of one organisation. The organisation in question is involved with private healthcare and owns over 30 hospitals situated around Britain. Facilities management exists at four levels within the organisation; board level, corporate level, regional level and hospital level. In broad terms, the director of facilities and the corporate facilities group are responsible for setting down facilities management policy, while the regional groups co-ordinate the day-to-day facilities management activities which are carried out at the different hospitals within their region.

The case studies are used to demonstrate how one particular organisation approaches the practices of briefing and building evaluation. The following summaries provide the reader with some background information on the organisation and these two areas.

Briefing – In order to remain competitive and meet healthcare legislation, the organisation is almost constantly involved with updating/altering its building stock. This means that the organisation is very familiar with the practice of briefing and hence, over the years have developed their own particular briefing method. Their approach is used in the case studies to highlight good briefing procedure as well as the occasional mistake.

Building evaluation – Whereas the organisation is well experienced in briefing terms it has only recently become involved with building evaluations. Therefore, the relevant case studies demonstrate why the organisation became involved in building evaluations and how it carried them out.

3.2 The Relationship Between the Facilities Management Function and User Needs Evaluation

3.2.1 Aims

Facilities managers should:

❏ understand how building evaluations can contribute to organisational effectiveness;
❏ be able to communicate the importance of building evaluations to other people within an organisation.

3.2.2 The importance of the design of buildings

The design of a building is very important, as it has the power to affect how well an organisation can perform its function. At its most fundamental level, a building provides its users with basic elements that maintain the necessary comfort which allow them to carry out their jobs. These elements are shelter, light, heat and sanitation. In addition, facilities provide spatial arrangements that can aid specific activities and hinder others. Ease of movement, ease of communication and privacy are all dependent upon the design of a building. Therefore, if a building is designed without these basic requirements in mind, it is unlikely to provide a suitable working environment.

There is more to the design of working spaces than the provision of these essentials. Changes occurring recently in office technology, business climates and human values have affected many things from organisational structures to the way people work. Consequently new managerial strategies are required to cope with these changes. To enable these strategic changes to take place, it will be necessary to rethink the way in which workspaces are designed. Workers now require far more from their workspaces than they have ever done before. This is due to the fact that workers are now better educated, have more job mobility and are more technically oriented. They are now concerned with the quality of work life and this includes the quality of their working environment.

Environmental planning was relatively simple in the past. It was based on the requirements of the organisation and management, not the requirements of the general employees. Buildings were designed to allow tasks to be carried out efficiently, with little concern for the comfort or needs of the workers. Organisations that consulted their staff about their preferences were few and far between.

In contrast, planning for today's ever-changing business operations requires organisations to think about the preferences of their workers, as well as their organisational objectives.

'Corporate environmental design must include an in-depth analysis of the corporation as a social organisation, the behaviour of the individuals within it, and the physical setting that houses it – a total system of interrelated parts.'[3]

3.2.3 *Value of user knowledge/involvement*

Users may be pressurising managers to take their design requirements into consideration, however, organisations should realise that there are definite benefits to be gained from employee participation. They fall into two basic categories:

❑   organisational development
❑   improvements to the built environment.

Organisational development – Participation encourages users to make decisions about their own environment. Employees realise that their views are important and this encourages feelings of personal responsibility, hence they become more motivated and committed to their jobs. If users are involved in the design of a facility, this can contribute to their understanding and acceptance of the final design. Alternatively, a lack of staff consultation may encourage feelings of rejection or hostility towards the new environment and the managers responsible for introducing it.

Improvement of the built environment – Users obviously come to know about the buildings that they work in; they are the experts on how well a facility works physically and operationally. Therefore, it makes sense to consult them, when either refurbishing facilities or designing new ones. When considering existing buildings, users can pinpoint areas which do not assist them in carrying out their work, enabling them to be corrected. Similarly, when thinking about a new facility, users can save an organisation money by identifying designs that have created problems in the past.

3.2.4 *The importance of building appraisals for organisations*

How do organisations know if their facilities are supporting organisational goals and user requirements? The key is to introduce regular building appraisals. However, in most organisations, building appraisal methods are not very well developed. Organisations tend to have far more information on items such as photocopiers than they do on their buildings. Organisations that are relatively good at managing the rest of their assets often have very little information concerning the performance of their buildings. Those that possess data on areas such as energy costs, could well have no information on how energy performance relates to employee comfort. Even if organisations have such information, it is unlikely that they will have tried to relate their present needs to what they are likely to require in a few years time.

The realisation that facilities may affect an organisation's effectiveness and its employees' welfare, makes it imperative that building appraisals are introduced on a regular basis.

'Facilities represent a new and untapped frontier for improving organisations performance.'[4]

3.2.5 Facilities management and building appraisals

Logically, the department that is most suited to carrying out building appraisal is the one that is responsible for an organisation's buildings; namely the facilities management department. All service groups within organisations today are being asked to demonstrate how their activities are helping the organisation to achieve its business objectives. Facilities represent a substantial percentage of most organisations' assets and also a substantial proportion of their operating costs, thus facilities managers have to justify why and how money is being spent.

When the FM unit lacks reliable and comparable data on building performance and costs, its ability to make its most basic decisions is impaired, as is its ability to make a convincing case for its recommendations. The ability to demonstrate the FM unit's organisational effectiveness is hampered without such information. Reporting to management is easier and more convincing when the consequences of decisions can be demonstrated. The FM unit should be able to show, for example, that the new planning processes, procedures, or space guidelines have lowered the cost or the number of renovations and have better enabled the building to accommodate organisational change, a new management style, or dramatic shifts in group size.

3.2.6 Uses and benefits of building appraisals

Building appraisals provide an opportunity for an organisation to see how well a particular facility meets their requirements from various viewpoints. In the most general terms, appraisals can serve two purposes:

❑   to improve the current situation; known as post-occupancy evaluation;
❑   to aid in the design of future buildings; known as briefing.

These two areas are covered in detail in sections 3.3 and 3.4; however, the following list gives an idea of just some of the more specific issues that appraisals can be applied to.

Appraisals can be valuable when organisations are either shrinking or expanding; when they are renovating or when building new. When deciding whether to lease or purchase new facilities, performance and cost data are invaluable. They can be used as a preliminary form of architectural briefing, to guide the search for design solutions. It is difficult to decide what is needed in a new building unless an organisation has assessed what it has at present.

For long-range strategic planning, building appraisal provides information about what kinds of buildings will be needed in the future to accommodate the organisation's expected development. Knowledge of which buildings are performing poorly and which buildings are performing well is an important consideration of long-term strategy.

Decisions about managing the occupancy of the building stock require comparable and reliable data. Which buildings or which areas within the current stock of buildings have the best location for a particular unit? Which building will best meet the needs of that unit over the next several years so that disruption and cost incurred by frequent relocations or renovations can be minimised?

Operational and maintenance decisions can also benefit from building performance data. Which types of buildings or which elements within buildings require the least maintenance, are the most energy efficient, and incur the fewest breakdowns and repairs? Which are the easiest to clean? What cleaning or maintenance strategies work best for particular buildings?

The above examples demonstrate the various ways that building appraisal can be used. It can be applied to existing buildings, proposed designs, cost or occupant satisfaction.

Case Study: Evaluation benefits

The organisation had been involved with many building projects over the years, both refurbishment and new-build. The organisation was typical, in that once building work was completed project managers would turn their attention to their next project. If problems occurred after occupation then a hospital manager would contact the project manager and the problem would be corrected as far as possible. No formal procedure existed for recording these problems, hence the different project managers were making similar mistakes on other projects. Thus the organisation was following a linear building programme, rather than a cyclical one where the organisation would learn from its mistakes.

Through informal discussions within the facilities department it became apparent that the lack of feedback could prove costly. If problems were not identified quickly there was the possibility that they could be repeated throughout the other thirty hospitals. Therefore, it was decided that a formal evaluation programme would be initiated so that mistakes could be identified and recorded to prevent the same thing happening again. In addition, the evaluations would be used to highlight successful designs so that these could be used again. The facilities manager suggested that the information collected during the evaluations could be used to compile guidelines for an ideal hospital, against which all future new build and refurbishment projects could be measured.

> ***Comment***
> The organisation initially decided to implement an evaluation programme to prevent costly mistakes from being repeated in other hospitals. However, the facilities manager realised that evaluations could be used to identify good points as well as bad, thus demonstrating the versatility of evaluations.

3.3 Briefing

3.3.1 Aims

Facilities managers should be able to :

❏ understand the possible communication problems that may hinder the briefing process, so that they can avoid them;
❏ successfully manage the briefing process;
❏ understand what information will need to be collected in order to produce a brief.

3.3.2 The importance of briefing

All organisations will at some time find it necessary to prepare a design brief. This may be because the company wants new, specially designed premises or wishes to upgrade its existing accommodation in some way. As was demonstrated in section 3.2, the design of buildings is a contributing factor which can affect an organisation's ability to achieve its goals. Therefore, when new building work is being considered, it follows that if an organisation wishes to obtain value for money and a building to meet their requirements, then time and effort should be put into the briefing process.

At its most basic level, a brief is essentially a statement setting out the client's requirements for a new building/refurbishment/room layout, however, there is more to a brief than just a list of space requirements. Several other aspects have to be taken into consideration if the briefing process is to result in a successful building. These aspects can be broken down as follows:

❏ communications and relationships between participants;
❏ management of the briefing process;
❏ information required during the briefing process.

Each of the above aspects is considered in more detail below.

3.3.3 Communications and briefing

Many of the problems encountered during the briefing process are the result of poor communications between participants. Clients and designers often misunderstand each other and this can result in a completed building which does not meet the client's expectations. The following list provides a guide to the most common communication problems and suggestions on how they can be solved or avoided.

Client organisation conflicts

The term 'client' is misleading, as in reality the client is not just one person, but an organisation comprised of different factions. Thus, a brief must satisfy the requirements of each of these groups, if the final project is to be successful. With so many different people involved, architects/designers may find that they are receiving contradictory information. Therefore, it is a good idea if the organisation appoints one representative who is responsible for co-ordinating all client requirements. The facilities manager is ideally suited to act in this capacity.

Client knowledge

A client's lack of experience is another area which may cause problems. Several studies have been undertaken where communication patterns between clients and professionals were analysed during the briefing process.[5-7] These studies found that the input from the parties varied considerably depending upon the client's previous experience of construction. In cases where the client had no previous knowledge or dealings with the building industry, the consultant (architect, quantity surveyor, structural engineer etc.) tended to dominate any discussions. Whereas the opposite was found to be the case where the clients had previous experience. Therefore, it is important to establish at the outset what level of experience the client possesses. If a consultant is dealing with an inexperienced client it is important that a common language is established between participants to avoid misunderstandings.

The potential benefit of increasing communication between the different parties is shown in Figure 3.3 by the Johari Window[8].

The public area represents the client communicating his initial requirements without difficulty to the design team. The blind area can be seen to be the needs of the client that are identified by the consultant (architect, engineer etc.) through two-way discussion. The private area relates to information that is not disclosed by the client, whether intentionally or not, until a good level of trust has developed. The unknown area is initially hidden from both parties, but may reveal itself through joint discussion once a good working relationship has been established. The more information a consultant has about a client the better the final brief is likely to be, as it will be tailor made for that specific organisation.

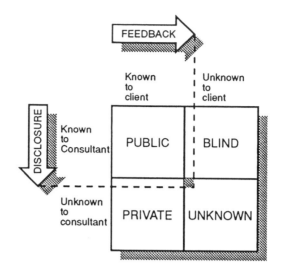

Figure 3.3   Johari Window as used in the briefing process.

Forming a design team

As buildings increase in complexity, it becomes less likely that a single person could possess all the knowledge required to design a new building. Therefore, most projects will require a team of designers if all the different factions in a client group are to be satisfied. As design teams increase in size, communication within the design team becomes as important as communication between the designer and the client. The following groups of people may need to be consulted during the briefing process.

❑   Architects
❑   Project managers
❑   Quantity surveyors
❑   Structural engineers
❑   Town planners.

❑   Mechanical engineers
❑   Building surveyors
❑   Electrical engineers
❑   Interior designers
❑   Landscape architects.

The choice of a design team is critical to the success of a project. Clients should take time to select an appropriate team and try to achieve a balance between technical knowledge and team skills.

> 'The prime objectives of clients should be to understand their own needs first and then to secure a design team who will reflect their view of the world. Clients who choose a team at odds with their own world view run the risk of being swept away by the design team's own enthusiasm down inappropriate directions. The client has a real choice and he should use it.' [9]

Lack of involvement of end users

When considering the building process, there are normally three different factions involved: designers, paying clients and end users. Traditionally, as shown in Figure 3.4, there has been very little communication between the end users and the other two groups.[10] The designers and paying clients have made the users' decisions for them without proper consultation. Hence, the final users have often found that the new building does not meet their true needs. This has resulted in costly alterations after a project has been completed. Such problems lead to the conclusion that end users should be involved in the briefing process. Many studies have been carried out on design projects where users have participated in the briefing process. It has generally been concluded that users were happier with buildings where they had been involved in decision making.[7]

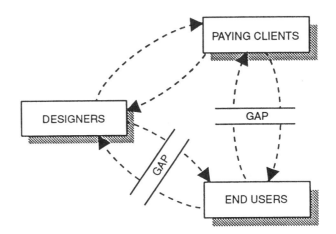

Figure 3.4   The user-needs gap.

Summary

(1)   One person should be appointed from within the facilities department to act as project manager. This person should be responsible for co-ordinating all client requirements and liaising with consultants. This will prevent the consultants from being given contradictory information.
(2)   If the facilities manager is inexperienced with construction issues he should ensure that the consultants are aware of this. However, the facilities manager should not allow consultants to take control of the project or the organisation may end up with a building that does not suit their requirements.
(3)   The facilities manager should choose the design team carefully and ensure that each team member understands his responsibilities.

(4)   The facilities manager should ensure that users are consulted so that the new building/refurbished rooms meet their requirements, as well as those of higher management.

Case Study: Communication

Over the years the organisation had used a number of different building consultants. As hospitals are such specialised buildings, it was corporate policy to reuse good consultants as they would already be familiar with the difficulties of healthcare design. In theory this seemed sensible, however, in practice it created problems. As the consultants were normally only recalled every few years, the specific individuals who had worked on previous projects had often moved to different consulting firms. This meant that the appointed consultants had to go through the learning process again.

Comment

This example demonstrates the importance of communication within the design team. The organisation relied on the fact that the consulting firms possessed the necessary knowledge, when really it was only the individual.

3.3.4 Management of the briefing process

Briefing is not a rigid process, each person who deals with briefs will use a slightly different approach or emphasis. Also every project is different and hence, any briefing model will require alteration to suit a particular situation. However, there are some basic guidelines that should be considered during the briefing process. The following examples can be used to demonstrate these important points:

❑   Traditional briefing process
❑   Phased briefing process.

Traditional briefing process

The RIBA Plan of Work, shown in Figure 3.5, outlines the building procedure and associated briefing process that is generally followed in the UK (other countries adopt similar procedures).[10]

It can be seen that the main brief is developed through the four initial stages: inception, feasibility, outline design and scheme design. A breakdown of what is included in each of these stages can be seen in Table 3.1.[11]

As a process model, the RIBA Plan of Work is helpful to a client or facilities manager, as it demonstrates the various steps that they should go through. However, this method is not actually very realistic. It does not make it clear enough that the client will be required to make frequent evaluations during the process. It mentions amendments and appraisals, but it does not suggest that the client may be forced to rethink some of his requirements quite late on in the briefing process. It is not always possible to achieve a perfect match between the design of a building and the brief requirements. Conflicts may occur between space requirements or the budget may not allow for all briefing requirements to be included.

It should also be taken into consideration that the actual process of collecting briefing information may raise users' awareness of their situation. For example, while considering their requirements, clients/users may begin to question how logical their working practices actually are and decide to change how they operate. Therefore, if a brief is fixed early on, as it is in this example, major changes in work practices can be difficult to achieve. In using this method, clients are encouraged to obtain as much information as they can early in the process; consequently the brief can become too detailed too soon. Over-detailed briefs sometimes preclude creative solutions that were not obvious early on in design development.

Table 3.1 attempts to cure the above problems.

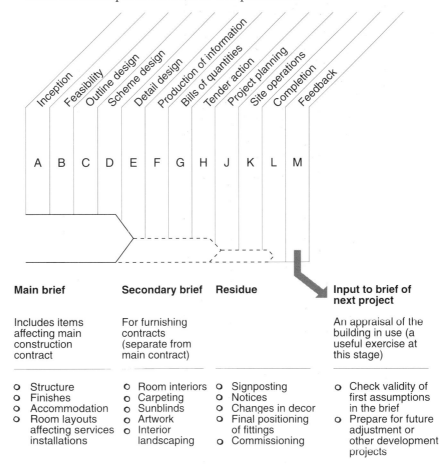

Figure 3.5   Development of the brief with regard to the RIBA Plan of Work.

Table 3.1   Development of the brief through RIBA initial stages A–D

Client action	Material for brief	Consultants action
Stage A – Inception		
❑ Considers need to build ❑ Sets up supporting organisation (working party, committee or representative) ❑ Appoints consultants ❑ Commences exchange with consultants ❑ Provides information for outline brief	❑ History of events leading to decision to build ❑ Details of client and consultant firms, personnel ❑ Timescale for the project *Outline brief* ❑ Policy decisions ❑ Purpose and function of project ❑ Details of site and services ❑ Basic details of building requirements, and cost limit	❑ Carry out preliminary consultations and appraisals of buildings or sites ❑ Receive and examine outline brief
Stage B – Feasibility		
❑ Conducts user studies ❑ Considers feasibility results and analytical studies and reports ❑ Develops brief	❑ Additions/amendments to outline brief in as much detail as possible about: site conditions; space requirements; relationships and activities; interior environment; operational factors ❑ More precise information about client's financial arrangements	❑ Survey and study site and locality ❑ Consult statutory authorities ❑ Conduct feasibility exercises and studies of features of the brief ❑ Advise about meeting of cost time limits ❑ Elicit information required, and guide and assist with collection of briefing material
Stage C – Outline proposals		
❑ Receives and appraises designs and reports ❑ Receives and approves outline designs and costs	❑ Amendments and additions to brief as a result of appraisals ❑ Completed room data sheets	❑ Produce first sketch designs for analysis ❑ Complete outline design and cost plan ❑ Complete informal negotiations with statutory authorities

Table 3.1 Continued

Stage D – Scheme design		
❑ Receives and approves full scheme designs and costs (if satisfactory) ❑ Instructs preparation of presentation drawings ❑ Authorises formal submission for required statutory consents	❑ Amendments and more details ❑ Layouts etc. of furniture and equipment in special rooms and areas	❑ Prepare full scheme designs and estimate of costs ❑ If approved, prepare presentation drawings, perspective sketches and/or models ❑ Apply for planning consents
After the completion of Stage D correlation between the brief and the scheme design should be complete.		

Phased briefing process

This method follows similar steps to the traditional method, however, the importance of evaluation is made explicit. The phased method was developed by the Stichting Bouwresearch (Building Research Board) in Rotterdam, as the result of a research project into client briefing.[12] The basic principle of the system is that the brief contains, prior to each new planning phase, only the minimum amount of information necessary to be able to direct the plan in the next phase. Hence, the project is considered in very general terms during the initial phase, working towards greater detail with every respective phase, see Figure 3.6. For example, if the subject of location/spatial relations was being examined, the following issues would be considered in each phase:

❑ Phase 1 – the relationship between the proposed site and the rest of the town;
❑ Phase 2 – the relationship between the proposed site and the immediate neighbourhood;
❑ Phase 3 – the relationships between different departments;
❑ Phase 4 – the relationships between people or spaces within a department;
❑ Phase 5 – the relationships between furniture in a specific workspace.

Such a phased development results in a number of advantages for clients and users. A series of phases allows clients and users to become familiar with problems and to become aware of new possibilities which new or refurbished buildings could provide for them, including changes to their own organisation. In addition, this means that users and clients can introduce their requirements at strategic moments, rather than having to consider all their options from the outset.

It is imperative that the process is tightly controlled; a situation whereby clients introduce requirements at the wrong time must be avoided. Once

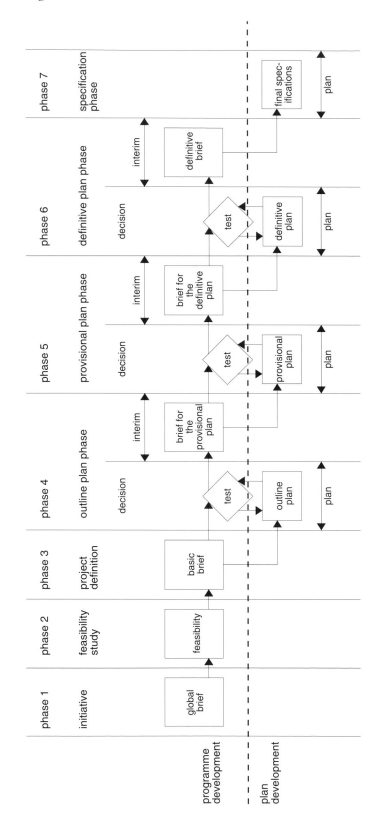

Figure 3.6   Phased briefing process.

major planning decisions have been made they should stay fixed. Process control makes it necessary to ask the right questions at the right time. Hence, this briefing technique can be seen as a process of two-way communication between parties. Phasing offers clients and users the opportunity to assess the new building several times before the design is firmly fixed, allowing adjustments to be made if necessary.

Summary

The facility manager should implement an iterative staged briefing programme, where the brief is assessed frequently to ensure that it still matches the organisation's requirements.

Case Study: Management of the briefing process

The following description outlines the organisation's method of briefing. The different stages are detailed below and relate to Figure 3.7.

Normally the hospital manager will *identify the need* (1) to improve a hospital and will contact the regional facilities manager to discuss what work is necessary. Their proposals will then be put to the corporate facilities manager who will *appoint a project manager (2)*. The latter works with the hospital manager to produce a *feasibility study* which demonstrates the financial implications (3).

Once the feasibility study has been approved the project manager works with the hospital manager and the matron to produce a *general policy statement* which describes which parts of the hospital are to be altered and why (4).

Discussions then take place between the project manager and the relevant departmental heads to obtain an overview of each department, a policy statement is completed which describes how the department will be run. The project manager then produces an *outline brief* which is tested at a series of meetings to ensure that the overall approach has been agreed (5).

Departmental heads are then asked to complete room schedules for their department, stating what rooms are required and what each room will contain. The project manager tests these requirements against a set of documents called the Health Building Notes which contain preferred sizes for specific rooms, as well as comparing them to plans of existing hospitals. All of this information is then fed into the *provisional brief*, from which the project manager produces a provisional plan which shows the location and sizes of all rooms (6).

At this stage department heads will often pin up relevant parts of the provisional brief on the notice board so that they can obtain staff views on the proposals. The brief is amended as necessary, resulting in a *definitive brief*. It is only at this stage that the architect is brought in to produce presentation drawings. The quantity surveyor is also engaged to advise on costs (7).

The definitive brief and scheme are then reviewed at regional and corporate level. If they are approved the scheme is worked up in detail in *preparation for tender* (8).

Comment
The organisation has developed an approach over the years that allows them to build up the brief in stages ensuring that the views of all interested parties are taken into consideration. By following this method the project manager is not overloaded with all of the information at once. People are asked for their opinions at the most appropriate stage; only the hospital manager and department heads are allowed to comment on general policy, while nursing staff are asked for their opinion on the workings of specific rooms. This process is very similar to the phased briefing process described earlier.

3.3.5 Information required during the briefing process

Once a suitable process for briefing has been selected it is necessary to establish what information needs to be collected. Obviously every building project is different, an organisation may only want to refurbish existing offices or else they may wish to commission a new prestigious headquarters. In both cases it is necessary to collect a certain amount of data in order to be able to prepare a good brief so that the organisation gets the exact design they wanted. This section provides a guide to the information that facilities managers should collect during the briefing process.

There are four distinct areas where information may need to be collected:

❑   organisational concerns
❑   external influences
❑   individuals and work styles
❑   physical environment.

These are listed out in more detail in Table 3.2. These lists are by no means exhaustive and should be regarded more as a prompt or checklist to ensure that nothing has been forgotten. It should be remembered that allowances should be made for future use, as well as present requirements.

It should be pointed out that various processes exist for collecting data, however, because the same methods are used in evaluation, the different examples are described in section 3.5.

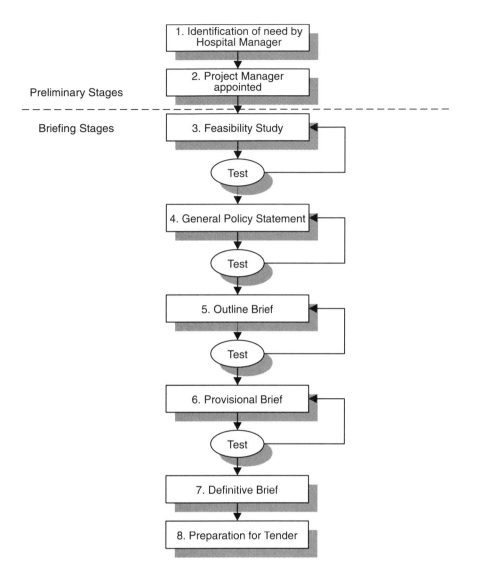

Figure 3.7 Briefing method as discussed in case study.

Table 3.2   Information to be collected during briefing

Organisational concerns

❑ *Future plans/objectives* – What are the organisation's plans for the future? Are there any initiatives already in place that the general workforce are not aware of? Does management intend to alter the structure of the organisation, resulting in a reduction of the workforce? If so, how does this affect space requirements?

❑ *Fixed constraints* – What decisions are fixed before briefing even starts. What finances are available for the project? What is the intended time span of the project? How many people does the building need to accommodate? Will the old furniture be utilised? Establishing what things are fixed will enable facilities managers to direct their data collection efforts towards areas where future decisions will need to be made.

❑ *Corporate culture* – Every organisation will have a different culture, which affects how the organisation operates. It will be reflected in the daily actions of management and staff: how do people interact with one another, who makes what kinds of decisions, how do people use their time/space ? It provides clues during interviews, for example, whether peoples' opinions reflect those of others or whether they hold conflicting views. Data collection methods can also be influenced; interview data may be useful in one company, whereas quantitative survey data may be the norm in another.

❑ *Organisational structure* – The briefing team needs to know how an organisation is structured. What sort of decisions are taken at which level? Who has to report to whom? This kind of information can determine from whom information is collected and about what.

❑ *Staff* – Headcount projections for the next few years, are of course a necessity. However, it is also helpful to know what sort of employees make up an organisation. Are the staff professional people who have very high workplace expectations?

❑ *Image expectations* – Organisations may wish to project a specific image to the outside world, and hence will require certain aesthetic qualities from their building.

External influences

❑ *Laws and codes* – It is necessary to be aware of any government legislation etc. that is likely to have an effect on the design of the building. This could include zoning plans, environmental legislation and fire regulations.

❑ *New technologies* – Changes are occurring in technology all the time; what is today's standard may have been superseded tomorrow. Organisations should seriously think about what is likely to happen over the next few years, so that the new building design can accommodate changes without major constructional alterations.

❑ *Labour force patterns*–Changes have been predicted in the labour force over the next decade. There are likely to be, for example, far more female workers, perhaps resulting in increased safety requirements within workplaces. Alternatively an increase in older workers could lead to concerns about health, fitness, lighting and air temperature.

Table 3.2 Continued

> ❏ *Competitors' actions and plans* – How does the organisation compare to its competitors? Are their facilities better equipped to do the job? If so, are they likely to attract our customers or employees? It is also useful to learn from competitors' experiences; has their new approach to space planning improved their service?

Individuals and work styles

> ❏ *Task analysis* – What exactly do different members of staff do? Specific job descriptions are useful for understanding how people fit into an organisation.
>
> ❏ *Environmental satisfaction* – How satisfied are staff with their current environment? Does their immediate environment enable them to work effectively and productively or have they just learnt to adapt to an environment that was poorly designed in the first place.
>
> ❏ *Communication and adjacency patterns* – Who communicates with whom, where, when, and how often? Does the environment assist with communication or hinder it? Are the right departments/people situated together?
>
> ❏ *Space, furniture and equipment requirements* – what furniture and equipment is necessary in order for an individual to perform his job? Has enough space been allocated for specific tasks?

Physical environment

> ❏ *As-built plans* – These are useful as a comparison tool. They can be used to test how proposed space requirements relate to existing ones. Can a department justify its requests for twice as much space as they occupy at present?
>
> ❏ *Space standards* – Space requirements should be recorded for all proposed areas. Remember to include support spaces, such as conference rooms, break areas, etc.
>
> ❏ *Furniture and equipment inventory* – Can any of the existing furniture be utilised in the proposed new building? Which pieces can be used in their present form? Which will require refurbishment?
>
> ❏ *Amount, type and variety of IT* – This again requires an inventory to establish what exists at present. What is to be relocated? Do any pieces of equipment require special environmental conditions?
>
> ❏ *Circulation requirements* – This applies to both people and objects. Do corridors have to be a certain width? Hospital corridors, for example, need to be wide enough to accommodate patient trolleys. What about ramps, staircases, lifts and hoists?
>
> ❏ *Transportation and parking* – How often do deliveries take place? Is a special loading bay necessary? How many car parking spaces are required for staff? How many people use public transport instead?

Table 3.2   Continued

❑   *Surrounding amenities* – Information about the external environment will govern what services are provided on site. It is important to understand how the surrounding area may change in the near future. Is a public car park being planned? Are there so many local facilities for food, that staff are unlikely to use a cafeteria.

❑   *Appearance* – Factors relating to preferred form, scale, texture, colour, proportion and style of building, both internal and external.

The client should be able to collect the necessary information on most of the above topics, aided by his consultants where necessary, however, there are certain specialist areas where consultants will have to advise the client. These areas are covered in Table 3.3 below so that the client can ensure that they have been considered.

Table 3.3   Information to be considered by specialist consultants during briefing

Specialist considerations

❑   *Loading requirements* – Superimposed loads, wind loads acceptable limits of structural deformation.

❑   *Fire protection* – Legislative requirements; means of escape, fire-fighting installations and equipment; spread of flame prevention.

❑   *Contamination protection* – ventilation, humidity, proofing against contamination and damage, security installations.

❑   *Heating/cooling* – Thermal factors, temperature requirements.

❑   *Lighting* – Natural and artificial lighting requirements, emergency lighting, display lighting.

❑   *Acoustics* – Factors affecting sound attenuation, sound insulation.

❑   *Energy demands* – Services required, standby systems, solar energy requirements.

❑   *Maintenance needs* – Maintenance programme demands, quality of structure, materials and installations.

Summary

(1)   The facilities manager should collect information in the following four areas:

   (a)   organisational issues
   (b)   external influences
   (c)   individuals and work styles
   (d)   physical environment.

(2)   The facilities manager should check that consultants have addressed all of the relevant specialist issues.

(3)   The facilities manager should ensure that the information collected relates to future as well as present use.

Case Study: Collection of information for briefing

In order to provide the best possible service, hospital managers constantly monitor their establishments to see where improvements could be made. Recently, in one particular case, the hospital manager was finding it increasingly difficult to staff the two operating theatres, as they were located one above the other and so had to be staffed separately. The facilities department was asked to investigate the problem and suggest alternative plans. During their investigation it was discovered that the local National Health hospital possessed a clean air enclosure; a facility which was not provided in this particular hospital. Therefore, the facilities department proposed that this would be a necessary addition to any refurbishment work, in order for the organisation to remain competitive.

Comment
The above example demonstrates that it is essential to consider external factors as well as internal ones. If the organisation had failed to identify the need for a clean air enclosure, then it is possible that consultants would have chosen to send their patients to the National Health hospital instead.

3.4 Post-Occupancy Evaluation (POE)

3.4.1 Aims

Facilities managers should:

❑ understand the potential benefits that an organisation can gain through the use of building evaluations
❑ be able to learn the necessary skills to enable them to conduct their own building evaluations.

3.4.2 Building evaluation systems

Various methods for building evaluations exist, however, they can broadly be divided into two categories: user-based systems or expert-based systems. The first system uses a building's occupants to evaluate the suitability of a building for their particular needs and hence, is also known as post-occupancy evaluation (POE). The second method relies on experts' assessments and typically covers far more areas, such as: provision for information technology; organisational growth; changes in staff work style; and energy efficiency.

As this book is directed towards good practice in facilities management, only POE methods are described in this section, as these can be carried out by the facilities management department, whereas expert assessments cannot. However, facilities managers should recognise that expert assistance may be necessary if post-occupancy evaluations highlight problems that are outside the capabilities of the organisation.[13] For example, various expert systems have been developed and a selection are described in *The Total Workplace.*[3]

3.4.3 POE methods

Users of buildings often complain that their workplace is not designed to meet all of their work needs. Facilities are designed by professionals who believe that they understand how people use buildings. Unfortunately this is rarely the case and issues that are important to users are often overlooked by designers. In post-occupancy evaluation methods, the focus is on user satisfaction.

At its most basic level, post-occupancy evaluation is a formal evaluation of a building by its occupants after it has been completed, to identify areas that do not meet users' requirements. However, despite its title, post-occupancy evaluation is also a useful tool when planning new facilities, as data generated during an evaluation can be used in the briefing process for a new building (see Section 3.2).

Potential benefits arising from the use of post-occupancy evaluations range from short term through to long term, as Table 3.4 illustrates.[14]

Table 3.4   Benefits of POE

Short-term benefits
- Identification of and solutions to problems in facilities.
- Proactive facility management responsive to building user values.
- Improved space utilisation and feedback on building performance.
- Improved attitude of building occupants through active involvement in the evaluation process.
- Understanding of the performance implications of changes dictated by budget cuts.
- Informed decision making and better understanding of consequences of design.

Medium-term benefits
- Built-in capacity for facility adaptation to organisational change and growth over time, including recycling of facilities into new uses.
- Significant cost savings in the building process and throughout the building life cycle.
- Accountability for building performance by design professionals and owners.

Long-term benefits
- Long-term improvements in building performance.
- Improvement of design databases, standards, criteria and guidance literature.
- Improved measurement of building performance through quantification.

Various methods for POE have been developed, however, the three examples which follow have been selected because they demonstrate the different techniques and uses of POE. It is hoped that these examples will provide the facilities manager with enough information, so that he is able to conduct his own POEs.

❑ partial user participation
❑ full user participation
❑ management POE.

Partial user participation

The following model was developed by Preiser *et al.*[13] It is an example of a POE whereby users are only partially involved in the evaluation process. Experienced evaluators conduct the process and users only participate at the request of these evaluators.

Three levels of effort are proposed in this model (Figure 3.8); the process selected depends upon finances, time, manpower and the required outcome. However, each level contains the same procedures of planning, conducting and applying.

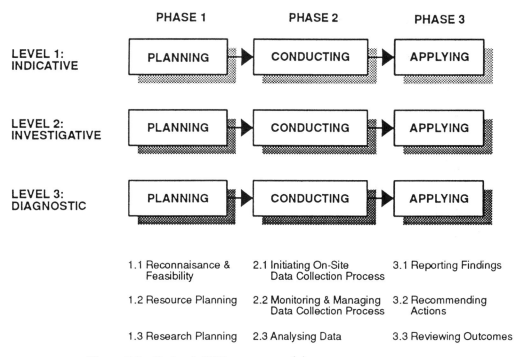

Figure 3.8   Preiser's POE process model.

Level 1: Indicative POE

This POE provides an indication of major successes and failures of a building's overall performance. It is normally carried out by an experienced evaluator, who should ideally be familiar with the building type being evaluated and is completed in a very short time span. Thus, data collection needs to be quick and easily accessible. Methods used include: archival document evaluation, walk-through evaluations and interviews with staff. The findings are usually presented in the form of a short report, outlining the purpose of the evaluation, the data collection methods used, findings and recommendations.

Level 2: Investigative POE

This is often instigated as a result of a problem identified during an indicative POE. It is likely that before a solution can be proposed, the problem needs to be studied in more detail. Unlike the indicative method, whereby the evaluators make judgements themselves due to a lack of time, this system relies on more sophisticated data collection methods to produce results. Initially the evaluators undertake state-of-the-art literature reviews and study recent, similar facilities. Then comparisons are made between these and the building being assessed, to see why problems may have occurred and to identify possible solutions. The findings are normally presented in a report which identifies the specific problems studied and proposes recommendations for action. Annotated plans and photographs may be used to clarify findings.

Level 3: Diagnostic POE

This type of POE aims to improve not only the particular facility being evaluated, but also to influence the future design of similar facilities. Typically it will follow a multi-method strategy, including questionnaires, surveys, observations and physical measurements. All of which will allow comparisons to be made with other facilities. A diagnostic POE is likely to take several months at a minimum to complete. The results drawn from such research are long-term oriented, relating not only to the improvement of a particular facility, but also to improvement of a specific building type.

Full user participation

In this type of POE, users are fully involved throughout the evaluation. People experienced in the process of evaluation are still involved, but their function is purely to guide the participants through the process rather than to make judgements. An example of this type of POE has been developed by Kernohan *et al.* [15] Every evaluation will include the same three core events, which are described in more detail later, namely:

- ❑ introductory meeting
- ❑ touring interview
- ❑ review meeting.

It is also fundamental to the process that the following groups are involved with the evaluation:

- ❑ *Participant groups* – who evaluate the building. Participant groups represent the different interests in a building, both users and providers. The interests typically include those of occupants, visitors, owners, tenant organisations, makers, traders and maintainers. Representatives from each of these interests should be selected to form small groups that can participate in the evaluation. Each participant group is involved in the three stage process and evaluates the building, taking into account the particular interests represented in the group.

❑ *Facilitators* – who assist participants to make their evaluations. Facilitators are there solely to support participants in their assessment. They do not evaluate the building or do any other kind of evaluation. Facilitators have a neutral role throughout. For the purpose of this book, it is assumed that members of the facilities management group will take on the role of the facilitators, (see next section on facilitation training). Both participants and facilitators may play a part in initiating evaluations and monitoring outcomes, but their prime activity is the evaluation itself. It is only participants and facilitators who are concerned with the on-site activities of the generic evaluation process.

❑ *Managers* – who authorise the evaluation. Managers are not normally concerned with the on-site activities, although they may be represented in a participant group. Their role is administrative and supportive. They may initiate, approve and authorise an evaluation, and they have the responsibility for ensuring there is action on the outcomes and for the ongoing management of that action.

Training in facilitation skills

The skills needed to be able to facilitate an evaluation can be acquired through practice. However, facilitators need specific attitudinal and communication skills. They should be good at listening and be able to discard their own personal and professional attitudes during evaluations. They should be clear that it is the participant groups who evaluate the facility and not the facilitators.

Before conducting proper evaluations, it is a good idea to perform a test run within the facilities management department. Run through the three generic evaluation activities, but concentrate on a just a few rooms. Try to formulate a couple of recommendations from the issues that are raised during the tour. Going through this exercise will provide the facilitator with a good insight into what it is like to be a member of a participant group.

The generic evaluation process

The generic evaluation process is outlined in Figure 3.9. The three core stages mentioned previously are highlighted and will be conducted in the same manner for every evaluation. The other stages are likely to differ from evaluation to evaluation. Hence, the three core stages are now described, whilst the other stages will be looked at later.

(1) *Introductory meeting* – The facilitators meet with participant group to explain the evaluation process and the procedures of the touring interview and review. Group members are encouraged to discuss their connection with the facility and raise topics that they feel are important. The route to be taken on the tour is then discussed, so that areas of concern can be visited. Each group does not have to follow the same route, obviously different groups will be worried about different aspects.

(2)   *Touring interview* – Each participant group walks through the building with the facilitators, following the agreed route. Group members should discuss their views of the facility during the tour. The facilitator can use standard open-ended questions as prompts, but should be careful not to ask direct questions – in this type of evaluation the objective is to obtain users' views and not the views of the facilitator. Topics raised during the discussions are noted so that they can be discussed during the review meeting.

(3)   *Review meeting* – At this meeting, the different issues raised during the tour are discussed. It is helpful if the facilitator produces a record of the meeting, e.g. on a flip chart, so that it can be referred to later. The participant group should prioritise its concerns, so that their major problems can be looked at first; this is obviously critical if only limited finances are available.

Facilitation guidelines

The facilities manager should now understand how the three core stages are conducted. The other stages will vary depending upon the required

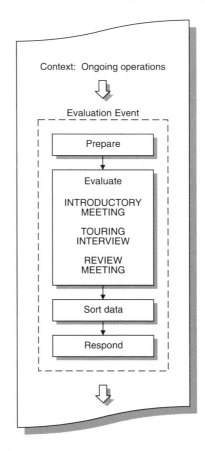

Figure 3.9   The Generic evaluation process.

output of the project. Table 3.5 summarises what activities may be included in the stages before and after the core. These activities are then described in detail in the following pages.

When preparing an evaluation the facilitator may find it useful to use Table 3.5 as a checklist to ensure that nothing has been omitted.

(1)   *Preparation* – It is important to ascertain why an evaluation is being conducted and on whose authority. Evaluations obviously need to be directed towards an outcome, so check what results are expected. Check time and budget allowances, who will pay for reports, etc. Try

Table 3.5   Facilitation tasks

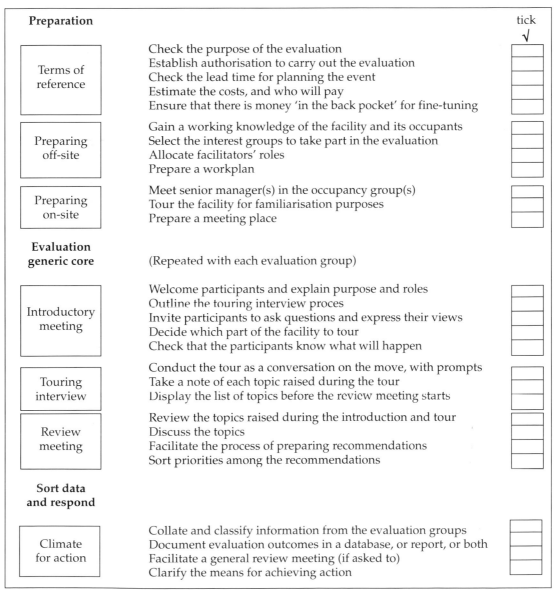

Preparation		tick √
Terms of reference	Check the purpose of the evaluation Establish authorisation to carry out the evaluation Check the lead time for planning the event Estimate the costs, and who will pay Ensure that there is money 'in the back pocket' for fine-tuning	
Preparing off-site	Gain a working knowledge of the facility and its occupants Select the interest groups to take part in the evaluation Allocate facilitators' roles Prepare a workplan	
Preparing on-site	Meet senior manager(s) in the occupancy group(s) Tour the facility for familiarisation purposes Prepare a meeting place	
Evaluation generic core	(Repeated with each evaluation group)	
Introductory meeting	Welcome participants and explain purpose and roles Outline the touring interview proces Invite participants to ask questions and express their views Decide which part of the facility to tour Check that the participants know what will happen	
Touring interview	Conduct the tour as a conversation on the move, with prompts Take a note of each topic raised during the tour Display the list of topics before the review meeting starts	
Review meeting	Review the topics raised during the introduction and tour Discuss the topics Facilitate the process of preparing recommendations Sort priorities among the recommendations	
Sort data and respond		
Climate for action	Collate and classify information from the evaluation groups Document evaluation outcomes in a database, or report, or both Facilitate a general review meeting (if asked to) Clarify the means for achieving action	

to ensure that some finances will be available on the completion of the evaluation, so that certain items can be dealt with immediately. If nothing changes as a result of an evaluation, both users and management will wonder why they agreed to participate.

(2)   *Selection of interest groups* – It is best to keep the size of participant groups small, between 3–7 people, for practical reasons. People must be able to hear what is going on during the touring interview. Groups can either be made up of single or mixed interests. However, the latter is not a good idea unless the facilitator is experienced, as there may be too many conflicting views or people may be afraid to express their views in front of people they do not know. Similarly people may feel intimidated if their managers are present.

(3)   *Allocation of facilitators' roles* – Most evaluations should have at least two facilitators, one to guide the process and one to take notes. Decide beforehand who will do what. Will anybody take photographs or slides of relevant areas?

(4)   *Workplan preparation* – It is essential that a workplan is prepared before the evaluation. This should ensure that all aspects of the evaluation are planned for. Check that all participant groups are available on the date of the evaluation. Decide in which order groups are to be dealt with. Check that managers are informed of the agenda and appropriate times when their workers will be involved. Ensure that a room will be set aside for the meetings.

(5)   *Post-evaluation activities* – It is a good idea to produce a report following the evaluation, so that people can see that their recommendations have been recorded accurately. Do not try to include every comment that was made during the process. A typical report may consist of:

(a)   a cover sheet
(b)   a contents list
(c)   summary of the evaluation method
(d)   a brief background to building project
(e)   a photographic, drawn and written description of the building
(f)   the main recommendations that were proposed during the review meetings
(g)   photographs where appropriate to illustrate recommendations or particular problems.

Sometimes the distribution of a report may be enough to promote action. If this is the case it is important to make sure that all participants are kept informed of any agreed action. However, in most cases a general review meeting is held to agree on how the recommendations should be dealt with.

Before a general meeting is held it is a good idea to discuss with the appropriate managers, their attitudes to the recommendations. There is no point in formulating proposals at a meeting if managers are likely to veto them at a later stage. It is also sensible to distribute copies of the report prior to a meeting, so that everyone understands what issues will be discussed.

(6) *General review meeting* – The purpose of a general review meeting is to discuss and agree recommendations for action. Participants should be reminded of the various proposals made previously by each of the groups. It may be useful to display these on the wall, so that they can be addressed during the meeting.

During the meeting, facilitators should help the participants to establish which recommendations have priority. Obviously different groups may feel that different issues are important, so it is necessary to ensure that one group does not dominate the meeting. The final outcome should be an agreed list of priorities. If possible, conclude with an explanation of what action will now be taken. Management may have already given authority for certain problems to be dealt with; if so inform the participants so that they can see management is committed to improving problem areas. Finally, the mechanism for keeping staff informed of further actions should be made clear.

POE as a management aid

It should be remembered that POEs not only serve to improve physical conditions, but can also act as an aid to management. In POEs, the process of consultation can be as important as the information collected. Facilities managers will realise the benefits of staff participation and feedback, as these have already been discussed in previous chapters. POEs can be used to gain the trust and support of staff, so that when changes are necessary people may be more co-operative.

POEs can also serve to highlight general management or personnel problems. 'It is a psychological fact that people often unconsciously blame their visible or tangible surroundings for problems which have intangible or invisible causes.'[16] If a facilities manager takes environmental complaints at face value, he may spend a lot of money on physical solutions which are not going to solve the real underlying problems. A complaint about bad air, for example, could actually stem from dissatisfaction about overcrowding. In such a case, investment in a new air conditioning system would still not solve the real issue. If a facilities manager suspects that environmental problems are not the real cause of complaints, then he should try to investigate further. A good technique for this is to hold a small group meeting, whereby those involved are encouraged to discuss their problems. Again the actual process of taking part may help to defuse the situation. If people are allowed to discuss their problems freely, it is likely that any personnel problems will become apparent. Obviously, if it appears that the environmental complaint is based on fact, it is up to the facilities manager to initiate any necessary actions.

Summary

(1) POEs can be used for different purposes. It is up to the facilities manager to identify the purpose of an evaluation before selecting a suitable method. Is the POE to be used to:

❑ improve the physical surroundings?
❑ gain the support of staff through participation?
❑ collect information to be fed into future building designs?

(2) If staff are to be involved in a POE, the facilities manager should ensure that there are visible results or else staff will lose confidence in the facilities department.

(3) Before conducting a POE, the facilities manager should check that all the different stages have been planned for. Figure 3.10 can be used as a reminder of the major stages which are applicable to all of the POE methods described in this section.

(4) The POE process, like the briefing process, should be regarded as cyclical, as shown in Figure 3.10. If, after any stage, information seems to be missing then the facilities manager should be able to step back and collect the necessary information. In addition, after a POE has been completed, the facilities manager should review the project to see if any part of the process could be improved upon next time.

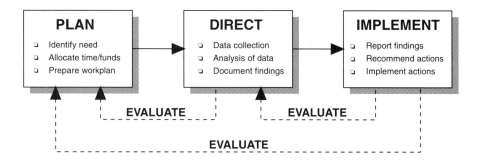

Figure 3.10   POE Composite Process Diagram.

Case Study: POE

As stated earlier, (section 3.2.7, Case study – evaluation benefits), no formal feedback procedures were undertaken by the facilities department to see what users thought of new building work. Problems with newly completed projects were dealt with promptly if they were reported, but users' views were not actively sought after each project.

Last year, however, five major refurbishment projects were completed and so the facilities manager decided that it might be a good time to actually introduce a formal post-occupancy evaluation programme. Not only would this ensure that all problems were addressed, but it would also enable the department to identify which design solutions were preferred by the users. Previously, even though the three project managers all worked in the same room, they each had their own way of doing things that the others did not necessarily agree with. The facilities manager suggested that the information arising from the evaluations could be used to compile guidelines for an ideal hospital, against which all future new build and refurbishment projects could be measured; thus ensuring a more unified approach to specific situations.

So that similar information could be collected at each site, a standard approach was agreed upon. A questionnaire would be completed for each new/refurbished room by the appropriate departmental head in conjunction with a project manager. The former would act as a representative for the whole department and discuss any problems/good solutions before the evaluation exercise. Consequently, one of the project managers was assigned to design a post-occupancy evaluation questionnaire. Once he had compiled a nine page form, it was suggested (by the author) that it would be sensible to conduct a pilot test to see if the document was easy to use and promoted useful responses. However, it was decided that this was an unnecessary waste of time and so the project manager went straight to one of the five hospitals to conduct the first evaluation.

It very quickly became apparent that the document was far too long, as it took over an hour to complete each room. In addition, many of the questions were unnecessary and users believed they had to try to find a fault with each listed component, even if there was nothing wrong. Thus if the same questionnaire were to remain in use, it could take weeks to do just one hospital! So the project manager designed a new three page questionnaire in consultation with the author, which was intended to act as a prompt rather than having to complete every section, (see appendix).

Even though the evaluations have not yet been completed, attention has already been drawn to a number of features that could be improved in future designs. In an operating theatre department, for example, it is essential that dust and dirt are kept to an absolute minimum. However, these requirements have been overlooked in a number of ways, including unnecessary skirting boards, pipework that has not been enclosed and corridor walls that are falling to pieces as they are too narrow for the easy movement of trolleys. Further problems have been encountered in an X-ray department, where several rooms were just too small to be used properly. However, perhaps the worst case was not providing a bathroom close enough for patients who had been given a barium meal!

Comment
The above example demonstrates the importance of the planning stage in any post-occupancy evaluation exercise. By not conducting a pilot test, the department wasted both time and resources redesigning the questionnaire.

The problems that have been identified above may seem relatively minor, but such mistakes could prove very costly to correct if they were repeated throughout the organisation's thirty hospitals.

3.5 Data Collection: Methods, Analysis and Presentation

3.5.1 Aims

The facilities manager should:

- ❑ be aware of the various methods that exist for data collection
- ❑ understand the benefits and drawbacks of the different collection methods
- ❑ understand how to approach data analysis
- ❑ know the various techniques available for the presentation of results.

3.5.2 Context

Data collection and analysis are obviously a very important part of both briefing and evaluation; without sufficient data it is difficult to make informed decisions. The techniques covered in this chapter can be used during either process.

3.5.3 Data collection methods

The different methods covered in this section are listed in Table 3.6. The associated benefits and drawbacks are described briefly so that facilities managers can quickly select the appropriate method for a particular situation.

This list is by no means exhaustive, however, these particular techniques have been selected as they are the most useful and well known ways of collecting data. [9]

Table 3.6　Data collection methods

Standardised questionnaires	Benefits:	• Generating quantitative data • Quickly tapping a broad cross section of employees • Enabling a statistical analysis of subgroups
	Drawbacks:	• Probing responses • Understanding complex non-statistical relationships • Generating goodwill and confidence in the process
Focused interviews	Benefits:	• Probing responses • Engendering goodwill • Understanding complex relationships
	Drawbacks:	• Developing quantitative data • Quickly tapping a broad sample of employees • Time consuming and expensive
Structured observation	Benefits:	• Checking information given in surveys and interviews • (If systematic) generating quantitative data • Generating visual evidence to support interviews and surveys • Getting at issues that employees have difficulty verbalising
	Drawbacks:	• Understanding why something is occurring • Generating goodwill, unless coupled with interviews
Tracing	Benefits:	• Unobtrusive • Inexpensive data collection
	Drawback:	• Understanding why something is occurring
Literature search	Benefits:	• Eliciting responses about other buildings • Stimulating the imagination
	Drawbacks:	• Understanding how well a building functions • Time consuming
Study visit	Benefits:	• Eliciting responses about existing buildings • Stimulating the imagination
	Drawbacks:	• Background research time consuming • Understanding complex relationships
Archival records	Benefits:	• Unobtrusive • Inexpensive data collection • A check on other sources of information
	Drawbacks:	• An understanding of why something is happening • A detailed look at an issue • An accurate interpretation of data
Simulation	Benefits:	• Exploring 'what if' possibilities • Eliciting responses to new designs or plans • Removing scepticism that something will happen • Avoiding costly mistakes • Stimulating the imagination • Generating enthusiasm and excitement
	Drawbacks:	• Getting a completely realistic response

Before embarking on any data collection programme, it is worth bearing in mind the following points:

❑ Using multiple methods is likely to produce better results than using one single technique. For example, structured observation will only highlight what is occurring, rather than why.
❑ Information should not be collected just for the current situation. Organisations are forever changing, therefore, possible future requirements should also be catered for.

Standardised questionnaires

Questionnaires are a very traditional method of obtaining data. They are often used to discover regularities among groups of people, by comparison of answers to the same set of questions. Analysis of questionnaire responses can provide precise numerical data, from which tables, graphs etc. can be produced.

Before writing a questionnaire, researchers should carry out preliminary investigations, such as focused interviews. This enables the researcher to establish what type of answers respondents will give to specific questions; people will not always react to a question in the way that was expected. Following this, a standardised questionnaire can be compiled. Once the questionnaire is written, it should be pretested to see how people react. This should draw out any potential problems and the questionnaire can be altered to take these into consideration. It is worth remembering that employees are busy people and will not want to waste their time filling in pages of answers, therefore, questionnaires should be kept as short and as simple as possible. It is helpful to outline at the start what the aim of the questionnaire is; if people can see that it will benefit them they are more likely to complete the form.

Data produced by this method is good for establishing trends, but does not necessarily go deep enough to find out why things have occurred. Therefore, used together with observation methods and focused interviews, standardised questionnaires will help produce a fuller picture of the situation being studied.

Focused interviews

A focused interview can be used to establish in depth, what individuals or groups think about a particular situation.

Before carrying out an interview, the researcher should undertake some basic groundwork. He should try to establish what topics are relevant to the situation. A questionnaire, for example, may have already been distributed, which highlighted several areas for concern. On the basis of this analysis, the researcher develops an 'interview guide', which lays down the topics that should be covered during an interview. Whilst conducting the interview the researcher can ask further questions to clarify points or to enlarge on specific issues. However, the interviewer should ensure that he does not influence the answers in any way, it is his job to keep the interview flowing without directing it.

Structured observation

There are several methods of structured observation also called direct observation. However, a technique that is both systematic and quantitative is known as *behavioural mapping*. This is when an observer records where and when certain behaviour occurs in a specific setting. Used over a day, week or month, such behaviour records allow the observer to build up a picture of which areas within a building are being used by what sort of people, in what ways and at what times. If, for example, a lounge at the end of a corridor is hardly used, compared to one in the middle of a circulation route, then a facilities manager could ask if this space could be used more productively for something else.

Tracing (unobtrusive observation)

'Observing physical traces means systematically looking at physical surroundings to find reflections of previous activity not produced in order to be measured by researchers.'[9]

Traces may have been unconsciously left behind (for example, paths across a field), or may be conscious changes people have made to their surroundings (for example, a curtain hung over an open doorway). From such traces, researchers can ascertain how people actually use the environments that they work/live in. Facilities managers could use the technique to see how many changes staff make to their workspaces etc. in order for them to meet their particular needs.

This method is unobtrusive and inexpensive. However, it also has its drawbacks, as without consultation with the users, researchers may make false assumptions. So again it should be used in conjunction with another technique. Methods of recording observations include: annotated diagrams, drawings, photographs and counting.

Traces can be divided into the following four groups:

- ❑ by-products of use
- ❑ adaptations for use
- ❑ displays of self
- ❑ public messages.

Examples of these different traces are presented in Table 3.7.

Table 3.7   Physical traces

By-products of use	These can be useful to the facilities manager to establish if people use spaces for the purposes they were initially designed for.
Erosions	Parts of the environment can be worn away indicating that an area has had more use than it was originally designed for. New routes may become apparent across a section of grass, indicating that the original design did not take into account how often people in one building would need to cross to another.
Leftovers	These are physical objects that may be left behind indicating how people have made use of a setting. Cigarette stubs, for example, left behind in a washroom may indicate that there is a need for a dedicated smoking room. Leftovers help to differentiate between places where planned activities have occurred and places where unplanned activities have taken place.
Missing traces	A lack of erosions or traces may help to identify areas which are being underused. A coffee/rest area without any empty cups or magazines etc. may demonstrate to the facilities manager that the space could be put to better use.
Adaptations for use	**When people find that their physical environment does not allow them to do something they want to do, they change their surroundings; they become de signers. Adaptive traces are significant for facilities managers and designers because they demonstrate how people would choose to design their own environments if consulted.**
Props	New props are often added to a setting to allow for new activities. This may be due to a change in the function of a room or may be because certain activities were considered too expensive to allow for during the original design stage. Comfortable chairs and a low table may have been added to allow informal meetings to take place in someone's office, rather than having to occupy an official meeting room.
Separations	Changes may have been made to separate spaces that were previously together. A large open plan office, for example, may have been divided up by partitions to increase privacy.
Connections	Adaptations may have been made to allow for increased movement or communication between spaces that were designed to be physically separate. A door, for instance, between two offices may be permanently fixed ajar as the users work together as a team.
Displays of self	**People change their environments so that a place can be associated with them in particular. An environment which allows for no personalization may result in workers that are unhappy with their surroundings, which may have a detrimental effect on how they view their organisation.**
Personalization	In work environments people often utilise space for their personal possessions, such as family photos or certificates. Facilities managers should bear this in mind when considering new designs.
Identification	People use their environments to enable others to identify them more easily. If employees have placed temporary name plates on partitions etc. it may suggest that a new design should provide fixed name plates as standard.

Table 3.7 Continued

Public messages	Physical environments can be used to communicate a specific message to the public at large.	
Official	How often does the name of an organisation appear around a building? How important is corporate image to the organisation? Are visitors prevented from going in certain areas by the use of *private* signs?
Unofficial	Are there a number of unofficial direction signs written on paper distributed around the building? If so, perhaps the official direction signs are inadequate.

Literature search

This method enables the client/designer to identify similar buildings and organisations, which may provide useful information on how other people have approached similar issues. The designer may use this method to ascertain the client's reactions to different architectural styles before any initial designing occurs.

Study visit

This method enables users, clients and designers to learn from the experiences of others. Study visits can be thought of as POEs of other peoples' facilities. Visits to similar organisations and buildings can make people aware of the different ways in which other people have designed buildings for the same use. Study visits may highlight problems with a particular building type or design solution, allowing designers and clients to avoid similar costly mistakes in the future. A building that seems impressive in a photograph, will not necessarily function very well from its users' point of view. Obviously it will be impossible to visit too many buildings, so try to visit the ones that are the most comparable.

Archival records

This method is inexpensive, but again will only relate to what happened, rather than why. In this case, researchers consult records that have been collected by the organisation as part of its regular record keeping. Medical records, staff turnover and rates of absenteeism could all be used to assess satisfaction with a building. If, for example, staff turnover is higher in one building than another, could the old HVAC system be responsible? Of all the methods considered this is probably the least reliable and should really only be used to verify the results from another technique.

Simulation

Simulation is not a method for initial data collection, however, it can be a useful tool for obtaining reactions to new proposals. Simulation techniques include, photographs, models, drawings, full-scale mock ups, computer drawings, games and video animation. The method selected will depend upon the resources available. However, the cost of the simulation should be considered in relation to the cost of making a major mistake. A full-size mock-up of a new workstation may seem expensive, but it is better to get negative feedback at this stage, rather then when 40 new workstations have been installed that do not meet users' requirements.

Case Study: Use of multiple data collection methods

One of the office based departments within the organisation felt that it might be able to reduce costs through a revised use of space. Hence an external space planning consultant was engaged to propose an alternative solution. Before any decisions could be made it was necessary to assess how the space was used at present, therefore the consultants conducted a post-occupancy evaluation.

During their evaluation, the consultants employed four different data collection methods:

❑ Questionnaires – All staff were asked to complete a short questionnaire which established general trends throughout the department.
❑ Diary completion – A cross-section of employees were asked to complete a diary for a week, which looked at how they used their time and how often they were at their own desks or elsewhere.
❑ Interviews – These were held with a cross section of the staff to follow up certain issues in more depth.
❑ Room usage schedule – These were focused on enclosed offices to see how often they were unoccupied.

Once completed, the post-occupancy evaluation allowed the consultants to identify rooms and areas that were underused. They were then able to make proposals for a revised departmental layout.

Comment
By using multiple methods, the consultants were able to establish which rooms/spaces were not being used to their full capacity, but more importantly they were able to question why this was happening. If they had used questionnaires or observational methods only, they may have drawn different conclusions. This could have resulted in a revised layout that did not meet the requirements of the department.

3.5.4 Data analysis

The overall objective of data analysis is to interpret the collected information, so that useful recommendations can be made for existing or future buildings.

Various methods for analysis of data exist; however, for most POEs and briefing projects simple techniques can produce useful results.

Data analysis cannot be left to the final stages of a project; it must be thought of early on in the process, as it will have implications throughout. Facilities managers should establish at the outset how final results are likely to be presented, as this will effect data collection methods and data analysis. If an organisations' managers, for example, like to have graphs to demonstrate results; then this suggests that questionnaires may be used, so that quantitative information can be manipulated to produce graphs. Budget and time schedules should also be considered to ensure that allowances for data analysis have been included.

Once data has been collected it can be analysed in various ways, either by hand or through the use of computers. At the most basic level, questionnaire responses can often be analysed simply by counting how many people answer in the same way. Alternatively if the project team wants to do more sophisticated analysis, a simple statistical package can be employed. The choice of method depends upon the required output.

When interpreting results try to identify areas where people agree and areas where people disagree, so that appropriate action can be initiated. If the majority of people in one building complain about the heat then there is likely to be a problem. However, if there is a certain amount of contradiction about a subject it is necessary to try to establish why contradictions exist. This may mean re-examining the data or performing further data collection. Once all of the data has been analysed try to prioritise the findings so that the most problematic or important areas are dealt with first.

3.5.5 Presentation techniques

Once data has been collected and analysed it will be necessary to present the findings in an appropriate format. The format selected will be dependent on how the information will be used. Some organisations will require the findings to be presented in a report that they can distribute to managers. Others will want a demonstration with overheads or flip charts. The facilities manager should really decide what method of presentation is suitable for his particular organisation. However, when presenting any findings it is helpful to bear the following in mind:

❑ Try to prioritise the findings so that the most important items are dealt with first.
❑ Present the findings as simply as possible; over-detailed presentations will leave the reader/observer unsure of what the results are.
❑ Charts and tables help to get points across quickly and easily.
❑ Photos or videos can be useful to illustrate problem areas within existing buildings.

3.6 References

1. Preiser, W., Vischer, J. & White, E. (1991) *Design Intervention: Toward a More Humane Architecture*. Van Nostrand Reinhold, New York.
2. Sanoff, H., (1968) *Techniques of Evaluation for Designers*. Raleigh, NC: Design Research Laboratory, School of Design, North Carolina State University, USA.
3. Moleski, W. H. & Lang, Jon T. (1986) Organisational goals and human needs in office planning. In: Wineman J.D. (ed.) *Behavioral Issues in Office Design*, Van Nostrand Reinhold, New York, p.40.
4. Becker, F. (1990) *The Total Workplace*. Van Nostrand Reinhold, New York, p.263.
5. Gameson, R. (1991) Clients and professionals: the interface. In: *Practice Management. New Perspectives for the Construction Professional,* eds. P. Barrett & A.R Males. E.and F.N. Spon, London, p.165–174.
6. Newman, R., Jenks M., Bacon V. & Dawson, S. (1981) Brief Formulation and the Design of Buildings. Oxford Brookes University, Oxford.
7. Farbstein, J. (1993) The impact of the client organization on the programming process. In: W. F. E. Preiser, *Facility Programming*, Van Nostrand Reinhold, New York, p. 383–403.
8. Bedjer, E.(1991) From client's brief to end use: the pursuit of quality. In: P. Barrett & A.R. Males, *Practice Management: New Perspectives for the Construction Professional,* E.and F. N. Spon, London, p.193–203.
9. Powell J. (1991) Clients, designers and contractors: the harmony of able design teams. In: Barrett, P. & A. R. Males, *Practice Management: New Perspectives for the Construction Professional,* E.and F. N. Spon, London, p.137–148.
10. Zeisel, J. (1984) *Inquiry By Design*. Cambridge University Press, Cambridge.
11. Salisbury, F. (1990) *Architect's Handbook for Client Briefing*. Butterworth Architecture, London.
12. Spekkink, D. & Smits, F. J. (1993) *The Client's Brief: More Than a Questionnaire*. Stichting Bouwresearch, Rotterdam, The Netherlands.
13. Bruhns, H. & Isaacs, N. (1992) The role of quality assessment in facilities management. In: *Facilities Management: Research Directions,* (ed. P. Barrett) Department of Surveying, Salford University, 105–115.
14. Preiser, W. F. E., Rabinowitz, H. Z. & White, T. E. (1988) *Post-Occupancy Evaluation*. Van Nostrand Reinhold, New York.
15. Kernohan, D., Gray, J., Daish, J. & Joiner, D. (1992) *User Participation in Building Design and Management*. Butterworth Architecture, Oxford.
16 Ellis, P. (1987) Post–occupancy evaluation. *Facilities*, 5.11, 12–14.

Appendix A: Post-Occupancy Evaluation Data Sheets

Date:	POST-OCCUPANCY EVALUATION DATA SHEETS	Ref:
	General information	
Building and department		
Room name/ no.		
Purpose of room		
Brief description		
Is room size appropriate?		
Location within dept.		
Overall suitability		
Names of users		
	Sketch of room	
User's additional comments	**Facilitator's comments**	

Date:	POST-OCCUPANCY EVALUATION DATA SHEETS	Ref:

Wall finish	
Description	
Suitability	
Durability	
Maintenance	
Aesthetics	

Floor finish	
Description	
Suitability	
Durability	
Maintenance	
Aesthetics	

Ceiling finish	
Description	
Suitability	
Durability	
Maintenance	
Aesthetics	

Doors	
Description	
Suitability	
Durability	
Maintenance	
Aesthetics	

Date:	POST-OCCUPANCY EVALUATION DATA SHEETS	Ref:
	Windows	
Description		
Suitability		
Durability		
Maintenance		
Aesthetics		
	Lighting	
Description		
Suitability		
Durability		
Maintenance		
Aesthetics		
	Power, communications and safety	
Name of item	Consider provision and location of following elements: electrical power outlets, data outlets, telephone points, fire alarms etc.	
	Furniture and equipment	
Name of item	What items of furniture/equipment are contained in the room? Are they well positioned? Does the room require further items of furniture/equipment?	

Chapter 4
Contracting-out

4.1 Introduction

4.1.1 Aims

This chapter aims to help the facilities manager make consistently good quality contracting-out decisions. It has been observed through extensive fieldwork that facilities managers often only take into account 'tangible' economic and functional variables when considering and making these increasingly crucial decisions. This chapter will contend that this decision-making process is too simplistic and promotes the argument that if better contracting-out decisions are to be made, then the facilities managers should incorporate the equally important 'intangible' variable of organisational 'culture' or 'environment' into the decision-making process.

This way of looking at the contrating-out decision-making process requires the facilities manager to 'unlearn' well-established ideas about contracting-out, and to learn and adopt new managerial perspectives and processes. The chapter, therefore, will have more of an argument style than other chapters, to assist the reader in making the required reorientation in the way facilities managers should view contracting-out. A rigorous understanding of the underlying reasons for the adoption of this more holistic and sophisticated contracting-out decision-making process will assist the facilities manager in making better quality decisions.

4.1.2 Summary of the different sections

- ❑ Section 4.1 – Provides a brief introduction of the aims of the Chapter.
- ❑ Section 4.2 – Seeks to achieve an understanding of contracting-out in the context of facilities management services. First the terminology used is clarified, then the influences responsible for the emergence and success of contracting-out are examined. The scope, scale and potential for contracting-out are explored and the importance of recognising a difference between management and operational services explained.
- ❑ Section 4.3 – Tackles the shortcoming of relating facilities management

to the non-core business of an organisation. Encouragement is given to adopt a more flexible approach, which is considered vital if the full added-value potential of facilities management is to be realised. This becomes an important prerequisite to facilities management resource decision-making.

❑   Section 4.4 – Seeks to determine how to decide whether to contract-out, or whether to resource facilities management services in-house. A structured, rather than an intuitive, approach to this decision-making process is promoted.

❑   Appendix A – Reviews the current state of flux that contracting-out decision makers find themselves in, due to confusion over whether European and British legislation applies. Until clarity is brought to the legal framework, the section concludes that each case has to be examined individually; but goes on to suggest that recent experience of applying the legislation may help to overcome some of the problems. This appendix should be considered as being self-contained, as it is not an explicit part of the decision-marking.

❑   Appendix B – Describes two case study organisations.

4.2 Understanding Contracting-out in a Facilities Management Context

4.2.1 Aims

The aim of section 4.2 is to assist facilities managers to understand the overall nature of contracting-out. Firstly, the concept of contracting-out will be described. Secondly, the scope for contracting-out in facilities management is analysed. Thirdly, the issue of contracting-out services separately or in varying bundles is discussed. Finally, this section examines how to determine the potential for contracting-out within an organisation.

4.2.2 Concept

Terminology

The first matter to resolve is the question of terminology that will be used in this chapter. The subject of this chapter is 'contracting-out'. This is employed as the generic term to describe the process by which a user employs a separate organisation (the supplier), under a contract, to perform a function, which could, alternatively, have been performed by in-house staff.

Many readers will be equally happy to use the term 'outsourcing' to describe this process. However, this chapter reserves 'outsourcing' to denote one type of contracting-out; namely, the process by which a user employs a separate company (the supplier), under a contract, to perform a function, which had *previously* been carried out in-house; and *transfers* to that supplier assets, including people and management responsibility. The various alternative terms, and in particular 'outsourcing', do have tighter meanings, which have largely become lost due to common usage.

What is important for readers of this chapter to understand is the relevance of contracting-out as far as facilities management is concerned because, clearly, contracting-out applies to other management sectors of an organisation, not least to the core business activity. To achieve this understanding, the reasons for the current popularity of contracting-out in facilities management will be briefly discussed, along with an overview of its scale and scope.

What has caused this contracting-out fashion?

For macro-economic reasons beyond the scope of this chapter, organisations began a drastic downsizing transition during the 1980s. Large organisations contracted-out more and more functions to external suppliers. At about the same time the facilities management function was emerging, and with its arrival the contracting-out exercise was extended from core business functions to this 'non-core' business activity. 'Core' and 'non-core' business are used here in a general sense. We will look at this aspect of organisational structure later in more detail.

Flexibility to meet changing market conditions became fundamental to business thinking. Facilities management – the management concept of co-ordinating many previously disparate support functions – tended to solve one problem, but create another. The internal bundling of services associated with facilities management spawned empire-building. An organisation's internal empires are not known for their flexibility, having a tendency to solve problems by recruiting more staff. To maximise the benefits of facilities management it was discovered, by some organisations, that the downside of inflexibility and empire-building could be overcome by the external procurement of services. Furthermore, intensifying competition, together with a global recession, placed increasing pressure on organisations to reduce total operating costs and concentrate on core business functions. Contracting-out apparently offered the solution to these demands, facilitating both efficiency gains and cost-effectiveness. For suppliers, the growth in acceptance of contracting-out strategies by users has come as a major business opportunity.

4.2.3 The scope and scale of contracting-out

Contracting-out trends

Most, if not all, facilities management services can be procured externally by an organisation. Further, most, if not all, companies will contract-out some facilities management functions, probably on a regular basis. This is without including the need to resource one-off project work, such as a major building scheme, or the search for new premises.

The trend is also toward increasing the scale of contracting-out undertaken. For instance, data from the Computer Services Corporation Index Survey (1992)[1] of European information systems executives showed that 71% of these executives were planning to contract-out some information technology operations by 1995, compared with 36% in 1990/91. This will boost the value of contracted-out information technology from US$1.6bn in 1990 to approximately US$10bn by 1996.

Moreover, the scope of contracting-out is increasing. According to a report P&O commissioned, 70% of facilities managers in the UK expanded their contracting-out operations in the period 1988–1990. The scope of contracting-out included:

> 'A broad range of support services, mechanical/electrical and fabric maintenance, internal planting and landscaping, security, cleaning, catering, vending and the supply of general clerical staff, telephonists, receptionists, mailroom, messengers, chauffeurs – in fact all non-core business activity.'[2]

In order to place this rapidly expanding phenomenon of contracting-out into focus, it is necessary to divide the facilities management 'umbrella' into its constituent parts of:

❑ user sector components
❑ participant function.

User sector components

Examining the scope of facilities management by reference to user sectors first requires the principal components to be identified. The components can be described as:

❑ the premises
❑ the support services
❑ the information services/information technology.

These components are brought together under a co-ordinated facilities management system to provide support to the core business. Figure 4.1. illustrates this idea, still at this stage using the general core versus non-core split. Further, by including personnel in the model, as another support for the core, but not (necessarily) as part of facilities management, the point is made that other functions may interrelate.

It is interesting to note that a fourth sector of the facilities management market is currently emerging, namely *infrastructure*. This is mainly relevant to local authorities and the like, and refers to such matters as street lighting. It remains to be seen whether this categorisation will be accepted by the practitioners; but this typifies the *dynamic* nature of facilities management.

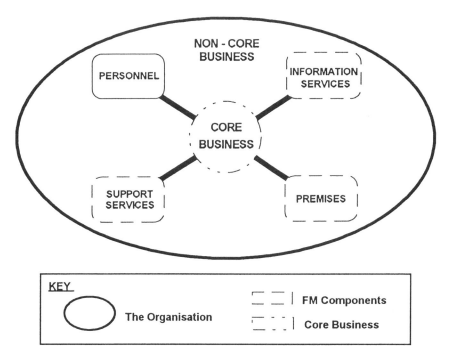

Figure 4.1 Facilities management supporting the organisation's core business.

Figure 4.2, and Tables 4.1 and 4.2 illustrate the elements covered by each group. The greater subdivision expressed in Figure 4.2 could, of course, be followed in the other two tables, and, thereafter, each subheading could itself be expressed according to its own multi-component parts. In this sense the figures are indicative of the scope of facilities management – and therefore the potential for contracting-out. It is certain that facilities managers will be able to embellish these lists, based on their own operations and experience.

However, whilst these three divisions certainly clarify the main umbrella groups of facilities, it is, as we have noted, not the only way they can be discussed. A valuable distinction is made by considering the function of the *participants*.

Participant function

The strategy of contracting-out can be applied to management functions and operational functions:

❑ *Management functions* comprise the 'thinkers': the managers, and planners, the consultants etc. with activities ranging from organising and strategic planning to staffing, directing and controlling.

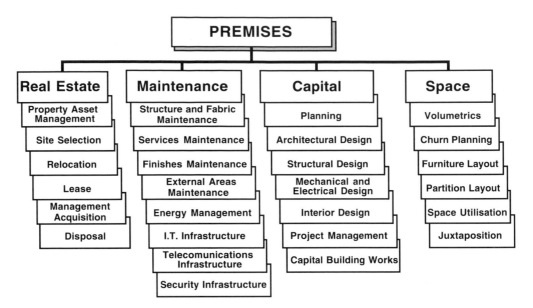

Figure 4.2   The premises component of facilities management.

Table 4.1   The support services component of facilities management

Support services	
❏ Mail services	❏ Refuse disposal
❏ Fleet car	❏ Reprographics
❏ Catering	❏ Security
❏ Reception	❏ Stationery
❏ Housekeeping	❏ Travel
❏ Office administration	❏ Vending
❏ Furniture	

Table 4.2   The information services component of facilities management

Information services	
❏ Data network	❏ Wiring installation
❏ Systems integration	❏ Planning and design studies
❏ Voice and data network	❏ Software development
❏ Network management	

❏ *Operational or implementation functions* comprise the 'doers': and may be thought of as the craftsmen, artisans, technicians or 'industrial staff'; i.e. they cover the operational and implementational aspects of service provision.

❏ For each management function, a reciprocal *operational* function is determinable.

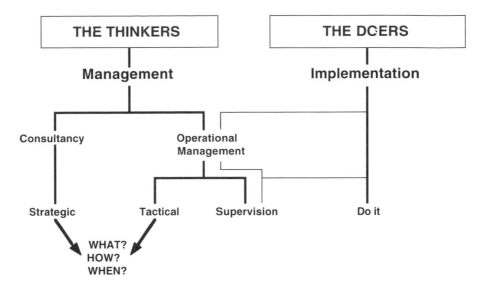

Figure 4.3 How facilities management works.

Figure 4.3 attempts to show how management can be divided into strategic, tactical and supervision; and how supervision ties in with the implementation aspects of 'operational'. There is no distinct boundary between the thinkers and doers, indeed the distinction can be particularly blurred where the supervision or monitoring of work is being carried out. For example, for some services the supplier on the doer side may be responsible for the supervision of work, whilst for other services the contrary may apply. The split between management and operational in the facilities management context will be seen to be of *particular* significance for contracting-out later in this chapter.

The division by function method allows a continuum to be developed between management and operational functions. The dotted line in Figure 4.4 indicates the variation in requirement for the mix of management and operational skills in the provision of any one service. For example, pure consultancy advice concerning a space planning exercise would require no 'artisan' skill (see Figure 4.4) e.g. FM service 9; whilst implementation of a furniture move would consist mainly of 'blue collar' involvement and a minimal degree of supervision e.g. FM service 4 or 5.

The next section looks at the manner in which facilities management contracts can be grouped.

4.2.4 *Grouping of facilities management contracts*

A range of contracting-out options can be considered by users. Taken to its logical extreme, the starting point could consist merely of one service being

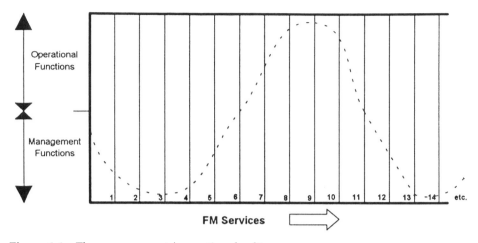

Figure 4.4   The management/operational split.

contracted-out, while all the remainder are retained in-house. A progression can then follow, whereby eventually all facilities management services could be contracted-out by *individual* contracts. The next stage would be to *group* some of the contracts together and place that group of services with one contractor; a concept known as *bundling*. Next several bundles could be let to the same contractor (supplier). Figure 4.5 demonstrates this range of alternatives by reference to just one sector of facilities management, namely building services.

The figure divides the activities up between the thinkers and doers; i.e. management and operational. Inherent in the model is the notion that 'bundling' of contracts tend to collect together groups of operational services separately from those of management services; with an advanced level of bundling being the groupings of all associated operational functions into one group, and of all associated management functions into one group. However, the reader's attention is drawn to the fact that Figure 4.5. is indicative only. It will be realised from the detail given above, describing the scope of facilities management and, hence, the scope for contracting-out, that Figure 4.5. could be expanded very significantly.

When all aspects of facilities management services are let to the one supplier, i.e. grouping all management *and* all operational roles into one contract, 'total facilities management' is the accepted descriptor, known by the acronym TFM. Experience of business generally indicates that TFM can never truly exist. It is not easy to envisage one supplier being able to adequately provide services ranging from audit and law through to providing cleaners and caterers. The term TFM itself should therefore be accepted as a continuum ranging from the grouping of bundles, which should include both management and operational, up to a theoretical extreme, which is unlikely to be achieved, where no in-house provision remains.

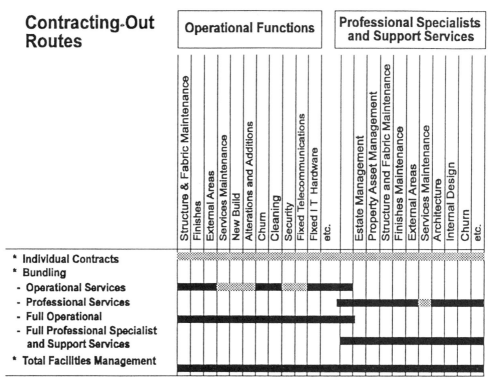

Figure 4.5 Methods of contracting-out building services packages.

The following section looks further at the potential for contracting-out and comments as to the likelihood of this potential being realised.

4.2.5 User's contracting-out potential

The potential for contracting-out from a user's point of view relates to the optimum balance between retained in-house facilities management services and those contracted-out. Following the method used above, this process can be discussed in terms of management and operational functions.

Taking the management function as an example, the minimum retained in-house component may equate to one member of staff acting in an 'unknowledgeable' capacity, as part only of his or her job description. For example, a bursar of a private school, with a wide range of responsibilities peripheral to his or her primary role (see Case Study 2 in Chapter 1). In many organisations, property matters are, for instance, delegated to the company secretary; while the personnel manager frequently becomes responsible for janitorial management. On this basis, a user would always have at least a minimal management role in facilities management, even if it is only an interface with a TFM contractor. The other extreme of the management continuum would be exemplified by a large and diverse team of managers, no doubt divided into departments. The large in-house teams employed by county councils in the 1970s would be an example but, again, it is improbable that the theoretical extreme of complete in-house resource could be reached, particularly if services such as audit are accepted as part of the facilities management role. A model of this continuum appears in Figure 4.6. It is important to recognise that this continuum model relates to *potential*. The larger the in-house resource, all other considerations being equal, the greater the potential the user displays for contracting-out.

The next section briefly examines one further concept that it is essential to understand, in order to make the right resource decision for facilities management services.

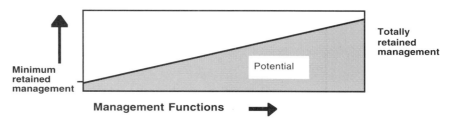

Figure 4.6   Potential for contracting-out.

4.3 Beyond Core Business

4.3.1 Aims

There is a perception that facilities management activities focus on non-core business only. This section aims to question that statement, recognising the very real restrictions it imposes on the development of facilities management, and especially contracting-out.

4.3.2 Core business

Facilities management is commonly described as the management, in a co-ordinated form, of all non-core business functions. This only aids understanding of facilities management and, hence, the opportunity for contracting-out, up to a certain point. The following examples highlight this limitation.

Example

The business of Case Study 1 (detailed in Appendix B) is the provision of healthcare.

The catering function of Case Study 1 serves both the staff and the customers (i.e. the patients).

For the patient who has elected to buy medical treatment, the obvious core business functions of a private hospital are largely taken for granted. Operating theatre equipment is expected to be fit for purpose; one X-ray machine looks remarkably like another, and clinical sterilizers are probably not thought about at all. The patient expects good medical care.

The patient also anticipates a good level of catering provision. This is an area he/she is familiar with, and consequently will have preconceived expectations. Customer satisfaction is much more likely to be evaluated upon experience of the catering services (and other hotel services such as cleaning and portering) than on the medical care – unless there has been a clinical problem.

Is catering core business or non-core business?

Example

For the office user described in Case Study 2 (detailed in Appendix B) catering services are largely provided to supply staff with meals and refreshment. At first glance a cut-and-dried support service.

However, the caterers also provide a service for clients of the firm, when being entertained in-house, and similarly for guests at Directors' lunches and dinners. Clients expect this mix of necessity and hospitality to be delivered at a standard commensurate with their esteem of the user. Core or non-core?

In a rational world, the second example probably describes a support service – but not as clear cut as originally anticipated. However, in the first example, catering performance becomes a prime indicator of customer satisfaction. Is this a core or non-core service? How does the answer affect (a) how the service is run/managed? (b) how the service is resourced?

The difficulty with the analysis is eased if a different view of core business is accepted. If core business is simply the revenue-producing part of an organisation, *part* of Case Study 1's catering fits. On the basis of producing income, running airports is BAA's core business, but retailing is one of their best revenue earners – can this be considered core business? The analysis becomes very muddled if one thinks only in terms of a function being identified purely as core or non-core. If such an all-or-nothing view of core business is allowed to dominate this analysis, much potential for added value will be lost. It is fruitful if a continuum view of core and non-core business is taken. For example, adopting this continuum view, running airports becomes the *raison d'être* of an organisation such as BAA, but only a part of its core business. Figure 4.7 demonstrates this philosophy.

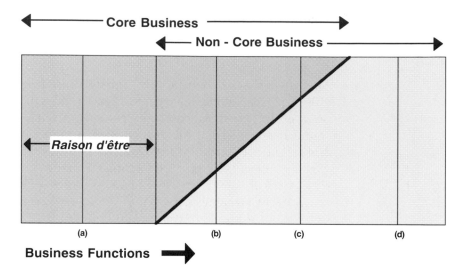

Figure 4.7   The core/non-core business continuum.

In the figure, an arbitrary interface between core and non-core business is used. The key point is that this interface is not shown as a vertical divide. This accommodates the notion that functions of the business can be:

❑   wholly core business
❑   wholly non-core business
❑   part core, part non-core.

On the diagram, wholly core business can be thought of as raison d'être functions of the given organisation. Reverting to our case studies, Case Study 1's raison d'être is clearly healthcare provision. So the function shown at point (a) in Figure 4.7. could be nursing, or provision of an operating theatre. Case Study 1's catering (b) is seen to be more core than non-core – but not raison d'être. Case Study 2's catering (c) on the other hand, is more non-core than core.

The important point is that facilities management – and hence the potential for contracting-out facilities management services – has, by this model, the ability to encompass more than pure support services (or non-core business activities), i.e. the potential is enlarged, and so is the flexibility to enable these services to be revenue-earning. To complete the picture, point (d) could relate to the maintenance of mechanical and electrical plant and machinery – a function which is likely to be a non-core support service for most users.

As has been shown, an adherence to a strict core versus non-core split can be a barrier to developing the full potential of facilities management to make an added-value contribution to the organisation. It is therefore a barrier to effective resource decision-making.

Having reviewed what contracting-out actually entails, and the importance of recognising a management: operational split, section 4.4. now focuses on how to approach the decision of whether or not to contract-out.

4.4 Facilities Management Resource Decision Making

4.4.1 Aims

The aim of this section is to present a decision-making framework which will enable the facilities manager to: firstly, decide whether or not to contract-out a given task or function; and secondly, to determine whether or not contracting-out is compatible with the organisation environment or culture. The section presents these two elements of the decision-making process as running sequentially, one after another. However, it should be noted that this is for the purpose of clarity of discussion only. It is perhaps intuitively obvious that a facilities manager would not carry out a careful deliberation of whether or not to contract-out a given function if he knows that the organisational environment would not allow contracting-out anyway.

Reference to the chapter on decision making will give facilities managers not only a structured approach to this aspect of problem solving, but will also provide the vital medium of communication – 'management speak' – in order for facilities managers to talk to their counterparts. This contracting-out chapter builds on that need to take a structured, rather than intuitive, approach to decision-making. This section concentrates on the considerations that have to be taken into account in order to make an 'acceptable' decision.

4.4.2 The shortcomings of the intuitive approach

Contracting-out is a relatively recent phenomena. One consequence of this is that there is relatively little data available from organisations concerning the effectiveness of contracting-out over a 'period'. If a typical contract is let on a three-year basis, a suitable 'period' would need to be at least one cycle, in order to take stock, both of the original decision to contract-out *and* the decision at the end of the cycle, where the options would be to:

❏ renew the contract with the same contractor;
❏ place a new contract with a different contractor;
❏ revert to in-house resources.

Until data of this nature is more available, the suppliers can make claims which are difficult to refute. Hence the risk of an intuitive approach; i.e. contracting-out being viewed as a simple choice between being either advantageous for an organisation or disadvantageous. We will show that decisions made on this basis are vulnerable and an alternative approach should be adopted. That is not to say that advantages/disadvantages of contracting-out do not play an important part in facilities management resource decision-making. They do, but it is not the whole picture.

To get to the whole picture we need to examine the driving *and* the constraining forces, which should be part of the process. To simplify the process we will consider two broad categories of forces which interrelate:

❑ *Primary* advantages and disadvantages of contracting-out.
❑ *Secondary* driving/constraining forces.

4.4.3 Primary advantages and disadvantages of contracting-out

Tables 4.3 and 4.4 list perceived advantages and disadvantages of contracting-out in the order research has shown them to be most frequently occurring in the literature on this subject.

Table 4.3   User-perceived advantages of contracting-out in ranking order

Ranking by weighted average	Categories of potential advantages
1	Reduced costs/economies of scale
2	Concentration on core business/strategic appreciation of service
3	Right-sized headcount/reduce space
4	Improved productivity/operational efficiencies
5	Increased flexibility/workload pattern
6	No obsolescence/latest technology/specialist knowledge/ current statutory knowledge
7	Overcome skills shortage/specialist equipment shortage
8	Added-value (at no extra cost)/quality/value for money
9	Reduced management burden
10	Career path development
11	Implementation speed (start-up)/response time
12	Improved management control/performance levels targeted
13	One-stop-shopping/one invoice/contractor acts as screen between user and suppliers
14	Improved accountability/performance levels monitored/user risk reduced
15	Optimal equipment configuration
16	Assist user to obtain competitive advantage in market-place
17	No operational headaches
18	No capital outlay/latest technology for least capital outlay
19	Tax gain

There are several important riders to make concerning this data:

❑ The categories are 'perceived' advantages and disadvantages. Suffice to say, actual experiences might not necessarily support the priorities shown. Indeed, it is possible to suggest that the advantages table can be read as the supplier's sales pitch, whilst the disadvantages table may be interpreted as the sceptical user's preconceived ideas. There is merit in both views, hence the need for a structured approach.

❑ The tables can appear contradictory; for instance, the perceived prime advantage of contracting-out is that it is a more cost-effective method of resourcing facilities management. However, the perceived prime shortcoming or disadvantage of contracting-out is that contracting-out is not always cost-effective.

Table 4.4 User-perceived disadvantages of contracting-out in ranking order.

Ranking by weighted average	Categories of potential disadvantages
1	Claimed savings = forecasted hopes/not always cost-effective
2	Personnel problem – shift from user to supplier/those leaving versus staying/unions/redundancies
3	Lack of control of suppliers
4	Risk of selecting a poor supplier/supplier market insufficiently competent
5	Personnel problem – loyalty to user
6	Confidentiality of data/security issues
7	New (different) management problems
8	Worse strategic focus/can't separate strategic from operational
9	Strategic risk/contracting-out critical segments may jeopardise user's organisation
10	Lose in-house expertise or capability
11	Long-term fixed contracts
12	Supplier's capacity
13	Contrary to culture of user's organisation
14	Ownership of new applications with supplier
15	Ignores in-house solution/in-house resource satisfactory
16	Supplier's commitment
17	Supplier's availability
18	Supplier's continuity
19	Hidden costs
20	Decision time required when considering contracting-out
21	Lack of independent advice by supplier (manufacturer)
22	Learning curve for supplier
23	Slower response time to problems
24	Lack of flexibility
25	User tends to wrongly rationalise contracting-out decision as correct
26	Taxation penalty (contracting-out supplier's fee taxable versus hardware capital allowable)
27	All eggs in one basket

These tables do provide a broad overview of the many considerations and issues involved in deciding to contract-out or not. However, it should be appreciated that the advantages and disadvantages of contracting-out only cover half the alternatives available.

Example

For Case Study 2, the fact that in-house catering staff accrued expensive employment packages, including perks, can be seen more readily as a disadvantage of *in-house* resourcing; rather than observing that contracting-out would be an advantageous alternative because of the absence of such 'corporate' benefits.

In this example, advantages of contracting-out and disadvantages of in-house resourcing are not synonymous, but have the same end result. Similarly, as shown in the next example, disadvantages of contracting-out are not necessarily synonymous with advantages of in-house resourcing.

Example

Case Study 1 contracted-out the role of the clinical sterilizer engineer in one region, not because it was advantageous to do so, but because of the in-house disadvantage of not being able to attract a suitable candidate.

Therefore, a matrix of alternatives (shown in Figure 4.8) should be considered, which can act as a helpful tool in the decision-making process.

Advantages of contracting - out	Disadvantages of contracting - out
Disadvantages of in - house resourcing	Advantages of in - house resourcing

Figure 4.8 Matrix of primary factors.

These primary advantage and disadvantage variables, when compared with what will be called secondary driving factors, can be seen to be:

❑ predictable: i.e. predictable in nature, though not in the effect they have on any given user;
❑ uncomplicated.

In essence, *primary* forces can be viewed as *influencing* resource decision making; while *secondary* forces generate incidental advantages or disadvantages, (i.e. they are a spin-off result of a decision).

Example

For Case Study 1, the electrical testing service was contracted-out because of the *primary* advantage that this delivered the service more efficiently. Previously, Case Study 1 had attempted to cover the electrical testing requirements, to all 32 locations, by providing one in-house electrical technician. It was found that the combination of excessive travel time, overnight accommodation requirement and away-from-home working, not only led to a gross inefficiency of resource, but also resulted in it becoming a difficult post to fill, due to the unsociable hours. By contracting-out to regional suppliers, these problems were overcome.

In this case, the advantages of contracting-out *directly* influenced the resource decision-making, and were therefore considered *primary*.

Example

In one of their four regions, Case Study 1 contracted-out the role of the clinical sterilizer engineer. This was against the wishes of senior management, who considered it both desirable and advantageous to directly-employ these engineers.

However, due to a combination of influences, which included:

(1) a general shortage of well-qualified sterilizer engineers; and,
(2) an unattractive work opportunity, when compared with the opportunities afforded by specialist maintenance contractors; i.e. long travel distances to locations, few clinical sterilizers to maintain and the requirement to undertake low skill fill-in work.

Case Study 1 was unable to fill their vacancy.

Contracting-out was, therefore, undertaken largely as a 'Hobson's choice' alternative, but one advantage of so doing was that it proved a more cost-efficient method.

This can be considered a *secondary* or spin-off advantage, because it did not influence the decision-making process.

4.4.4 Secondary driving and constraining forces

The matrix proposed in Figure 4.8. indicates a set of variables. The advantages and disadvantages can be predetermined, but *how* they affect a given organisation will depend on how they interrelate with other driving and constraining forces.

Example

Case Study 1 contracted-out some of their laundry services even though *more* expensive than their in-house operation; while they retained in-house the majority of their clinical sterilizer engineering capacity, even though *more* expensive than a contracted-out option.

Case Study 1 found that there were 'primary' advantages and disadvantages, and secondary 'spin-off' advantages and disadvantages of contracting-out. The former were considered 'powerful' enough to influence resource decision making, i.e. were capable of being *driving factors*; the latter accrued as a result, rather than influenced the result.

Example

Case Study 1 experimented with contracting-out the *management* of hotel services (principally the catering sector) while retaining the *operational* element in-house. This was found to be unsuccessful, but directed attention toward recognising a management/operational split as a variable factor.

❑ The organisation (as a healthcare provider) were very conscious of the interrelationship of staff with their customers/patients. It was part of their culture that staff, who had regular contact with patients, should be directly employed, in order to ensure they were inculcated with the personal service levels required. Consequently 'regular patient contact' versus 'infrequent patient contact' became an important variable.

❑ The organisation had 32 hospital locations at an average number of staff of only 100 per location, working three shifts. An acceptable over-simplification would be that there were approximately 30–35 staff per shift. This became rather akin to running a chain of corner shops rather than one hypermarket store.

❑ The organisation's geographic spread was an important influence. Because the locations were widely dispersed around the country, opportunities for co-operation between locations were minimal. This ratio of the number of locations plus the staffing levels at each location can be termed the 'scale of operation' and becomes a further variable. In addition, the ratio of contract workers to staff in small locations, was also seen to be a critical variable.

Figure 4.9 illustrates a structure for resource decision making which takes into account both primary and secondary factors. The figure collects the five variables of the foregoing example together as driving factors. Each variable is then applied to hotel services in turn. These are shown as influences upon resource decision-making:

I_1 *The influence of management/operational split:* The policy of contracting-out the *management* of hotel services was found to be unsatisfactory, and a decision was made to reject it as a method of resourcing. This leaves the possibility of contracting-out the operational aspects of hotel services.

I_2 *The influence of regular patient contact:* Case Study 1 found it unacceptable to contract-out tasks which included regular patient contact; i.e. they rejected the contracting-out of operational services with regular patient contact, leaving the remaining operational services available for resourcing by contracted-out means, if considered appropriate.

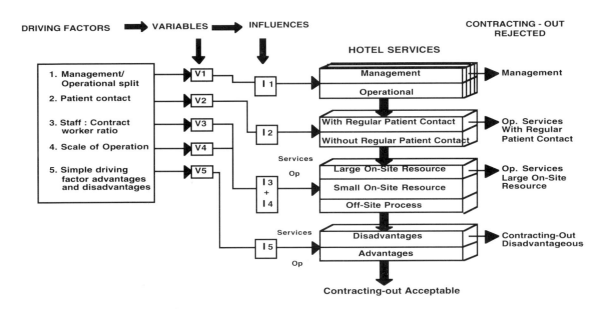

Figure 4.9   Contracting-out decision-making model.

I_{3-4} *The influence of staff : contract worker ratio:* These influences, in Case Study 1's case, had the effect of rejecting contracting-out as an option where the resourcing of operational services required a disproportionately large number of on-site contract workers, relative to the total workforce of a given location.

The 'sieves' of these four influences so far considered result in contracting-out being considered a viable option where:

❏   A small on-site human resource is required (relative to the total workforce), for operational services without regular patient contact; or
❏   work (i.e. an operational process) is carried out off-site.

I_5 The final 'sieve' in the decision making process, consisting of the primary advantages and disadvantages of contracting-out, is then applied to these two surviving groups.

This approach can be adapted to your specific case and produces a prima facie 'decision' about whether contracting-out is advantageous or not, which must then be considered further in the context of the organisational 'environment'.

4.4.5 Determining the user's 'environment' toward facilities management resourcing

The next important step in facilities management resource decision-making is to analyse whether the user is receptive to the strategy of contracting-out. The secondary variables, for a given user, collectively determine the *environment* presented *by* the user toward contracting-out. The environment can be described as ranging from being receptive or compatible with contracting-out (i.e. a friendly environment), to incompatible, (i.e. a hostile environment). Figure 4.10. is a model of this proposal showing a continuum existing, ranging from contracting-out *won't* occur, through contracting-out *may* occur and contracting-out *should* occur, to contracting-out *must* occur.

At the same time the *environment* presented by users is shown to range from hostile, through neutral, to a friendly environment. These stages equate to a range of influences impacting on contracting-out decision making:

❑ from the extreme of required rejection (e.g. a corporate decision against contracting-out);
❑ through acquiescence – where the user does not express strong preference either for or against contracting-out;
❑ through encouragement – where the user starts to promote contracting-out as the preferred method of resourcing; (e.g. an in-principle board decision to contract-out facilities management services where possible, or government policy for departments to market test);
❑ to the other extreme where the user requires contracting-out to be implemented (e.g. a corporate strategic decision).

The interface of the continuum is denoted by the dotted 'S-curve', which corresponds with the horizontal axes at both extremes. The exact position of this interface will vary from organisational setting to organisational setting; however, it should be consistently viewed that above the interface, contracting-out will not occur, and below the interface it will occur. To demonstrate the mechanics of the model, it follows that if a user presents an acquiescent environment (i.e. contracting-out is an acceptable tactic, but is not actively promoted) and the advantages and disadvantages balance, the position of the event on the model is likely to be above the interface and contracting-out won't happen. In a more encouraging environment, the same event is more likely to be below the interface and contracting-out will probably happen.

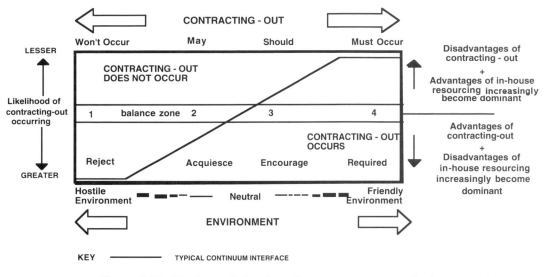

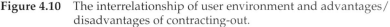

Figure 4.10 The interrelationship of user environment and advantages/ disadvantages of contracting-out.

For example, at Point (1): the user's strategy dictates contracting-out won't be allowed to happen; for instance, the board policy, reflecting the organisation's culture, is to resource facilities management services in-house. At Points (2) and (3) : contracting-out is more likely to happen at (3) in an encouraging environment than at Point (2). At Point (4) : contracting-out is enforced; e.g. by a main board strategic decision, for example by outsourcing facilities management services; or e.g. by government policy for central government departments.

The following examples show how the findings of the case studies can be analysed by employing this diagram.

Example

For Case Study 1, the management/operational split imposed after the lessons learned from contracting-out the management of catering services, conveys that the environment is now hostile to contracting-out management. i.e. contracting-out is rejected as an option, as a result of a corporately-made strategic decision, and therefore the event occurs to the left of the 'S-curve' of the model in Figure 4.11.

In addition, the findings show that for Case Study 1 it is also disadvantageous (as well as anti-policy) to contract-out management – the findings range from in-balance with advantages, to primarily disadvantageous. This positions the event from the central zone up toward the top axis.

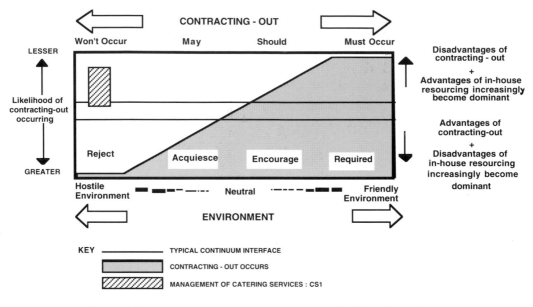

Figure 4.11 Management of catering services for Case Study 1.

Example

Within Case Study 1 some of the *operational* services of hotel services may be contracted-out; i.e. there is no overall anti-policy. Various services, e.g. catering services, window cleaning, etc. responded to *different* variables, forming different micro-environments, such that taken as *individual* services they were exposed to a range of user environments, as per Figure 4.12. Contracting-out of catering and cleaning were subjected to the hostile environment generated by the corporate decision to interface patients only with directly-employed staff, irrespective of the merits of contracting-out. Porterage attracted no driving factor advantages or disadvantages, but submitted to the corporate preference for roles which comprise full-time *local* involvement to be resourced in-house; i.e. a hostile–neutral environment, as far as contracting-out was concerned. Laundry and linen service was not 'governed' by the user's environment (i.e. a neutral environment existed) and was resourced differently according to the local preference. The remaining four services were contracted-out on a piece-meal basis primarily in an neutral environment (i.e. the user did not dictate circumstances, as a result of other influences). Because of distinct advantages of contracting-out, which amounted to primary driving factors, such as the efficient provision of: specialist skills and specialist equipment; part-time requirement; plus, off-site processes requiring specialist plant, etc., the dominance of advantages of contracting-out placed the events below the curve in the 'contracting-out will happen' sector. The position of hotel services operational services is shown on the model, together with hotel services management.

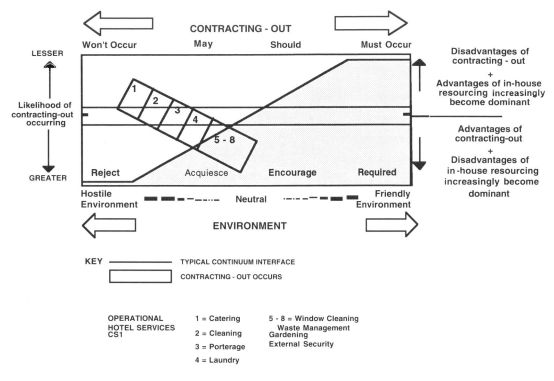

Figure 4.12   Management of hotel services for Case Study 1.

4.5 Summary

This chapter has identified and developed an approach to resolving contracting-out issues which demands from facilities managers the adoption of a new managerial perspective which both considers and integrates a diverse range of 'soft' as well as 'hard' variables. Sections 4.2 and 4.3 provided the context for this new way of thinking, by questioning the prevailing practice of limiting the facilities management sphere of responsibility to non-core or support activities only. It was argued that such a definition negated the enormous potential the facilities management function has in contributing substantial added-value to an organisation's core business activities. This widening of the facilities management function onto a more strategic plain was identified as providing a crucial managerial context to which the consideration of contracting-out issues should be firmly anchored.

Section 4.4 developed a contracting-out decision-making process which involved dual consideration of both the specific advantages and disadvantages of contracting-out for a given task or function, and the broader consideration of the compatibility of contracting-out of the given task or function with the organisation environment or culture. Both these decision-making process elements are depicted as models, in Figures 4.9 and 4.10 respectively, and are supported by explanatory case studies. The models allow the facilities manager to place the specific contracting-out issue within the overall organisational context; enabling a more holistic and balanced final choice on whether to contract-out or not. Finally, the facilities manager should appreciate that resources should be allocated to the creation of a monitoring and feedback mechanism to ensure that the outcome of the final decision is continually assessed and that any lessons learned as a result can be fed into future contracting-out decision making.

4.6 References

1. *Information Week* (1992) Share of (IT) contracts by country, 22 June, p.42.
2. Association of Facilities Managers (1990) Contracting-out – the P&O way. *AFM Newsletter*, (27), December.

Appendix A: Legal Considerations

Aims

The aim of this short section is to draw to the reader's attention the importance of including legal considerations in the contracting-out decision-making process. However, because of the fluidity of the situation, this section seeks only to point where to look, rather than to speculate on what the answers might be.

The problem area

Two factors combine to make the problem area complicated. First, there is a European Union Directive involved – the Acquired Rights Directive. Second, there is U.K. legislation, principally the Transfer of Undertakings (Protection of Employment Regulations), 1981, (TUPE), amended by the Trade Union Reform and Employment Rights Act, 1993.

At the time of preparing this chapter, the legislation dictating whether TUPE applies to contracting-out is still evolving through test cases and by due consideration by the Council of Ministers. In the meantime, it is left to British courts to resolve matters on a national basis, on the facts of individual cases.

The essence of TUPE

For employers, TUPE specifies their obligations to their staff. It protects employees' rights to security of employment, coupled with rights of compensation, together with rights such as salary, in the event of a Transfer of Undertaking.

The big question is: is contracting-out, or more accurately, *'outsourcing'*, as defined by this chapter, a Transfer of Undertaking? Remember, we have defined outsourcing as:

'the process by which a user employs a separate company (the supplier), under a contract, to perform a function, that had *previously* been carried out in-house, and (especially relevant for TUPE) *transfers* to that supplier assets, including people.'

In one recent case, cleaners at the Orsett Hospital, Basildon, UK were outsourced. The 'transfer of assets' was to a private cleaning company, who subsequently paid the cleaners what it considered to be the market rate. This was below the level of their previous remuneration. It took a High Court decision to resolve that the employees were not covered by TUPE.

If TUPE *had* applied, the cleaners would have been entitled to continuous employment rights, having transferred from the hospital to the cleaning contractor. This would have entitled them to the same terms of employment, including salary, but with the probable exception of their pension entitlements. A change in these rights or dismissal would, if TUPE applied, have enabled the cleaners to claim for unfair dismissal or redundancy payments against their new employer.

So how can a user, and a facilities manager in particular, determine whether outsourcing is a viable option? Because if TUPE applies, prospective suppliers are going to want to protect their interests, and that could easily affect viability. The following are merely listed as *considerations*.

Pointers as to whether TUPE applies

First and foremost, both parties to a transfer (the user and supplier, or transferor and transferee) must carry out a full analysis of the function or 'business' being transferred .

The following ten steps are an indicative list only of the issues which should be examined, and the questions which should be asked:

❑   Determine the type of 'business'.
❑   Are tangible assets to be transferred (e.g. buildings, equipment, etc.)?
❑   What is the value of intangible assets?
❑   Are intangible assets to be transferred (e.g. trade names, intellectual property rights, etc.)?
❑   Are the majority of the 'business's' employees being transferred to the supplier?
❑   Are the 'business's' customers being transferred?
❑   Will the function of the transferred 'business' be recognisably the same after transfer?
❑   Will the transfer include previously made contracts between the user and other contractors?

❑   Are trade debts being transferred?
❑   Are restrictive covenants being transferred?

Nota Bene:

❑   The foregoing list is *not* definitive.
❑   Where the questions can be answered 'Yes', this may only point toward TUPE applying, and *vice versa* for 'No'.

TUPE may be good news

Do, however, note that if TUPE is applicable, that does not necessarily mean that outsourcing is not viable. On the contrary. Consider, for example, those organisations who have recently circumvented TUPE, and subsequently made relevant staff redundant on the last day of the operation of the business under its old guise – often with well-publicised hefty redundancy payments – only to employ the same people the next morning in exactly the same jobs, but working under a different 'badge'. Is this more efficient than following TUPE?

The transfer of support services from Chase Farm Hospital, Enfield, North London, to the facilities management supplier company, Matthew Hall Limited, appears to be running successfully. Matthew Hall Limited accepted the contract for management responsibility of the support services, which were transferred to them, from the trust running the hospital, in 1994. The contract requires an integrated service, including the employment of 65 people, 40 specialist sub-contractors and over 300 specialist supply companies. This is, to date, the largest transfer in the health sector, and yet, precisely followed the requirements of the legislation. It is understood that reduced redundancy payments offset the necessarily higher bid made by the supplier (the transferee) – much of the extra cost being to resource the actual management of the transfer process. Further, by spreading the costs over the four year term of the contract a more efficient cash-flow profile was achieved.

Careful management, particularly man-management, to handle understandable concerns, is essential. If this can be achieved successfully, then the opportunity for added values comes from such factors as the once support staff having a clear career progression structure available, when they become core workers in the supplier company.

If the Chase Farm Hospital outsourcing experience does work, it will prove that the perceived problems associated with TUPE can be addressed successfully; but only if (as advocated in this chapter) a planned approach to facilities management resource decision-making is adopted.

Appendix B: Description of Case Study Organisations

Case Study 1
Description of the organisation

Case Study 1 is a private hospital group operating under a trust registered as a charity. The organisation comprises of 32 acute surgical hospital sites (plus one clinic), located in England and Scotland, divided for administration purposes into four regions of eight hospitals each, plus one day care centre. Each hospital provided a full range of consulting, diagnostic and treatment facilities for both in- and out-patients.

The following briefly sets the scene:

❑ There are 200 hospitals in the private sector. BUPA is the main competitor for Case Study 1 having 30 sites (but approximately 2000 beds to 1300). Five operators control 50% of these hospitals, leaving a large number as one-off enterprises.
❑ Case Study 1 employed approximately 3700 staff in 1992. (3100 whole-time equivalent).
❑ Consumable expenditure in 1991 was approximately £8 million.
❑ Capital expenditure in 1991 was £4.6 million.
❑ Revenue and capital expenditure in 1991 was £6.7 million.
❑ Case Study 1 owns all the buildings they occupied with the exception of a warehouse, workshop and the head office, which are leased.
❑ Typical maintenance spenditure was £11.5 million (1989).
❑ Projected refurbishment and capital expenditure was £7.3 million, plus minor capital works spenditure of £4.2 million.
❑ The capital asset register is approximately £100 million.
❑ Depreciation of buildings – 60 years.
❑ No completely new hospitals had been built for Case Study 1 since 1982.
❑ Because of the number of locations, Case Study 1's assets included: 32 diagnostic departments; 50 X-ray sets, 5 scanners, 70 theatres.

How is the facilities management function organised in Case Study 1?

The facilities management function consists of the following elements:

❑ Capital planning and development, including the acquisition and disposal of land and buildings;
❑ Building maintenance;
❑ Mechanical and electrical maintenance;
❑ Hotel services management;
❑ Utility services negotiations;
❑ Purchasing of specialist systems – nurse call, fire alarm, piped medical gas etc;

❑ Purchasing and maintenance of general hospital furniture and equipment;

❑ Purchasing and maintenance of medical, surgical and diagnostic plant and equipment;

❑ Purchasing of medical and surgical consumable products, including prostheses;

❑ Purchasing and maintenance of office furniture, equipment and stationery;

❑ Purchasing and maintenance of voice and data communication systems and computers.

Facilities management is being viewed as:

'The co-ordinated planning and management of the eleven elements (to) ensure that each of (the) 32 hospitals are designed, equipped and maintained to support hospital staff, who organise and deliver a range of health care services to (the) patients. (Source: Director of Planning and Facilities – internal paper used for training purposes.)'

Case Study 2
Description of the organisation

Case Study 2 is an international firm of accountants, represented in 670 offices located in 110 countries, and employing approximately 70 000 staff worldwide. The core business is the provision of professional accountancy services, including tax consultancy. In the UK there are 27 locations, of which six are in London. The UK staff roll is around 7000, half of which is located in the capital.

For the purposes of this chapter, the research was limited to Case Study 2's London locations.

How is Case Study 2 organised?

Case Study 2 is an accountancy and business management practice, structured within an international holding organisation. The UK operation's legal entity is based on a partnership.

The London presence are housed in a total of 14 buildings, recognised for organisational purposes, as six locations due to interlinking. These six locations are grouped together into two 'campuses' – namely London North and South. The former located in the City, the latter in the City of Westminster on the south bank of the Thames. The locations, within a campus, are all within short walking distance of each other. Total space provided approximated to 400 000 sq. ft., in buildings ranging in age from the late 1960s to early 1980s. All buildings are held on leaseholds.

How is facilities management organised in the London offices of Case Study 2?

Within Case Study 2, facilities management is seen as the grouping together of all support services. In London, this facilities management department is known as Central Support Services, and reports to the UK director of administration, who in turn reports direct to one of three managing partners.

The central support services comprises of 175 staff, of whom approximately 60 are contractors' implants. The annual budget, controlled by the director of administration, amounted to approximately £34m for 1993 (a figure which included allowances for building rents, rates and service charges).

Catering services in London reports to the client services manager, who in turn reports to the general services manager.

Chapter 5
Computer-based Information Systems

5.1 Introduction

5.1.1 Scope of the chapter

This chapter will examine the use of computer-based information systems (CIS) in support of the facilities management function within organisations. It is *not* about the management or installation of information technology (IT) facilities within an organisation. There will be nothing, for example, on cable management or the design of workstations. At present many facilities managers have problems surmounting the considerable difficulties associated with generating effective and efficient CISs. These problems are generally brought about by both a lack of proper understanding of how IT can support facilities management activities and by the adoption of a haphazard and fragmented approach to CIS development. These deficiencies will be addressed in this chapter; discussing the importance of developing and using a CIS which combines organisational, human and technological considerations and resources to stimulate and support effective facilities management.

Furthermore, the chapter is geared towards the premise that the facilities manager is generally a *user* of CIS, rather than a specialised developer. The chapter aims, therefore, to provide the facilities manager primarily with a business perspective of information systems and IT, although it is hoped that there will be sufficient technical detail to allow the facilities manager to meaningfully communicate with specialists (such as computer analysts and programmers) when required.

5.1.2 Summary of the different sections

This chapter is designed to be used in a number of different ways. It offers both a general discussion of the use of CISs in facilities management and specific advice on developing CISs. It is divided into four sections. Following the introduction; the second section will be of use to those readers who are interested in the general role of information in facilities management. The third section will be of use to those facilities managers who want advice on how to develop an information system. The final section will present a case study which illustrates many of the ideas and issues raised in the first two sections. These three sections are summarised below.

❏ Section 5.2 – This sets out the need for facilities managers to appreciate that if the enormous potential benefits of IT are to be realised, then it should be firmly anchored to, and integrated with, an information system. The importance of a decision-making orientation to the CIS is discussed, with particular emphasis being placed on the need for the system to be sensitive to the information requirements of the different types of decision the facilities manager makes.

❏ Section 5.3 – This presents a CIS design methodology which incorporates organisational, technological and people-related variables into a life cycle design process of system definition and outline, system development, system implementation and system maintenance. The reliance which facilities managers place on off-the-shelf application software packages is indicated. However, it is emphasised that even though an off-the-shelf application software package may be being used, the facilities manager should still rigorously pursue all stages of the design process.

❏ Section 5.4 – This presents a case study which describes an approach which was used to evaluate prospective computer aided facilities management (CAFM) application software packages. It is argued that the technique articulated should not be slavishly pursued by readers as *the* model of good practice. Indeed, it is argued within the case study that improvements can be made. However, it is stressed that the case study provides a useful vehicle to bring to life some of the concepts and mechanism described earlier in the chapter; and to stimulate the reader in constructing for himself a software evaluation technique which is more suited to his particular needs.

5.2 Information, Information Technology and Information Systems in Facilities Management

5.2.1 Computer-based information systems: what are they and why are they important?

Computer-based information systems (CIS) combine organisational, human and information technology-based resources to generate the effective and efficient collection, storage, retrieval, communication and use of information. Good quality systems provide appropriate, accurate and timely information which can pull together a potentially disparate facilities management function into an integrated and organised one which is explicitly geared towards strategic corporate objectives. This will promote and enable:

❑ more efficient use of information at all managerial levels;
❑ improved decision making;
❑ improved managerial responsiveness;
❑ improved learning capacity and capability.

These benefits will ultimately enhance both the quality and cost-effectiveness of the service provided by the facilities management function. This is of particular importance, of course, if the facilities management function is to elevate itself from a perceived 'overhead' to a valuable internal generator of sustainable competitive advantage for the organisation as a whole.

5.2.2 Information technology: what is its relationship with information systems?

Information systems and IT are not synonymous. This misconception is arguably one of the major reasons why the often considerable investment in both information systems and IT is wasted. For example, a partner of a commercial property management firm remarked that most of the firm's investment in IT over the previous ten years had completely failed to achieve the anticipated benefits, primarily because systems had been bought on the strength of their technical specifications rather than on the ability to support an information system which satisfied organisational needs. This poor track record made the firm myopically wary of introducing further new IT to the point where they are now considerably behind their competitors in the effective and efficient use of IT. Indeed, the partners are now diverting considerable resources into a more well thought out IT programme in an effort to avert commercial failure.

Facilities managers should view information systems as being directed towards the design of optimal *information frameworks* within the facilities management function in order to maximise the effectiveness and efficiency of the decision-making process. IT, in contrast, should generally be considered as subordinate to the information system in as much as it is concerned with the effective use of *technological tools* to facilitate and support the operation of the information system. This generalisation tends to neglect the mutually crafting interaction between the two; with IT not only serving CIS and supporting business operations, but at the same time having the potential to create new ways of carrying out organisational activities. It is the latter interaction which, if correctly managed, can lead to sustainable performance advantage within the facilities element of an organisation's value chain. However, the generalisation does provide a fruitful platform from which to understand and develop a facilities management CIS.

5.2.3 Information technology: how has it been applied to the facilities management function?

The facilities manager is being confronted with an increasingly bewildering array of information technologies and applications which can potentially support him in his role. For example, there are software packages which can support accommodation planning, heating and ventilation, asset tracking and capital project management. The somewhat debilitating complexity of IT can be reduced by viewing all information technologies as consisting of one or more of the following basic information handling capabilities: information *capture*, information *storage*, information *manipulation* and information *distribution*. Computer-aided design (CAD), for example, allows the facilities manager to capture, store, manipulate and distribute drawings and related information. This facility is particularly useful as it allows the facilities manager to maintain and standardise a complete set of plans for the organisation's building stock. Furthermore, many CAD systems can be linked to databases, allowing, for instance, an item of furniture in a drawing to be related to a description in a database giving size, specification, cost and so on. Most CAFM systems are in essence a CAD system linked with a database and combined with a set of functions to carry out various standard tasks, such as space planning and stock control.

To reiterate however, the introduction of such IT does not equate to the introduction of a high quality information system. The use of information technologies without the overarching direction of an information system, more often than not, leads to the generation of voluminous, poorly focused and irrelevant information. This situation is not only expensive in terms of the IT resources, but it also tends to significantly reduce the effectiveness of the decision making process through managers either basing their decisions on the wrong information, or not being able 'to see the wood for the trees' as they become overloaded with information. The creation of excess information in this way is a good reminder of the need to evaluate an information system on the basis of a cost-benefit analysis. The facilities manager needs to ensure that a balance is maintained between the capital and running costs of the information system and the value of the information generated. For example, the facilities manager should evaluate proposed information systems on the basis of a business investment, as well as making sure that the full benefit (financial return) is being gained from the systems already in operation.

It is suggested that a useful way of focusing information systems, and the IT that serve them, is to orientate them towards the facilities manager's decision-making processes. For this objective to be achieved, the information system should be sensitive not only to the facilities manager's responsibilities but to all organisational elements which have an indirect or direct impact upon the performance of the facilities management function. An integrated information system of this nature, which covers the totality of operations, helps the facilities manager to clearly see his place in the organisation and recognise the interdependence between the facilities management function and all the other aspects of an organisation. For this integration to be realised, the facilities manager should develop information systems and IT which appreciate the differing types of decision-making processes, and their associated information requirements. The generic model and six interactions at the end of Chapter 1 provide a useful mechanism to achieve this.

5.2.4 *The organisational context of information: what type of information is required by the facilities manager?*

Information systems, to reiterate, should be able to accommodate the varied types of decision that the facilities manager has to make. The nature of the decision is very much dependent upon what decision-making layer the facilities manager is engaged in: strategic, management or operational. The strategic layer can be viewed as consisting of a set of interrelated *objective-orientated* decisions that identify the facilities management function's future service offerings, as well as establishing strategic checkpoints to evaluate the facilities management function's progress toward the accomplishment of the given strategy. The operational layer relates to the *task-orientated* decisions that will be needed to execute the strategic plans. The managerial layer in between consists of *responsibility-orientated* decisions which support and remove obstacles from the paths of the other two systems, linking the strategic and management layers effectively and efficiently to ensure that actual outcomes conform to strategically intended outcomes. Taken together these three systems form a logical set of decisions for guiding and controlling the work of all facilities management functions.

This representation of the facilities manager's role readily identifies differing information needs depending on where the decision falls along the strategic – operational decision type continuum. The reader is referred to Chapter 7 on decision making for a comprehensive discussion of the characteristics of managerial decisions, along with a diagnostic checklist which may be used in any given problem situation (see Table 7.2). The importance of designing an effective information filtering mechanism is indicated in Chapter 1 on managing the steady state which warned of the danger of functional units supplying unprocessed information to facilities managers to the extent that they become bogged down in the sorting out of *operational* problems at the expense of dealing with more important *strategic* problems. Furthermore, it is argued that in order to prevent such an information processing problem occurring, methods for handling information should be introduced whereby the functional units only refer major *exceptions* to the facilities manager. This is an important issue if facilities managers are to generate a holistic perspective integrating both the strategic and operational aspects of their activities. It is proposed that before any meaningful CIS of this sort can be developed, it is imperative that the facilities manager can categorise issues into operational and strategic decision types.

It is interesting to note that most attempts at the development of IT in facilities management to date have taken place primarily at the operational level e.g. computer systems for asset tracking or maintenance management. Much less has been done at a strategic level. However, if the model suggested here is correct, then the long-term effectiveness of facilities management will depend upon the effective use of IT at a strategic level.

5.2.5 Computer-based information systems: how can they be developed?

It has been argued that the successful development and implementation of a decision making orientated CIS is central to the effectiveness of the facilities management function. The realisation of this vision into reality is plagued with organisational, technological and people-related difficulties. For example, the adage 'information is power' is particularly relevant with information systems, as their creation or modification can substantially change power structures within organisations. This change is often resisted strongly by politically orientated organisational members or functions who want to protect their information generation/processing, hence power, position. Such obstacles can be overcome if the facilities manager explicitly considers the organisational, technological and human elements within all aspects of the information system design, development and implementation. This multiple-perspective life-cycle approach can be a very fruitful mechanism which the facilities manager can employ, and is the subject of the next section.

5.3 The Development of Computer-based Information Systems

5.3.1 Introduction

It has been suggested that organisational, human and technological design variables be integrated into the CIS design process. This methodology is illustrated in Figure 5.1. The facilities manager should appreciate that the design process is not rigidly linear, and that there probably will always be loops backwards and forwards throughout any given system development. For example, if the system specification indicates that the system will be too expensive, the design process may return to the start and redefine the system objectives so that they are not so ambitious. The methodology is useful because of its flexibility in providing a prescription for the development of a complete organisational or functional information system, right down to the purchase of a single application software package. The remainder of the section will discuss this methodology at a single project level in response to the findings that this aspect is of particular use to the practising facilities manager.

The reader may appreciate the similarities of these system design process stages with the basic model of the problem solving process in Chapter 7 on decision making (see Figure 7.1). This similarity exists because, at its fundamental level, the CIS development life cycle is based on, and motivated by, the need to ensure that the IT solution adequately satisfies an accurately identified problem situation.

The design process	Design variables		
	Organisation (roles, relationships)	**People** (needs and positive expectations)	**Technology** (acceptable man/machine interface)
↓	↓ ↔	↓ ↔	↓
Stage 1: System definition and outline ❏ Analyse current information system ❏ Define new information system requirements	Set clear, precise, organisational, human and technical goals for the new information system		
↓	↓ ↔	↓ ↔	↓
Stage 2: System development ❏ Design new information system ❏ Develop new information system	The identification and development of a new system which will satisfy the formulated objectives		
↓	↓ ↔	↓ ↔	↓
Stage 3: System implementation ❏ Implement new information system	Strategies for implementation		
↓	↓ ↔	↓ ↔	↓
Stage 4: System maintenance and learning ❏ Evaluation and continuous improvement	The integration of the organisation, human and technical elements of the new information system to achieve high effectiveness and efficiency		

Figure 5.1   Computer-based information system design methodology.

5.3.2   *The project team*

Before proceeding with a brief discussion of these stages, it is important to establish who should manage the overall project. The *project management* should preferably be carried out by a team which consists of three groups of personnel: representatives of the facilities management staff (users), representatives of senior facilities management and (where applicable) information systems management (management), and technical staff (information technology specialists). It should be noted that outside consultants are increasingly taking the place of the information systems and IT specialists. If outside consultants are to be used the facilities manager should address the following areas to make sure that he gets the best out of them:

❏ *Commitment* – There must be firm and sustained commitment from senior facilities management for the proposed project.
❏ *Understanding* – The facilities management should have sufficient knowledge of the project in hand to be able to fully benefit from the consultants' advice.
❏ *Expectation* – The facilities management should have realistic expectations about the services the consultants can offer.
❏ *Preparation* – The facilities management should prepare thoroughly for the consultants in advance with, say, information on their working environment and reporting systems.
❏ *Integration* – It is important that the facilities management ensures that the consultants' efforts are integrated with those of permanent staff by making sure the permanent staff know what the consultants' role is and why they have been brought in.
❏ *Ownership* – It is important that the facilities management takes ownership of the consultants' efforts in order for the solutions to be accepted by the staff. The reader should be aware of the crucial importance of ensuring that the 'client' has ownership of the project, and is referred to Chapter 6 on managing people through change.

5.3.3 Stage 1: System definition and outline

The system outline stage concerns itself with the definition of the problem which the proposed system must satisfy, along with a broad outline of the proposed solution. This stage is the most important phase of the design process as, of course, it is imperative that the project management team knows what it is trying to achieve. This intuitively obvious prerequisite to the creation of a new information system is nonetheless frequently forgotten.

The first issue the project management team should consider and appreciate is the organisational context of introducing a new system. If the facilities management function is to benefit from the proposed new system, it is essential from the outset to realise that the benefit is not achieved simply by investing in computers. Explicit consideration, for example, has to be given throughout the design process to the likely reaction of people to changes in work practices and organisational culture. Furthermore, it is important from the inception of the project to make sure that the design process is carefully linked to both organisational and functional strategic objectives, as well as complying with the organisation's information technology strategy.

With these considerations in mind, the project management team should instigate a comprehensive analysis of the current information system. The aim of this phase of the design process is to gain a clear and holistic understanding of the existing system, establishing the system's goals and processes, as well as identifying strengths and weaknesses and exploring potential improvements. It is important that the facilities manager appreciates the importance of carrying out such an analysis regardless of whether it is manual or computer-based. For example, an organisation made an investigation of the facilities management information system within an old office building, with the initial intention of introducing a CAFM system. However, the investigation informed the facilities manager that in actual fact the existing paper-based system was perfectly adequate, and was in harmony with the expectations of the organisation and it was able to perform tasks appropriate to the degree of complexity of the facilities. This example indicates the importance of not automatically installing CISs when there is no clear advantage in doing so. If paper systems work then use them. If computers can support the paper system or replace it in part, then all well and good, but it is important to consider all the possibilities and evaluate the advantages and disadvantages.

Although the analysis task is usually carried out by a systems analyst, the facilities manager should keep in mind that, although systems analysts may be experts about IT systems, they are not necessarily knowledgeable about the many tasks carried out by the facilities management function. It is the facilities manager's responsibility to clearly explain the existing system to the systems analyst. Indeed, the facilities manager's knowledge may be essential in predicting the ramifications of the CIS in the new work roles which may be defined by it.

From this understanding of the existing system, the facilities manager, working closely with the systems analyst, should define the requirements that the new system must satisfy. As discussed earlier, it is important to carefully link system requirements to higher-order corporate or functional requirements. Once the systems requirements have been established, then both manual and computer-based alternatives should be generated and evaluated for their feasibility. The facilities manager should consider the following three tests of feasibility:

❑ *Technical* – Are manual systems adequate? Is existing hardware adequate? Can the needed software be obtained or developed?
❑ *Economic* – Will the economic benefits outweigh the costs of the new information system?
❑ *Operational* – Will the management and the workforce implement the system successfully?

Stage 1 concludes with the analyst's preparation of a systems requirements report and a presentation to the project management team. The report provides the basis for the final determination of the completeness and accuracy of the new information system requirements, as well as the technological, economic and operational feasibility of the new information system. After the project management team has reviewed and discussed the report, a final decision should be made as to whether to proceed and, if so, which alternatives to adopt. Table 5.1 indicates a possible format for this report.

5.3.4 *Stage 2: System development*

The process

The second stage traditionally concerns itself with the bespoke design and development of the application software based on the system requirements generated in Stage 1, along with the associated specification and (if applicable) acquisition of hardware. This phase is usually the domain of computer specialists, such as software analysts and programmers. However, it has been observed that this approach is of limited use to facilities managers who, especially in small-to-medium sized organisations, generally purchase 'off-the-shelf' packages, albeit sometimes in a customised form. The purchase of 'ready-made' packages does eliminate, to a great extent, the programming element of this stage; however, the need to generate accurate system specifications from the system requirements is still extremely important. Indeed the facilities manager, with the inherent compromises which must be made when using systems which have not been tailor-made for a specific need, should be extra vigilant in ensuring the best fit between system specifications and the application software package specifications through careful software evaluation.

The system design phase involves the operationalisation of the system requirements into a system specification which describes:

❑   a complete overview of the new information system;
❑   the major processing modules within the system (see Table 5.2 for a sample of modules required for a computer-aided facilities management package);
❑   the input, processing and output activities in each module;
❑   the storage requirements for the new information system;
❑   the application controls to be employed within the system to protect the system and data from damage, from input and output inaccuracies and from access by unauthorised persons.

Once these issues have been addressed the project management team is then in a position to instigate the acquisition of the application software, systems software and hardware. Ideally, the application software should be chosen first, and then compatible hardware and systems software selected around the application software in order for it to run efficiently and for the system to be more flexible to changing system requirements. To be realistic, however, the project management team will have to work within existing organisational IT standards, as well as with existing hardware. These constraints reduce the acquisition phase to one of compatibility and compromise, rather than optimisation. This, of course, is organisational reality and should not only be accepted, but be viewed as an opportunity to create information system benefits through integration with existing systems.

Table 5.1 Full system proposal format

(1) Title page
❑ report title and reference
❑ author and department
❑ date of publication
❑ distribution list
	(7) System requirements
	❑ outline
	❑ comparison of alternatives and reasons for rejection
	❑ managerial implications
	  – reorganisation
	  – computer facilities required
	  – supporting services required
	  – training
	  – accommodation
	  – staffing
	  – security and audit
	  – operating schedule

(2) Contents list	**(8) Development and implementation plans**
(3) Summary ❑ objectives and proposals ❑ costs ❑ benefits	**(9) Costs** ❑ to date ❑ to continue proposal ❑ operating costs

(4) Recommendations
❑ management decisions required
❑ draft terms of reference for further work
	(10) Benefits
	❑ tangible
	  – direct (staff, equipment, space etc.)
	  – indirect (better resource utilisation etc.)
	❑ intangible
	  – information (quality etc.)
	  – control

(5) Scope of study ❑ background ❑ terms of reference ❑ objectives of the study ❑ objectives to be met by the proposal ❑ security and audit considerations ❑ time and cost constraints	**(11) Appendices**
(6) Existing system ❑ the system under investigation ❑ description of system ❑ problem areas	**(12) Glossary of terms**

The discussion so far is indicating that there is no golden formula for acquiring software and hardware. Indeed, the 'formula' is dynamically dependent on ever changing organisational strategies, structures and processes, in addition to facilities management activities which are constantly evolving to new demands. This being said, much of the uncertainty should have been ironed out during the system requirements and system specifications phases. Furthermore, there are well established generic considerations which generate 'good practice' when acquiring software and hardware. The lists below aim to identify the main considerations which the project team should address. Suffice to say, they are not exhaustive; indeed, they are meant to stimulate a process of enquiry which can be tailor-made to a given information system project, rather than be a rigid checklist. In addition, many of the points raised in the system definition and outline stage will be summarised and included in the lists in order in provide the reader with a complete picture of the information system design process up to this point.

Key software considerations

- ☐ *Organisational change*: The facilities manager should be aware that with the current rate of change in the organisation's environment, that the requirements defined however comprehensive, may need revision. Therefore the software should be flexible enough to accommodate constantly changing demands. For example, will the software have to accommodate a transition from single to multi-users?
- ☐ *Technological change*: The facilities manager should appreciate that with the current rate of technological change, that hardware and software selected should be new enough to take advantage of technological breakthroughs whilst being old enough to be compatible to an existing industrial standard. The hardware/software is then less unlikely to be withdrawn (leaving no support or upgrades) or subjected to high cost support/upgrades as a consequence of manufacturers locking users into the technology. Furthermore, leading edge software will require increased training overheads for the staff
- ☐ *Define constraints*: The facilities manager should identify organisational (for example, cost constraints) technological (for example, hardware and operating system requirements) and people-related restraints (for example, human resource implications).
- ☐ *Completeness*: The facilities manager should recognise that some software systems come as a complete package while others come in modules.
- ☐ *User preferences*: The facilities manager should identify user needs. For example, are the users experienced perhaps, preferring command-driven software; or are they inexperienced, preferring menu driven software? Wherever possible and appropriate, the facilities manager should involve the users in the choice of software.
- ☐ *Functionality*: The facilities manager should make sure the software package offers the features and capabilities required.
- ☐ *System compatibility*: The facilities manager should check whether the proposed software package will be able to talk to other relevant systems within the organisation. This is of particular importance, as the nature of facilities management requires access and integration of data from a wide variety of sources throughout an organisation; for example, architect's drawings, personnel files and maintenance records. In addition, is the application software compatible with industry standards?

❑   *System suppliers*: The facilities manager should take his time with suppliers in order to establish a mutual understanding of what is required and to generate a good working relationship. For example, it is important to get a good demonstration of their systems, covering the facilities manager's concerns rather than the supplier's standard 'stage show'.

❑   *Support*: The facilities manager should make sure that the software is fully supported. For example, what kind of documentation and training is provided? What kind of warranty is offered?

❑   *Realism*: The facilities manager should appreciate that software, especially off-the-shelf packages, will not satisfy all the system requirements and that compromises will have to be made.

❑   *Operating systems*: The facilities manager should ensure that the operating system is compatible with industrial and organisational standards, the application software and the hardware. In addition, the availability of trained technical support personnel and manufacturer's hotline support should be available to assist in the solution of hardware and software problems.

❑   *Hardware*: The facilities manager should make sure that the software is suitable for existing hardware and/or new hardware.

Key hardware considerations

❑   *Future growth*: The facilities manager should anticipate future requirements. For example, the facilities manager should consider how many users the system will need to support now and for the next three to five years, and if any networks are required.

❑   *Compatibility*: The facilities manager should make sure that if existing hardware is being used along side new hardware, that they are compatible.

❑   *Operating system*: The facilities manager should determine the type of operating system required to ensure software compatibility and efficiency.

❑   *Memory*: The facilities manager should determine how much main memory (RAM) is required by finding out the minimum amount of memory to satisfy the process requirements of the proposed software applications.

❑   *System size*: The facilities manager should determine the required system size by establishing the software storage requirements.

❑   *Data output*: The facilities manager should determine the types of printers/plotters required by establishing the quality, volume and type of printed output to be produced.

❑   *Location*: The facilities manager should determine where the hardware is to be installed.

Lease, rent or purchase?

Another major consideration for the project team is whether to lease, rent or purchase the system components. Again, the decision may be dictated by organisational policy or budgetary constraints. Nonetheless, it is useful to consider the strengths and weaknesses (shown in the lists below) of each approach, as it provides a fruitful mechanism to assist in identifying the capital and running costs of a system.

Renting
Strengths:

❑ The equipment can be tested to find out whether it is appropriate and whether it improves facilities management services and 'profitability' without an expensive capital outlay.
❑ Suppliers will usually allow equipment to be exchanged when system requirements change.
❑ Renting requires the smallest up-front capital outlay.
❑ Short-term rental contracts avoids equipment obsolescence.
❑ Maintenance of rented equipment is usually supplied by the vendor.

Weaknesses:

❑ Renting is usually the most expensive option over the installed period.
❑ The tax benefits are not as good as leased or purchased equipment.
❑ Locked into the maintenance costs of the vendor.

Leasing
Strengths:

❑ Leasing is an alternative way of financing a computer system. Most lease contracts specify a purchase option when the lease expires.
❑ Leasing generally provides favourable tax advantages.

Weaknesses:

❑ It is more expensive to lease than to purchase outright.
❑ Leasing usually comes with a costly service contract.
❑ Price is usually harder to negotiate when leasing.
❑ The supplier usually does not provide support.

Purchasing
Strengths:

❑ Purchasing is usually the least expensive way to acquire a computer system.
❑ Well managed and serviced equipment will last a long time and can provide a growing organisation with additional data-processing capacity over time, as new equipment is brought in.
❑ The purchaser accrues all tax advantages.

Weaknesses:

❑ Support and maintenance for the equipment must be provided by the purchaser.
❑ The purchaser may get locked into equipment that is incompatible with future industry standards.
❑ The equipment can become technologically obsolete.
❑ Purchase usually requires the largest amount of capital outlay up-front.
❑ Computers have low re-sale values.

An example of an innovative solution to the rent-lease-buy conundrum was displayed by a general practice surveying firm. The firm had recently won a residential property management contract, which constituted a considerable move away from its traditional market of commercial property management. The contract required the firm to administer the service charge collection, as well as recording and monitoring expenditures. Owing to the large size of the residential complex, it was quickly identified that a manual information system was inadequate, and that a CIS was required. This decision necessitated the firm in acquiring new application software, as the firm's existing information systems were set up for incompatible commercial property management requirements. The precise system requirements were not readily identifiable, as the firm had no previous experience of the activities and information flows involved, and this knowledge would only be accrued through experience. This situation was viewed as a 'what came first, the chicken or the egg' dilemma, and certainly not the basis for making substantial outlays on new application software and perhaps associated operating systems software and hardware. Furthermore, the firm identified the residential management sector as a growth market for it, and wanted a system which had the flexibility and capacity to expand.

The firm's novel response to this problem was to approach a housing association which had an appropriate information system which was being under utilised. The housing association agreed to rent out some of the systems capacity and associated human resources. This solution is seen by the firm as only being short-term in nature, but allows it sufficient time to properly define its information system requirements and specifications before purchasing an off-the-shelf application software package.

5.3.5 Stage 3: System implementation

The implementation stage, unless properly carried out, can render an otherwise satisfactory system useless. The reader is referred to Chapter 6 on managing people through change for advice on how to manage the change process which is intrinsic to the introduction of a new CIS. It is important that the facilities manager prepares carefully for the implementation stage, with all aspects of the implementation planned and all operational documentation produced in advance. The implementation itself should then simply become the execution of these plans. Planning for the implementation stage should be explicit throughout the design process, and should consider the following issues:

(1) The preparation of physical plan layouts, with consideration of the following points:

- ❏ Determine who will be responsible for physical facilities planning.
- ❏ Determine how long it will take to create a physical facilities plan.
- ❏ Create a physical layout chart that specifies where all equipment and cabling will be located.
- ❏ Determine how long it will take to make site modifications.
- ❏ Make necessary floor plan modifications.
- ❏ Route all cabling safely.
- ❏ Run correct power to all computer equipment.
- ❏ Evaluate environmental factors, such as heat, air conditioning, humidity control, dust collection, lighting and sound proofing.
- ❏ Evaluate ergonomic factors, such as monitor and keyboard height and sources of glare.
- ❏ Consider access and security vision.
- ❏ Evaluate outside contractors, if necessary.
- ❏ Determine how the system will physically be moved to the desired installation site.
- ❏ Install appropriate fire protection and safety devices.

(2) The preparation of an implementation plan which all parties are happy with.
(3) The ordering of required software and hardware.
(4) The ordering of required communication lines and installations.
(5) The ordering of all required stationery and consumables.
(6) The notification of all users affected by the implementation.
(7) The determination of user training objectives.
(8) Determination of who needs to be trained.
(9) Determination of training method.
(10) Determination of implementation support requirements.

There are four basic approaches to implementing a new CIS: direct implementation, parallel implementation, phased implementation and pilot implementation. The particular characteristics of each approach are described below:

- ❏ *Direct implementation*. With this approach the change is made all at once. The old system is halted on a planned date and the new system is activated. This approach is particularly suitable for small systems. Simply halting the old system and starting up the new system carries both technical and people-related risks.

❑ *Parallel implementation*. This approach involves running the old system and the new system simultaneously for a specified period. This approach is the safest because operations do not have to be shut down if the new system has problems; however, it is by far the most expensive and difficult approach to co-ordinate.

❑ *Phased implementation*. This approach implements a new system in incremental steps to both accommodate technical problems and to avoid the traumatic effect on users of introducing a new system all at once.

❑ *Pilot implementation*. This approach involves implementing a new system in one location after another. This is useful in facilities management functions dispersed over a number of sites – especially as it enables any problems within the system to be ironed out before it is implemented on subsequent sites.

5.3.6 Stage 4: System maintenance and learning

This stage is often neglected, with a combination of inadequate resources being allocated and the habit of senior management walking away from the project, thinking that their task has been completed once a system is in place. The implications of these practices are twofold; firstly, the system in place will probably not run as effectively and efficiently as it could; and, secondly, the project management team will miss the chance to learn from the project, and to incorporate these lessons into future projects. The project team, therefore, should appreciate the importance of the system maintenance and learning stage, and pledge both commitment and resources to a post-implementation evaluation and maintenance program.

Post-implementation evaluation is a formal evaluation process that determines whether the new system is meeting its objectives or that system changes have been completed so that it will. The process is similar in rationale to the user needs evaluation process outlined in Chapter 3. This evaluation procedure culminates in the preparation of a new systems evaluation report. The report summarises the extent to which the system meets the original objectives and includes a list of enhancements to be considered for future development and implementation. Furthermore, the report should include an evaluation of the entire design process, identifying any strengths and weaknesses and making recommendations of modifications which can be made to the design process for other projects.

Systems maintenance refers to the ongoing adjustment of the system to cope with changing information needs, as well as modifications to support and training policies if needed and the rectifying of any technical bugs which emerge. The existence of this stage highlights that optimum systems are not static but evolve with time, as frequent usage identifies further improvements within the system. However, organisational and technological change will eventually render the system obsolete, triggering a need for a change in the system itself. This brings the CIS design methodology full circle as system definition and outline is instigated again.

Case Study: Computer-aided facilities management – a technique for system selection

Introduction

It has been argued that the successful use of IT is very much dependent upon explicit and careful consideration of organisational, technological and people-related variables within a life-cycle design process. This case study, in keeping with the scope of this book indicated in section 5.1, will examine the system selection technique which was used by a health authority to identify a suitable CAFM system for a large hospital undergoing major refurbishment. The implementation and maintenance stages will only be discussed briefly. The case study provides a useful vehicle for bringing together many of the ideas contained within the previous three sections.

Project management team

A project management team was set up which consisted of representatives from both the health authority and from an external firm of consultants. The consultants were brought in for their expertise in facilities management in general and CISs in particular. The consultants were instructed to assist in the identification and installation of a facilities management system which satisfied the specification of the client in terms of flexibility, economy and ease of use. The main aim of the consultants was to provide a professional service which would satisfy the facilities management requirements of the client (both now and in the future) in an efficient and cost effective manner.

System definition and outline

The project management team quickly determined that owing to the nature of the core business, as well as the complexity and size of the hospital, a CIS was essential (as opposed to paper-based systems). Furthermore, it was identified that the central task facing the project management team was the selection of a suitable CAFM package. Comprehensive and wide-ranging discussions between client representatives and the consultants, focusing on facilities management activities as well as the nature of the organisational and functional decision making processes, enabled the formulation of detailed system requirements. The project management team appreciated the need for the analysis to be guided by, and integrated with, the corporate policy. Indeed the corporate policy, which had evolved in a bureaucratic and fragmented fashion over time, was the source of considerable organisational and technological constraints. For example, the health authority used a wide range of software, hardware and operating systems throughout their numerous sites. This situation meant that there were possible integration problems with, for example, required operating systems being incompatible with existing hardware and software. With such considerations embodied within the analysis, the stage culminated in a set of requirements which centred around an extensive range of pre-programmed modules, a sample of which is presented in Table 5.2.

Table 5.2   CAFM software modules required

Module	Applications	Module	Applications
Space management	❏ Equipment ❏ Furniture ❏ Area values	*Emergency maintenance*	❏ Plan jobs ❏ Print dockets ❏ Track jobs ❏ Job history
Project management	❏ Planning ❏ Scheduling	*Spares management*	❏ Stock inventory ❏ Stock control ❏ Purchase requisitions
Asset management	❏ Asset register	*Resource planning*	❏ Equipment ❏ Craft ❏ Labour ❏ Management
Preventative maintenance	❏ Plan jobs ❏ Print dockets ❏ Track jobs ❏ Job history ❏ Monitor condition ❏ Monitor defects ❏ Failure analysis ❏ Trade contractors ❏ Manage budget	*Additional services*	❏ Consultations ❏ Training ❏ Support ❏ Maintenance

In addition, the project management team considered it essential from the outset that the consultants tightly monitored and controlled project costs. To achieve this requirement, the consultant set up a spreadsheet system which recorded estimates/quotes, purchase orders and invoices. The aim of this system was to monitor total expenditure, changes of item cost with time, and variations in costs of items ordered and the cost of supplying substitute goods.

System development

Once the system definition and outline had been completed, the task of generating a system specification (for both software and associated supporting hardware) was undertaken. The final system specification determined that the CAFM software package should:

❏ be written in a portable programming language (e.g. 'C') so that the software was not hardware dependent;

❏ contain a relational database written in a flexible language (e.g. a structured query language) to enable ease of cross-referencing and extraction of data;

❏ contain all the necessary modules and be sufficiently flexible to accommodate (anticipated) future needs;

❏ be easy to use with clear, understandable screen displays;

❏ be readily used by computer non-experts;

❑   support single data entry and hence the data of all modules to be inter-related; and,
❑   possess a menu driven CAD package which would engender ease of interrogation for non-CAD trained operators.

In addition the package should contain a:

❑   flexible report generator with user defined formats;
❑   flexible statistical graphics module;
❑   form of desk top publishing;
❑   bi-directional data interface between the CAD system and the database.

Once the specification had been established, a five stage 'sifting-out' selection process was carried out within which relevant data was collected and analysed against the specification in order to identify the optimum package. The five stages of the selection routine are detailed in Table 5.3.

The five-stage routine used a spreadsheet analytical technique to award points for successfully satisfying system specification parameters and requirements. Table 5.4 gives a sample of some of the parameters investigated and the specific aspects that were considered.

Table 5.3   Five stage software evalution process

Stage	Stage activities	Stage output
1	Data concerning software packages was obtained from various sources. For example literature surveys, company advertisements, lectures, seminars, general information and word of mouth.	A list of some 40 software packages.
2	Telephone conversations and interviews with the various companies were carried out to collect more project-specific information.	General quotes and cost estimates.
3	Company visits and demonstrations were carried out with the top eight companies. These visits assisted in evaluating the companies further. For example, in the elucidation of company policy towards general software development and the aspects of current and proposed research and development.	Detailed quotes and cost estimates.
4	Demonstrations at operational sites to the consultancy team – to observe the package in the industrial/business environment and witness the ease of use, problems, benefits etc. by 'real' operators.	A full report for the client including the final 'short list' of packages.
5	Client demonstrations of three top packages at operational sites. This stage enabled the client to observe the software package operating in a working environment.	The selected software package.

A score was awarded to each aspect according to usefulness, availability and compliance with the specification. The scoring system applied was simple. Generally, if a package had a facility it scored a '1'; otherwise it scored a '0'. Some aspects had weighted scores. For example, if the language in which the package was written was highly portable it scored '3'. Table 5.5 illustrates the scoring system.

At each stage the freshly acquired data is analysed and the accrued score is re-assessed. Summation of the aspect scores then indicated the suitability of each package. The resulting ranking enabled the formulation of a shortened list by discarding the least suitable systems. From this shortlist the final software package was chosen. The final spreadsheet format and content is indicated in Table 5.6.

Table 5.4   Software evaluation parameters

Parameter	Aspects
Type of company	Engineering, QS, M&E or dealership
Previous experience (in years)	Manual FM CAFM Health authority applications
Operating system	MS DOS MS Windows Xenix Unix etc.
General details	Program language Database language Screen display
System enhancements	CAD-based CAD link – graphic images only CAD link – data link Report generator + user-defined formats Statistical graphics – on board Statistical graphics link to external package Import/export of data Bar code link BMS link

System implementation

In addition to CAFM system selection, the consultancy team were contracted to take responsibility for the implementation and initial running of the system until the operational experience of the client was adequate for them to be independent. The project management team realised the importance of successful installation, not only in terms of physical installation, but also the management of the system installation organisational and people-related implications.

Table 5.5 Scoring process to assess system parameters

Is the package written in a portable programme language?			
High portability	3	*Moderate portability*	2
Used on a range of computers or computer systems with little or no programme modification. For example, it could easily be moved from an IBM PC to a 'Mac' or from a Microsoft DOS environment to a Unix system.		The package could be used on a range of computer systems but would require considerable programming modification – possibly expensive + time consuming.	
Low portability	1		
A package in this language may only be usable on a specific type of computer. High financial and time penalties to translate.			

Table 5.6 Final software selection spreadsheet presentation

Software package	Operating system DOS	Operating system UNIX	Can be net-worked	CAD based	Report generator	Etc.	Grand total
A	1	1	1	3	1	*	19
B	0	1	1	2	1	*	13
C	0	0	1	1	0	*	4

System maintenance and learning

The consultants appreciated the importance of ongoing support and maintenance for the installed system. After the initial training and support exercise was completed, a support infrastructure was used to assist users in solving many of the 'teething' problems. This support allowed the users to solve any problems quickly, freeing them to perform their role. Maintenance arrangements were set up to cover hardware breakdowns and software upgrades, as well as user support.

Conclusion

The software selection technique proved to be a useful mechanism for linking software package characteristics with organisational needs. In particular, it provided a structure to the software evaluation process which, as is discussed in Chapter 7 on decision making techniques, is essential if facilities managers are to come up with well balanced and successful, in this case, CIS solutions. Suffice to say, improvements can be made to the process. For example, it could be argued that the technique is somewhat technology-orientated, and could do with enhanced organisational and people-related dimensions. However, the technique certainly constitutes a substantial move in the right direction, and could be easily modified for different organisational settings.

Part 3

Enabling Capabilities

Chapter 6
Managing People Through Change

6.1 Introduction

6.1.1 The changing face of the work environment

The creation and maintenance of a working environment which supports an organisation's core activities is the overriding objective for the facilities manager. Although the accomplishment of such an objective is tricky enough; the task is being made much more difficult because of the ever accelerating rate of change throughout all aspects of the work environment. Whether it is the current transition to flatter, leaner and more flexible organisational structures, or the quite staggering rate of obsolescence in information technology, the facilities manager has the unenviable task of not only keeping abreast of such changes, but effectively and efficiently integrating them into the work environment. For the facilities manager, the capacity to manage change successfully is becoming one of the most important management skills for the 1990s and beyond.

6.1.2 Putting the human element into change

Right from the outset, facilities managers should view managing change as being synonymous with managing *people* through change. The management of change should not be restricted to administrative or technical considerations alone. For example, when changing from a traditional office layout to an open office environment, the facilities manager should not only take into account technical and administrative considerations, (such as optimal layout of workstations and building services provision), but also the human ramifications of the change, such as staff perhaps feeling that:

❏ the atmosphere of the working environment has become impersonal, compared to that of traditional individual offices;
❏ they are distracted either by too much movement around them or by the level of noise;
❏ there is a lack of privacy.

Similarly, when introducing new information technology into the work environment, the facilities manager may have to take into account such issues as:

❑ *the design of work stations in the new office*; for example it has been shown that when workstations are poorly designed, staff working with VDUs can experience discomfort and fatigue;
❑ *the organisational changes which occur as a result of the introduction of information technology*; for example, the introduction of information technology has typically resulted in more decentralised organisational structures;
❑ *the personal anxieties resulting from such change*; for example the introduction of information technology can change the nature of work in many jobs, influencing people's morale, affecting relations with co-workers, and improving (or worsening), levels of work performance.

These issues have focused managerial attention to the change *process* itself, with facilities managers increasingly realising the importance of empowering end-users to influence the way information technology is introduced and used. By doing this the potential benefits of information technology, to both the individual and the organisation, can be better realised.

To generalise from these specific examples, if facilities managers are to manage change successfully, they must integrate employees into the change process. However, as many facilities managers will know all too well, change, (or the methods used for its implementation), is often resisted by those people impacted by it. The reason for resistance to change, as hinted above, is that change is perceived by many people, quite naturally, as a threat to their existing way of working and their general *status quo*. For example, when the facilities management function of a large organisation proposed a space layout change for one of its departments, considerable resistance was shown from the staff to be affected. This resistance was centered around two main areas:

❑ *Self-Interest* – many of the staff felt that their *habits* and sense of *security* were being threatened by the change. For example, some people feared losing a window office and being moved into the centre of the floor plan; while others resisted the idea of losing their individual office and having to share a workstation.
❑ *Disruption of work flow* – many of the staff resisted what they perceived to be the never ending stream of change. One member of staff stated they had been moved five times in one year, while another said that each move was a '... nightmare', resulting in a '... lost week's work packing and unpacking'. Other staff said that previous changes, 'just happened', with one employee saying that there was, 'no period of transition between changes'.

6.1.3 Managing people through change objectives

The facilities manager should be aware that the higher a person's level of resistance to change, the lower their *level of motivation* and subsequent *work performance* tends to be. Therefore, the primary objective for the facilities manager when managing people through change is to:

'realise the potential benefits of change by proactively ensuring that resistance to change is kept to a minimum'.

The facilities manager should recognise that people generally pass through identifiable 'motivational moods' within a change process, which in turn influences the level of motivation and work performance:

❑ People tend to generate *over-ambitious expectations* of the final outcome of the change.
❑ However, as the full realisation of the limitations of any change objectives comes 'home to roost', people often become filled with *feelings of doom and gloom* about the whole change process.
❑ In time, if and when people begin to perceive a 'light at the end of the tunnel', they *regain their enthusiasm* for the whole thing.

With this in mind, as shown in Figure 6.1, the facilities manager should aim to *reduce* the motivational swings which are experienced by people undergoing change (from $Y^1 \rightarrow Y^2$, and $Y^4 \rightarrow Y^3$) and in so doing *shorten* the duration of the change process (from $X^1 \rightarrow X^2$). The net effect will be not only to return employee performance to pre-change levels earlier, but also to provide a platform from which employee performance can be improved to new levels.

The time axis refers to the duration of the *managing people through change process*, rather than the duration of the *'physical' change* itself. For example, it would take a comparatively short time for a facilities manager to introduce new software packages into the workplace. However, the facilities manager will have to manage people through the change in order to ensure their readiness to adopt the new technology. It is this 'people management' phase, as discussed earlier, which is the key as to whether the organisation gains the full advantage of the new information technology; and it is generally started before the physical move, and may well continue long after it. Therefore, a beneficial spin-off from improving the managing people through change process, is that the facilities manager will have a corresponding *reduction* in the amount of their time which is taken up in managing change.

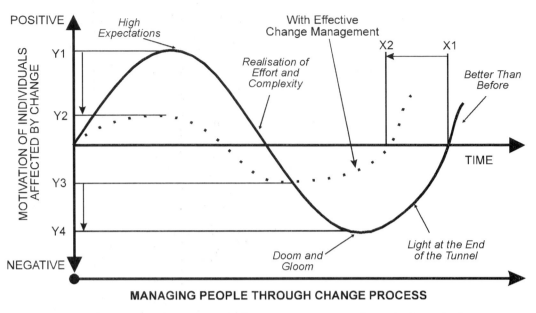

Figure 6.1   The impact of effective management of people through change.

6.1.4 Organisation development approach to managing people through change

People often find it very difficult to change long-established attitudes and behaviour. Even if changes are introduced, people tend to return to their old ways quickly if the new changes are not adequately reinforced and supported. For example, after implementing a hotelling system (where employees are allocated a temporary work space by the 'hotelling staff' upon arrival to the office, there being no permanently dedicated workspaces); people began to revert to their old 'dedicated desk' behaviour. This resistance to change manifested itself by such practices as purposely misrepresenting their length of stay in order to have a 'permanent' workstation, while others consistently 'squat' in vacant offices and workstations so they would not be disturbed. To help prevent this, facilities managers should adopt the following three-step philosophy when introducing change within a group of people (hereafter to be expressed as the 'client group'):

❏   Step 1 – *Unfreeze* existing behaviour; by helping employees identify and come to terms with the proposed change.
❏   Step 2 – *Implement* changes.
❏   Step 3 – *Refreeze* the new changes by consolidating and 'locking in' the changes as they are being implemented.

This philosophy for successful change management is present within the *organisation development* approach. The methodology has the infrastructure to:

❑ Create an awareness within the client group of the need to change.
❑ Provide the tools to diagnose change requirements.
❑ Provide the participation element to enhance internal commitment within the client group to the change.
❑ Provide the project management skills to ensure the change project runs smoothly.

These elements within the organisation approach can be operationalised within the change management process shown in Table 6.1. It will be readily appreciated by the reader however, that in reality these phases will tend to merge and/or swap around. However, for the purposes of simplification, this chapter will consider each stage as a self-contained process.

Table 6.1 Stages in the organisation development approach to managing people through change

Stage	Description
Initiating the change	Establishing a collaborative relationship between the facilities manager and the client group, carrying out an initial exploration of change objectives and the establishment of how the change process should proceed.
Collecting information on the change situation	Selecting, sequencing and carrying out information collection methods.
Diagnosis and action planning	Interpreting and organising the information, feeding it back to those people undergoing change and developing a shared understanding of the required change. From this, an action plan is developed.
Implementing and evaluating the change	Carrying out, and learning from, the action plans.

6.1.5 The role of the facilities manager within the change process

The facilities manager should see his role as helping the client group through the change project. The facilities manager should aim to move change along but should not control the change process. By creating this organisational buffer between the facilities management function and the client group, a sense of empowerment can be transferred to the client group, thereby instilling responsibility and commitment within the client group for the change to succeed.

6.1.6 Chapter aim and structure

The aim of this chapter is to structure the change process into a series of stages which gives the facilities manager guidance on 'good practice' when managing people through change. Each of the four separate stages (set out in Table 6.1) will be discussed in turn, with the use of relevant theory, managerial tools and case study material. The stages will be broken down into the following sections:

- ❏ *Stage objectives* – The purpose of the stage.
- ❏ *Stage rationale and context* – How the stage fits into the overall managing people through change process.
- ❏ *Tasks* – The individual tasks to be completed within the stage.
- ❏ *Tools* – Managerial techniques which can be used to accomplish the tasks. These tools are intended to give ideas only. It is accepted that they may be modified or rejected depending on the organisational situation, and the nature of the change.
- ❏ *Input* – The information required to carry out the stage.
- ❏ *Output* – The tangible product of the stage.
- ❏ *Case study* – Case study material will be presented to illustrate and expand upon the issues. The background to the case study is given below.

Case Study: Setting the scene

The organisation

The organisation is a major professional service organisation.

The space project

The case study deals with the consolidation and reorganisation of a department's space towards greater use of shared workstations. The change to shared workstations was primarily in response to the 'out on-site' nature of the work carried out by the department, which meant that the organisation could no longer justify the cost of fixed space for those employees who were not office bound. Prior to the change, the department was located on two floors in one building, and one floor in another. The number of staff involved was around 370.

Aims of the change

The aims of the change were to:

- ❏ Improve communication flows and increase productivity by consolidating all of the department onto one floor.
- ❏ Decrease facility costs through a reduction in space requirements.

Background to the change

Part of the department had already undergone a transition towards shared assigned office space in 1989. The change was very much owned by the facilities management function, rather than by the department itself. As a result, the 96 people involved were generally dissatisfied with both the change *process*, feeling that little regard had been taken for determining user needs; and the change *outcome*, with the new work environment not supporting their work patterns.

6.2 Stage 1: How to Get the Change Process Started

6.2.1 Stage objectives

- ❏   To encourage the client group to want to change themselves.
- ❏   To establish ground rules for the relationship between the facilities manager and the client group.

6.2.2 Stage rationale and context

The starting point for any change process is the perceived need or desire for change. Change may be in response to a functional situation, such as additional space requirements for an expanding department; or a more strategic change, such as the consolidation of several offices into one new building. Even though change may be essential, to recapitulate, the facilities manager should be aware that the motivation for the change should come predominantly from within the *client group* in order to overcome resistance to change. In other words, the client group senior management should perceive that they have 'selected' *themselves* for change, rather than be targeted for change by the facilities manager or top management. Nothing annoys people more than being autocratically told to do something, even if in their heart of hearts they know it's a good idea.

To create this sense of *ownership* for the change, the facilities manager may need to *persuade* the client group's senior management that change is in their best interests. For example, a facilities manager 'imported' the hotelling concept of space usage from the United States into an organisational department within the United Kingdom. The diffusion of the space usage innovation throughout other departments was encouraged by the facilities manager internally marketing the advantages of the hotelling concept through both formal communication networks and the informal grapevine. By doing this, departmental senior managers took it upon themselves to approach the facilities management function in order to have the hotelling system introduced within their departments. In contrast, when a local authority wanted to introduce teleworking, a more formal approach was used to persuade managers of the benefits of teleworking, with information packs being distributed to managers, as well as the teleworking concept being introduced in management and staff training courses.

Once an impetus to change has been established, the facilities manager and the client group senior management should begin to develop a working relationship. The first stages of this working relationship are perhaps the most crucial part of the change process, as it sets the tone for the whole project. Right from the outset, the facilities manager and client group senior management team should strive to create a culture of self-examination and problem solving, which will:

❑   help members of the client group determine its readiness to change.
❑   give the facilities manager an opportunity to learn about the client group's culture and change requirements.

Within these initial discussions, there should be a *contracting stage* where ground rules for the change project are established by exchanging expectations and coming to an agreement about outline change objectives, procedures and time frames. In addition, the team should ensure that there will be sufficient 'slack' within the allocated human and financial resources so that the change plan can be developed and implemented without undue pressure being placed on continuing day-to-day activities. Finally, the facilities manager should be particularly wary of the natural tendency at the beginning of any change process for those involved to become over-enthusiastic and rush into the remainder of the change process without first setting up the evaluation mechanisms to measure the actual performance of the change project over time. Such mechanisms should be set up at this early stage. In doing so, both parties are effectively 'locked in', preventing the client group senior management or the facilities manager from reducing organisational resources committed for evaluation, or changing the focus of the evaluation stage to serve political agendas that may emerge as the change project progresses. In combination, the decisions within the contracting stage allow the facilities manager and the client group senior management to be in a better position to anticipate problems that might later endanger the change process.

An example of a change process which encountered problems because of an initial lack of understanding between the facilities manager and the client group, occurred when a department replaced existing office furniture with system furniture. The change objectives from the client group's senior manager's perspective was to increase the *work* efficiency through improved layout of the working area. However, as the change process progressed, conflict between the client and the facilities manager developed, as it became obvious to the client group that the facilities manager was evaluating the success of the change on the increase in *space* efficiency through improved layout of the working area.

6.2.3 Tasks

❑   Establish a plan for the initial stages of the change process.
❑   Establish an effective relationship with the client group senior management.

❑   Set outline change objectives.
❑   Set up an evaluation procedure.

6.2.4 Tools

Initiation of change process flowchart

The facilities manager may find following the stages outlined in the flowchart shown in Figure 6.2 helpful. The flowchart represents a series of steps starting with the first contact and ending up with a plan of how the remainder of the change process should proceed.

Effective relationship with the client group checklist

The facilities manager should make sure the initial discussions with the client group senior management are focused towards forming an effective relationship. Table 6.2 gives an indication of the sort of issues which should be addressed at this stage.

Table 6.2   Client group: Facilities manager relationship checklist

Relationship issues	Comments
Which budget will any costs come out of?	
How is sensitive information to be handled?	
Who exactly is the client?	
What is the role of the client?	
How much responsibility for the change is the facilities manager going to take and how much is the client group going to take? Establishing shared responsibility is critical.	
What is the role of the facilities manager?	

Outline change objectives checklist

A useful method for producing good quality outline objectives for the change project is to consider proposed objectives against a 'SMART' checklist, (see Chapter 7 on decision making). The client group senior management and the facilities manager, by working through the checklist, can carry out a critical analysis of the usefulness of any initial change objectives suggested.

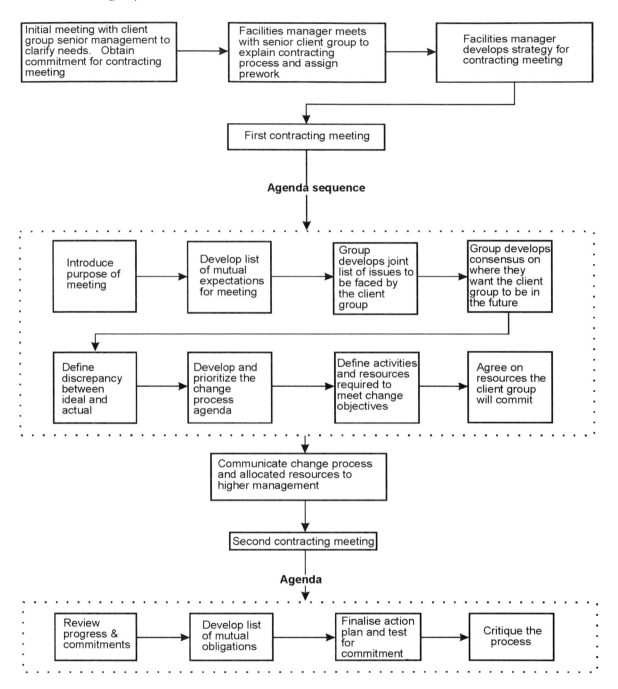

Figure 6.2   Initiation of change process flowchart.

Evaluation procedure checklist

In order to make sure that all the important considerations concerning the evaluation procedure are made at this early stage, the facilities manager may find it helpful to refer to the checklist contained in Table 6.3.

Table 6.3   Evaluation procedure checklist

Evaluation procedure issues	Comments
What should be evaluated?	
Why is it important?	
What will be gained from measuring the results?	
What will be the time and money costs?	
Who will conduct evaluations?	
How will the change process be evaluated?	
When will it be evaluated?	
What will be done with the evaluation results?	

6.2.5 Input

At this stage the input is information about the client group and the anticipated type of change. This information usually lies in the facilities manager's informal communication network, and from previous experience dealing with the same (or similar) client group, or from similar change processes.

6.2.6 Output

The initiation of change provides broad plans for the change process. However, these plans will only be based on initial information which will nearly always be incomplete. A more detailed change process requires further information. This collection of information forms the next stage of the change process.

Case Study: Initiating the change

The space project was viewed by both the client group senior management and the facilities management function as a natural progression from the earlier, partial transition to shared office space in 1989. In response to the dissatisfaction brought about by the lack of client group ownership from the previous change, the facilities management function decided to stay out of the initial planning phase as much as possible because they did not feel that they were the appropriate people to assess user needs and determine what their work environment should be. Instead of being 'informed' of how they would work, it was the facilities management's intention to allow the department to have free rein to determine their own working environment.

Towards this aim, the change process was set in motion through the setting up of a strong collaborative management structure. Firstly, a steering committee (made up of representatives from the department, personnel and facilities), was formed to head the space project. Secondly, two additional committees, accommodation and advisory, were created to involve and inform users in the change process. The accommodation group comprised senior management, while the advisory group was made up of some 20 departmental employees randomly selected. It was anticipated that the accommodation and advisory groups would be given copies of all reports, allowed to discuss recommendations and have some influence over planning.

The initial change objectives decided upon by the steering group were to create an effective office environment which would provide good working conditions with the optimal type and amount of space. The change process to achieve this was a modified survey-feedback approach, as shown in Figure 6.3.

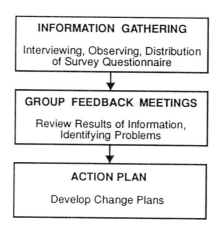

Figure 6.3   Initial space project change process.

Discussion

The incremental approach to change, with the 1989 change paving the way for the subsequent larger scale change, is very common within all organisations. The approach allows managers to reduce the inherent risk in change by providing the opportunity to assess, evaluate and learn from the performance of small changes before committing the organisation to larger scale changes. On the downside, however, the facilities manager should appreciate that such an incremental approach to change can produce a fragmented and unfocused solution. Therefore, if at all possible, any changes which are carried out should be done under the umbrella of a carefully thought out long-term strategy.

In this particular organisation, the corporate and facilities management strategies are in the process of becoming more integrated, allowing a more stable platform from which to perform well-focused incremental change. In the past, the facilities management strategy was very much dictated by corporate strategy which had been developed without consideration of its implications upon the performance of the organisation's facilities. This one-way flow of communication and influence had often resulted in the effectiveness and efficiency of the organisation's facilities being unduly compromised. The tide is changing however, as partners and senior management within the organisation have begun to increasingly realise the strategic importance of facilities to the organisation's overall competitiveness. In response, the facilities management function is beginning to have a strategic input into corporate strategy; and in so doing, the corporate and facilities strategies are being simultaneously developed to their mutual benefit.

The space project made a positive attempt to involve the people within the department in the change. The approach benefited from the incorporation of ideas which had been learnt about the importance of ownership and participation from the 1989 change. However, as will become clear as the case study unfolds, the user involvement element of the change process was perceived by the staff to be symbolic only, with staff feeling they were kept very much in the dark and had little meaningful involvement in determining their own work environment. As a result, staff exhibited a similar sense of dissatisfaction with the final work environment, and the change process used to achieve it, as in the 1989 change.

At this early stage, it could be argued that the seeds of problems to come could be seen in three closely related areas.

Unclear ownership

The facilities management function had taken pains to transfer ownership of the change from themselves, but failed to make it clear to the staff who in actual fact now had that ownership. As a consequence, staff often expressed concern over who was directing and controlling the space project.

The facilities management and client senior management team may well have been advised to have appointed a 'visible' manager within the client group as the project leader and central point of contact, and communicated the identity of the project manager to all members of the client group.

Lack of meaningful empowerment

As the change process progressed, staff quickly felt that the managerial infrastructure set up for the space project did not devolve real empowerment to the majority of the staff involved within the change. As a result, staff did not feel that their input would positively contribute to the space project, or that they had any self-determination in performing change process tasks.

The solution to this problem is extremely difficult. The facilities manager could well argue that an organisation-wide cultural change to a more participative form of management is required for empowerment to be effective. Needless to say, such a large cultural change is generally beyond the scope of the facilities manager! Instead, the facilities manager will have to settle for trying to create meaningful empowerment within a change project in collaboration with the client group's senior management.

Ambiguous change objectives

Many staff thought that the aims of the space project were not specific enough, being:

> '...just another meaningless project because of its vague objectives.'

While other staff considered the official objectives of the space project to be a ploy to disguise the ulterior motive of cost cutting through space reduction. This fear was expressed by one member of staff, when they felt that the change was:

> '... more about reducing the amount of space available to staff rather than producing a better working environment'.

In addition, support staff resisted the change, fearing the change objectives were wrongly focused with:

> '... the emphasis appearing to be more on staff who spend most of their time working in client's offices and therefore do not need as many office facilities'.

This lack of belief in the initial objectives was reflected in the staff's poor acceptance and commitment to the change, with a lack of associated identification, involvement and loyalty to the change. The facilities manager should aim to get the right balance when setting initial change objectives. They should be specific enough to have real meaning to employees; but not so specific as to prove inflexible and restrictive as the change project progresses. In addition, the objectives should be realistic; it is far better to understate the possible benefits of a change project to employees, than it is to create false hopes. In this particular case, unbeknown to the staff, the change project was under extreme budgetary constraints, effectively preventing the proposed objectives from being satisfied from the start.

6.3 Stage 2: How to Collect Information for the Change Project

6.3.1 Stage objectives

❑   To collect information on the client group and the change situation.

6.3.2 Stage rationale and context

The rest of the change process is based upon the raw material produced from this stage. The information collection stage allows:

- ❑ The *facilities manager* to develop an understanding of the client group's change requirements.
- ❑ The *client group* to learn about the change project and the role of the facilities manager, and to begin to develop their own ideas on how the change process should be carried out.

As with all stages of the change process, it is important that the client group are involved in the development and implementation of the information collection stage. In most organisations, employees feel that information collection exercises are a 'bureaucratic waste of time'. This attitude is very much a legacy of the over use of often poorly focused and constructed questionnaires and interviews in the past. To overcome this negative attitude, the employees should be empowered to the extent they feel that any information they provide will positively contribute to the change process, and that the information collection process has relevance to both the particular change project and to them. For example, staff resisted the efforts of a consultant who was trying to collect information for a proposed space layout change, because they felt aggrieved that the consultant had left the previous client's name on the questionnaire!

The information collecting phase can be expensive and the facilities manager should pay attention to the required scale and scope of the information collecting effort. There are four basic methods for collecting information: interviews, questionnaires, observations and secondary information sources. In order to maximise the strengths of each of these information collection methods, it is best if a combination of them is used. Proper sequencing of the use of these methods improves the efficiency and accuracy of the information collection process. The optimum sequence is as follows:

- ❑ *Observation and secondary information sources.* The facilities manager can build up a picture of the client group's needs by collecting information from informal communication networks, through direct observation and through analysing organisational records. Through this process, the facilities manager will be in a position to ask more relevant and focused questions at the interview stage.
- ❑ *Interviews.* The facilities manager can further develop his understanding of the critical areas of the client group's situation by building upon the issues indicated as important by the observation phase. Together, the observation and interview elements of the information collection stage allows the facilities manager to make a detailed diagnosis of the client group's needs, problems, interrelationships and so on.

❑   *Questionnaires.* The facilities manager is now at a stage where questionnaires can be developed which will be far more attuned to the special needs of the change project at hand than if the questionnaires were used first off.

6.3.3 Tasks

❑   Develop and carry out properly sequenced observations, interviews and questionnaires in collaboration with the client group.

6.3.4 Tools

Scale of information collection phase checklist

The facilities manager may find it useful to consider the questions contained in Table 6.4 when deciding upon the scale of the information collecting effort.

Interview checklist

The facilities manager may find it helpful, when scheduling and carrying out interviews, to refer to the checklist contained in Table 6.5.

Questionnaire checklist

The facilities manager, when constructing both questionnaire and interview questions, may find it useful to address the issues indicated in the checklist contained in Table 6.6. On point 7 in the checklist it should be noted that a dry run on a small scale is almost always to be recommended.

Table 6.4   Scale of information collection stage checklist

Criteria forming questions	Comments
Is there a clearly defined and agreed upon change project area for which information can be effectively collected?	
Are there existing information sources which can be tapped into to reduce the burden on the present information collection effort?	
Is there a favourable cost-benefit potential for the proposed scale of the information collection phase?	
Is there sufficient in-house expertise and resources to carry out the proposed information collection stage?	
Will the proposed effort produce information that is relevant to the decisions the facilities manager and client group will need to make?	
Is there potential for combining various information collection processes taking place in different change projects going on throughout the organisation to reduce unit costs?	

Table 6.5   Interview checklist

Interview checklist	Comments
Arrange the interview as early as possible at a mutually convenient time.	
Create a friendly atmosphere and encourage co-operation of the interviewee.	
Remove the mystery from the interview immediately by stating its objectives.	
If at all possible, conduct the interview at the interviewee's desk both for the psychological reason that the person will feel at home and for the practical reason that working documents and files will be near at hand for reference.	
The interviewer should ensure that not too many facts and details are collected and should be sure that they are relevant to the change project.	
Technical terms should only be used if understood by all concerned otherwise misunderstandings may arise which may cause problems at a later stage.	

Table 6.6   Questionnaire checklist

Questionnaire checklist	Comments
Initial decisions	
Exactly what information is required? Exactly who are the target respondents?	
Decision about question content	
Is this question really needed? Will this question produce the required information?	
Decisions concerning question phrasing	
Do the words used have but one meaning to all the respondents? Are any of the words or phrases loaded or leading in any way? Are there any unstated assumptions related to the question?	
Decisions about the response format	
Can this question best be asked as an open-ended, multiple-choice or dichotomous yes/no question?	
Decisions concerning the question sequence	
Are the questions organised logically to avoid introducing errors?	
Decisions on the layout of the questionnaire	
Is the questionnaire designed in a manner to avoid confusion and minimise recording errors?	
Decisions about the pilot study	
Does the questionnaire require a pre-test to ensure its design and content are correct?	

6.3.5 Input

The collection of information phase should progress from a sound understanding between the client group senior management and the facilities manager developed from the initial stages of the change process.

6.3.6 Output

An enhanced understanding of the client's way of working, as well as a broadening of the facilities manager's relationships with members of the client group. In unison, these activities enable both parties to begin the collaborative generation of an appropriate solution and development of an action plan ready for implementation.

Case Study: Collection of information on the change situation

The steering group, in contrast to the 1989 change, engaged an external space design consultant to carry out the survey-feedback phase of the change process and to draw up possible space layout solutions. The information was collected through the following techniques:

❑ *Questionnaires* were distributed to all members of the department to determine existing work practices and perceived change requirements. There was a 50% return rate.
❑ *Semi-structured interviews* were carried out with 30 representative members of staff to determine the user activities, needs and preferences.
❑ *Diaries* were distributed to 43 people to determine work patterns.
❑ *Office occupancy monitoring* was carried out every hour for two weeks between 9.00 a.m. and 5.00 p.m., to determine work patterns.

The consultant then prepared a summary of the results for the group feedback sessions.

Discussion

The use of external consultants is an increasingly common organisational practice. The perceived advantages of bringing in consultants for the space project included:

❑ The enhancement of the credibility of the space project, with the image of objectivity and expertise associated with consultants.
❑ The reinforcement of the organisation's in-house space planning capability.

The facilities manager should remember that to get the most out of consultants, they should be properly integrated into the change process and not left to work in isolation. This integration stimulates involvement and commitment on both sides, as well as allowing the host organisation to learn from the consultant to improve the in-house capability for subsequent change projects. For a fuller discission on the use of consultants, see section 5.3.2 in Chapter 5.

On the positive side, the consultant used multiple information collection techniques. This was very important, as it allowed the consultant to investigate existing behaviour and user needs from many different perspectives, therefore increasing both the richness and validity of the information produced. On the down side, however, the information collection stage lacked commitment from the client group, and could have been better sequenced. These failings can be pinpointed to three areas:

Lack of collaboration
The gaining of motivation within the client group for change is an accumulative process. Commitment to the change process from client group members was already weak due to their adverse reaction to the initiating stage of the change process. This lack of commitment was compounded at the information stage by staff feeling they had not been sufficiently involved in the development and implementation of the information collection stage. In particular, staff felt that the techniques used by the consultant were not sufficiently attuned to their particular needs with, for example, obviously standardised questionnaire and interview formats being used.

Lack of sequencing
The multiple information collecting techniques were used simultaneously. It is appreciated that there are usually tremendous time pressures, but it could be well argued that the extra resources needed to properly sequence the collection of information techniques would be well rewarded with highly focused and relevant information from which to base the action plan on.

Lack of process diagnosis
The surveys and interviews concentrated solely on the present office and work arrangements, and did not take advantage of the valuable opportunity to evaluate the *managing people through change process* to date. This, potentially, would have allowed staff to feel more involved in the change process; as well as providing valuable process improvement information which could have been fed into the diagnosis and action planning stage.

6.4 Stage 3: How to Develop an Action Plan

6.4.1 Stage objectives

- ❑   To diagnose change needs from the collected information.
- ❑   To develop an appropriate action plan based on a sound diagnosis.

6.4.2 Stage rationale and context

The degree of involvement in the diagnosis and action planning process generally improves the chances that the change project will be successful. With this in mind the facilities manager should process and summarise the collected information, and feed it back to the client group. The feedback should be made through a *series of interlocking feedback meetings*, starting at the senior management level and going down to the lower levels. The group setting not only ensures that discussions needed to resolve issues occur, but it can stimulate enthusiasm for change.

The facilities manager should appreciate that a frequent failure in feedback meetings is a lack of common ground between the client group and the facilities manager, culminating in a *communication gap* whereby the client group representatives are sometimes unwilling to believe the information, diagnosis or recommendations placed before them. To help overcome this problem it is advisable that a member of the client group leads the meetings, rather than the facilities manager, so that the *ownership of the information is transferred to the client group*. To accomplish this, the facilities manager should brief a senior manager of the client group on the content and process of the feedback meeting so that it has a participative atmosphere designed to lead to innovation and commitment. The facilities manager should be present at the meeting to interpret information, assist in solving change problems and to act as a process consultant to help the group examine and critique how they are working in the meeting.

Once the information has been fed back through the client group and the information examined and analysed to a stage where a solution has been agreed, the facilities manager and client group should translate the chosen solution into an action plan. The facilities manager should make sure that the action plan is developed as soon as possible, as there is a tendency, unless the energy generated from the feedback meetings is not quickly channelled towards an action plan, for the whole change process to drift and lose momentum.

An important part of the action plan is scheduling the sequence of activities which must be completed within the change project. For example, making the plan visible by means of a bar chart or network diagram, and clearly showing important milestones on it, can induce the effort required to achieve the change objectives. In addition, it is important that the action plan strikes the correct balance. It should be not so vague that the plan is effectively useless. Conversely, it should not be so detailed to the extent that it becomes inflexible to ongoing changes. For example, in a large office move, which was to be implemented over some 23 consecutive weekends, the facilities management function made sure that all move planning tasks were thoroughly, but flexibly, detailed and defined, with individual checklists and countdowns being created to keep the action plan on track.

6.4.3 Tasks

❑   Carry out feedback sessions.
❑   Generation of possible solutions.
❑   Develop an action plan.

6.4.4 Tools

Feedback meeting checklist

The checklist contained within Table 6.7 enables the facilities manager to make sure that consideration is given to the major issues which must be addressed if the feedback phase is to be successful.

Table 6.7   Feedback checklist

Feedback issues	Comments	☑
Has there been agreement about the information to be collected and the method of feedback?		
Will the feedback be consistent with the expectations of the client group developed in the agreement above?		
Will the feedback be given in a group setting where open discussion can be promoted?		
How much attention should be given to validating the content of the information, rather than analysing its implications?		
To what degree should the meeting allow for the opening up of related issues, rather than channelling the discussion within predetermined boundaries?		
Is the feedback information relevant and understandable?		
Will the group be able to do something about the information themselves?		
Will the process of the meeting be managed in such a way that the client group will participate in problem solving, rather than be defensive about any proposed changes?		

Solution generation techniques

A useful way of producing innovative solutions for the change project is for the feedback meeting to adopt creative techniques (see Chapter 7 on decision making, section 7.3.3.).

Action plan checklist

The checklist contained within Table 6.8 indicates some of the major issues which the facilities manager should identify and address if the action planning phase is to be successful.

Table 6.8   Action plan checklist

Action plan issues	Comments	☑
Is the action plan formally recorded and a copy provided to all client group members?		
Are individual responsibilities and dates specified?		
Is there advanced agreement about review dates?		
Are individuals given sufficient time to carry out their allotted tasks?		
Are individuals rewarded for accomplishing their change goals?		

6.4.5 Input

The diagnosis and action planning stage requires an appropriately unbiased but focused summary of the data collected during the information collection phase.

6.4.6 Output

An action plan which has been based on a thorough examination of the information collected. However, the facilities manager will appreciate that successful change is more than a good action plan. Once made, the action plan must be implemented and evaluated efficiently and effectively.

Case Study: Diagnosis and action planning

Following the information collection stage, the consultant analysed and summarised the data, and presented it back to the client group through feedback meetings with the steering group and the space planning advisory group. The remainder of the department was informed of events through a three page internal memorandum. The final space planning arrangements evolved over a period of weeks, through a collaborative effort between the facilities management function and the steering group.

The steering group feedback session comprised a presentation by the consultant, followed by a group discussion, culminating in the request for various floor plan arrangements to be drawn up by the consultant. The advisory group meeting was limited to a presentation by the consultant, followed by a general review and discussion of the initial space planning considerations and proposals made by the steering group.

Discussion

The diagnosis and action planning stage of the space project was a major cause of staff dissatisfaction and helped considerably to reinforce the resistance to the change. Many staff perceived that the user involvement element was finally ushered out of the side exit of the change process, with the traditional bureaucratic management style taking centre stage. Many staff felt that senior management had roller-coastered their way through the participative mechanisms that they themselves had set up. As a result, employees felt they were unable to influence the planning or the design of the new office environment. The reasons for this sense of alienation from the diagnosis and action planning stage include the following.

The role of the consultant in the feedback meetings
The presentation of the information was carried out by the external consultant. This arrangement was not conducive to the transfer of ownership of the information to the client group. To recapitulate, the facilities manager may find it fruitful to ensure that a senior member of the client group presents the information, and is briefed prior to a feedback meeting about the content of the findings and how the meeting should be conducted. The facilities manager should have instructed the consultant to have been present at the meeting only as a resource in interpreting the information and as an expert to assist in the solution of space planning problems.

Many staff felt that this lack of ownership prevented them from having the opportunity and authority to contribute to the diagnostic and action planning stage of the space project. This was particularly evident in the space advisory group, where one of its members commented:

> '...there has been one meeting of the Advisory Committee where the findings of the consultant were read between the lines, almost a 'faît accompli'.'

while another member of the group said:

> '...the space advisory group were told what their decisions were going to be by the consultant.'

The repackaging of the space project's objectives

At this stage of the change process, many staff were becoming very disillusioned with the space project. This feeling of disillusionment was certainly not helped by senior management seemingly making excuses for why the space project would not come up to staff's expectations when, in an internal memorandum distributed after the feedback meetings to all of the staff, it was stated that:

> 'To give you some of the background, the main constraint on better use of the building is ... air conditioning ... cabling channels and outlets ... lighting runs ... When you consider these constraints in total, you will begin to appreciate the degree of inflexibility to the use of the building.'

Such space planning limitations are common knowledge and should have been communicated right at the start of the space project, thereby avoiding the creation of overambitious expectations of the change by staff. As it was, the overall feeling of the staff at this stage of the space project was summed up by one senior manager who said:

> '...I'm bored with the whole thing, yet again false promises, yet again my staff feel demoralised and fed up. It would be far better to inform us that our next 'home' will be the stairs. At least they'll believe it ...'

This feeling of ridicule of the space project by staff was hinted at in a private internal memorandum from a senior manager:

> 'I am concerned that we may be trying to move too fast on the new space plan. The re-layout needs time to ensure we are making best use of the available space and are offering the improvements needed to gain *credibility*.' (Emphasis added).

Suffice to say, the 'people' phase of the space project, by this stage, was in very murky waters indeed. The facilities manager and client group senior management team had all but lost any commitment of the staff to the space project. From here on in the *managing* of people through change was replaced by the *pushing* of people through change.

6.5 Stage 4: How to Implement and Evaluate the Change Project

6.5.1 Stage objectives

- ❑ To carry out the action plan efficiently and effectively.
- ❑ To learn lessons from the change project to improve future change processes.

6.5.2 Stage rationale and context

The facilities manager will be all too familiar with the implementation phase letting the whole change process down, with what actually happens being far removed from what should have happened. Common reasons for implementation problems include:

- ❑ implementation taking more time than originally planned;
- ❑ major problems coming to light during the implementation stage which had not been identified during the diagnosis and action planning stage;
- ❑ failure to ensure an understanding of what needs to be done within the client group;
- ❑ inadequate co-ordination and control of implementation tasks;
- ❑ failure to gain acceptance or motivation for what needs to be done within the client group;
- ❑ inadequate resources allocated for the implementation process.
- ❑ competing, and often conflicting, demands upon the facilities manager, distracting their attention from the implementation stage;

To a great extent, all of these problems can be proactively avoided if the facilities manager and the client group have carried out the previous stages in the change process carefully. Moreover, the general theme of the change process to date, participation and empowerment, should be continued to obtain employee commitment and involvement. If employees are permitted to be involved with the detailed implementation planning, their commitment will tend to increase. For example, in an organisation where non-territorial space usage was being introduced, collaboratively developed implementation plans were hung up for employees to review and comment on two months before the change. This mechanism proved effective in winning support for the implementation process.

No matter how good an action plan is, unforeseen problems will more often than not occur. It is imperative that when such implementation hiccups occur, the facilities manager is in a position to take quick action to address and resolve problems as they occur. Obviously, the speedier the corrective action is initiated during implementation, the more likely it can be resolved before it impacts adversely on the change project. In addition, the facilities manager should be aware that attention needs to be paid to consolidating the changes within the client group as they occur. In particular, the facilities manager should appreciate that people need time to get to grips with any changes introduced. Employees may become overwhelmed with the rate or scale of change. Thus the pace of change and the extent to which changes are introduced should be addressed by the facilities manager and client group.

The accomplishment of the implementation phase, above all, depends on the facilities manager ensuring that there is an effective two-way *communication* process with the client group. The facilities manager should not restrict communication to the traditional one-way office memorandums, but expand the communication process to widely distributed feedback, to continuous written follow-up on action plans, to daily and weekly bulletins and so on. For example, when a phased office relocation was being implemented, the facilities manager placed great emphasis on giving feedback to those undergoing change regarding how the action plan was functioning. Newsletters were regularly distributed, giving details of who would move where and when, and of the new working environment. In addition, relocated staff, upon arrival to the new office, received a 'welcome pack'.

The final stage of the change process is the *evaluation* stage. This stage is extremely important to:

❑   ensure the change has been implemented satisfactorily;
❑   iron out teething problems with the change;
❑   provide lessons for future change projects;
❑   make any modifications which prove necessary;
❑   measure the change outcomes being achieved against those expected;
❑   satisfy the client group of the usefulness of the change.

However, this stage is often missed out due to lack of time and money. Obviously, it is difficult (if not impossible), to estimate whether the change project has been successful if an evaluation of outcomes is not carried out. To overcome this common problem, it is essential that the evaluation plans are considered during the initial planning phase, (see section 6.2). The methods for collecting information for evaluation are the same as those for the initial information collection phase: namely, observations and secondary sources, questionnaires and interviews.

6.5.3 Tasks

❑   Carry out action plan.
❑   Evaluate, and learn from, the change project.

6.5.4 Tools

Communication checklist

It is important that the facilities manager appreciates the essential role of communication in managing the implementation stage. The facilities manager may find it useful to check all communication against the guidelines in Table 6.9.

Table 6.9   Good communication checklist

Good communication guideline	Comments
Is a two-way communication process encouraged within the implementation stage?	
Is the need for accuracy and mutual understanding emphasised?	
Is relevant information for key change members provided on a timely basis?	
Are several communication channels used to help get the message across? Back up written messages with verbal elaboration; conversely, back up verbal messages with written confirmation.	
Is sufficient information released into the 'grapevine' to reduce the risk of inaccurate and distorting rumours?	
Are different points of view on a particular issue being elicited?	
Are measures being taken to avoid to the tendency for people to filter out negative information from upward flowing communication?	

Evaluation checklist

The facilities manager and client group team should, if at all possible, carry out the evaluation process established at the start of the change process, (see section 6.2).

6.5.5 Input

The implementation phase requires top management support and the evaluation infrastructure established at the beginning of the change process, as well as a carefully developed action plan.

6.5.6 Output

The final output from the change process is an outcome which satisfies the original objectives of the change project. In addition, the evaluation phase of the change process provides a useful way of continually learning how to improve the change management process in subsequent projects.

Case Study: Implementation and evaluation

The implementation was carried out in a short time frame to minimise the disruption to the department. During the implementation period, temporary 'doubling up' of office accommodation was carried out, as well as temporary holding areas being provided. The evaluation of the change project took the form of a conventional post occupancy evaluation, carried out by an external consultant two months after the change. The report, while discussing the employees' work performance as a result of the new working environment, concluded:

> 'Employees' overall effectiveness in the office appears to have suffered as a result of the renovation. The quality and the quantity of work they are able to perform, as well as their ability to concentrate in the office, were rated below that in the original office environment.'

Discussion

The implementation phase, in this particular instance, was of such short duration, that it has little implications for the managing people through change process. The evaluation phase, however, was of critical importance as it provided the facilities manager with feedback on how well the change was managed. This information should have been the catalyst for introducing improvements into future change processes. However, the evaluation concentrated on the space project *output*, in terms of such issues as overall satisfaction and physical design; with little consideration being given to change *process* issues. The continuous learning dimension to the change process would have been enhanced considerably if staff were asked their views on the strengths and weaknesses of the change process, and how the process could have been improved.

6.6 Concluding Remarks

The most significant part of the case study which readers should note, is the way that the facilities managers involved in the space project appreciated the importance of managing people through change and made a real effort to improve their performance in this area. The case study has illustrated that, as with any new managerial competence, learning is never easy and that many mistakes will be made along the way. In this particular organisation, the vision and commitment to persevere with this difficult learning curve is being pursued by the director of administration, who is championing a strategic initiative to generate a supportive and creative climate where facilities managers are encouraged to question the existing use of facilities and experiment with new ways of introducing and managing change. The development of such a capability and capacity for continuous learning and innovation may prove to be an important source of competitive advantage for the organisation in the future.

6.7 References

1. Beer, M. (1986) *Organization Change and Development: A System View*. Goodyear, California.

Chapter 7
Decision Making

7.1 Introduction

7.1.1 The importance of decision making

Decision making is an integral part of the facilities manager's role. Facilities managers have to continuously process information and make decisions concerning all aspects of the work environment. For example, the information produced from a post-occupancy evaluation should be analysed and fed back into the decision-making process for future space planning policies and so on. Cumulatively such decisions plan, organise, and control an organisation's facilities so that they support the organisation's primary business needs.

Managers generally concentrate on decision *output*; for example, the decision to install a building management system is often assessed on such variables as its impact on fuel costs. But such a preoccupation with assessing the decision output tends to underplay the role of how decisions are made. It can be readily appreciated that the *effectiveness* of decisions is determined predominately by the quality of the decision-making *process* used to generate it. For instance, decisions geared towards controlling occupancy costs are only as good as the process used to collect and analyse the occupancy cost information. Improvement in the decision-making process is therefore a very good opportunity for facilities managers to consistently improve the decisions they make.

7.1.2 The myth and reality of decision making

In general, much is assumed but little is known about this important managerial activity. The opinions of a facilities manager regarding their own decision-making abilities are conditioned strongly by what they consider a satisfactory decision to be. In consequence, when it is suggested to a facilities manager that he might be able to improve his decision-making techniques, he often responds with a highly defensive reaction. For example, who among the readers of this chapter would admit that they are not a good decision maker?

However, it has been observed that decision making is a complex, irrational process. Decision makers generally:

(1) *apply few special decision making procedures when arriving at their choice.* For example, facilities managers often do not use a systematic procedure to assess the impact of an office layout change upon related building elements, such as raised floor systems, floor service outlets and air conditioning systems;

(2) *lack information about the merits and consequences of alternatives.* For example, in matters of facilities planning and furniture allocation, facilities managers often fail to consider alternatives. Instead, facilities managers apply predetermined organisational standards without question. Such a stance runs the risk of alienating individual user needs, potentially generating all the problems associated with resistance to change, (see Chapter 6 on managing people through change and Chapter 3 on user needs evaluation for further discussion on the importance of participation).

7.1.3 The need to rationalise the decision-making process

In spite of the apparently chaotic nature of the decision-making process, it is essential to the overall success of the facilities management function that its managers develop more rational decision-making procedures and generally strive to improve their decision-making capabilities. Experience has demonstrated that being more rational improves managerial decision making of all types and considerable benefits can be reaped, including:

❑ providing more structure to poorly structured problems;
❑ extending the manager's information processing ability;
❑ providing cues to the manager of the critical factors in the problem, their importance, and the relationships between them;
❑ breaking out from 'blinkered' frames of mind to view problems from new perspectives.

For example, the facilities manager can provide a more *structured* base from which to make better energy management decisions if he has the benefit of systematic procedures for the collection, recording and evaluation of energy use information. By providing timely and useful information, the facilities manager can *process* more information, as he is not hampered by first having to sort out the relevant from the irrelevant information. As the information is more focused to the facilities manager's needs, he is in a better position to identify the *critical factors*, and observe trends more readily. For instance, fuel consumption trends can be an indication that heating and ventilation plant requires maintenance. Finally, the facilities manager will be in a better position to view occupancy costs from a proactive, rather than reactive, *perspective*. Such a perspective for energy management can allow greater accuracy in scheduling preventive maintenance and thus reduce costly equipment failures.

However, facilities managers have been known to dismiss any rationalisation of the decision-making process. Instead, managers frequently maintain that experience alone is sufficient to achieve good decisions. It is suggested that such reasoning is a dangerous path to follow, as :

> '.... past experience in decision making is no guarantee that our experiences have taught us the best possible methods of ... decision making and problem solving. Learning from experience is usually random. Furthermore, although we all learn experiences, there is no guarantee that we learn *from* experiences. In fact, it is possible to learn downright errors and second-rate methods from experience, as in playing golf without taking lessons from a professional. As with the golfer, so with the manager: it is only training in systematic method which enables us to correctly analyze situations so that we can truly learn from experience in those situations.'[1]

This is not to dismiss experience as worthless. Experience has its own essential role to play within the rationalised decision making structure. Moreover, the facilities manager should view decision making as a process which can be improved by working on integrating rational decision making with his own *intuitive* and *common sense* approach to decision making.

7.1.4 The decision-making process

In developing structured approaches to the decision-making process, the facilities manager should appreciate the relationship between the *decision-making* process and the *problem-solving* process. In this chapter, the decision-making process will be considered as *part* of the larger process of problem solving. The decision-making process focuses around the managerial tasks of sensing problems and choosing between possible solutions. Problem solving is a broader process which includes the implementation of the solution, along with the solution's follow-up and control. Figure 7.1 shows the stages of the problem-solving process and separates those stages which form the sub-process of decision making and which are largely the concern of this chapter.

The decision-making process begins with the exploration of the nature of the problem, continues through the generation and evaluation of possible solutions, culminating in the choice of an option. For the purposes of simplification, the chapter will consider each element as a self-contained phase. It will be readily appreciated by the reader however, that in reality there is not a simple sequential relationship between them. The predominant objective of delineating distinct phases is to help ensure that the facilities manager has considered the most relevant factors and all necessary actions have been taken. In addition, it is hoped that it will enable the reader to easily enter the decision-making process at what ever stage they want to for a given problem situation. However, the facilities manager should appreciate that such an approach only states what he *should* do; it does not specify *why* it should be solved, or its priority within the organisation. This is where experience and knowledge of the unique situation comes in.

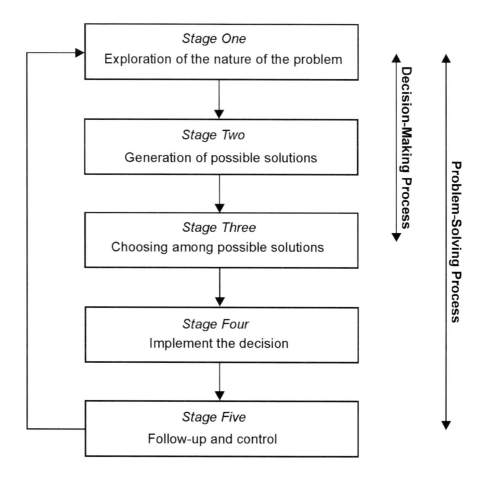

Figure 7.1   The basic model of the problem-solving process.

7.1.5 Chapter structure

Each of the separate decision-making process *stages* will be discussed in turn, in the remainder of this chapter, with the use of relevant theory, managerial tools and case study material. Each stage has been split into *steps*, which in turn have been examined under a standard format of *sections*.

These sections are:

- ❏ *Step objectives* – The purpose of the step.
- ❏ *Step rationale and context* – How the step fits into the overall decision-making process.
- ❏ *Tasks* – The individual tasks to be completed within the step.
- ❏ *Tools* – Managerial techniques which can be used to accomplish the tasks. These tools are intended to give ideas only. It is accepted that they may be modified or rejected depending on the organisational situation, and the nature of the decision.
- ❏ *Input* – The information required to carry out the step.
- ❏ *Output* – The tangible product of the step.

7.2 Stage 1: What is the Nature of the Problem?

7.2.1 Introduction

The objective of this stage is to provide the remainder of the decision-making process with a sound foundation, reducing the risk of generating an inappropriate solution and/or excessive use of organisational resources. In essence, the exploration stage gives overall direction, and builds in the potential for added value where the benefits of the *outcome* of the decision making process exceeds the required *input* of organisational resources. Figure 7.2. shows the steps in the exploration of the problem stage.

7.2.2 Step 1: Sense problem

Step objective

- ❏ To detect problems effectively and efficiently.

Step rationale and context

Problem sensing is where managers detect a *problem gap* between a present situation and a desired situation, (see Figure 7.3). A manager usually detects problems when:

- ❏ there is a deviation from past experience;
- ❏ there is a deviation from a set plan;
- ❏ other people present problems to him;
- ❏ competitors outperform his organisation.

For example, the decision to relocate may be triggered off in response to the need to provide expansion space, to check rising occupancy costs, or because of changing markets in which the organisation operates.

The problems detected from these sources can be viewed as falling along a continuum. At one end there are *opportunity* problems, whose solution is initiated on a voluntary basis to improve an already secure situation. At the other end are *crisis* problems, where a situation arises which requires immediate attention. An obvious example of this is the relationship between planned and day-to-day maintenance. Planned maintenance can be viewed as the opportunity end of the continuum, while the day-to-day maintenance can be seen as the crisis end of the continuum.

With the rapid change being experienced by organisations, there is an increasing tendency for problems to be detected only towards the crisis end of the continuum. The aim for the facilities manager is to develop problem sensing mechanisms which will enable him to detect problems early, so that the problem is nearer the opportunity end of the continuum. This will give the facilities manager more time to come up with a high quality solution. To come back to the example of planned versus day-to-day maintenance, it is generally the aim of all facilities managers to place increasing emphasis on the planned maintenance function in pursuit of medium to long term cost benefits.

Tasks

❑   Monitor the organisational environment for problem gaps.

Tools

Environmental scanning techniques
The facilities manager will generally have scanning techniques which survey the external and internal environment for potential problems. Optimal scanning techniques should aim to:

❑   interpret information quickly and in a meaningful way;
❑   maximise the information yield from the information which is collected, and thus minimise the costs of the scanning technique.

For example, an increasingly common way for facilities managers to effectively and efficiently sense problems is to employ benchmarking techniques. This process of comparing an organisation's facilities performance with other similar organisations can be a positive, structured method of identifying and assessing an organisation's strengths and weaknesses.

Input

The input required for this stage is the output from a management information system, (MIS). It is suggested that any MIS should embody a critical success factor approach to enable the establishment of performance indicators. This is where a MIS is developed around strategic control points which are considered essential for the successful running of the facilities management function. This allows the facilities manager to reduce the potentially overwhelming amount of information available to him to a subset of information which monitors the most crucial areas only. By streamlining information acquisition in this way, the facilities manager can be more perceptive to the more critical problem gaps as they occur.

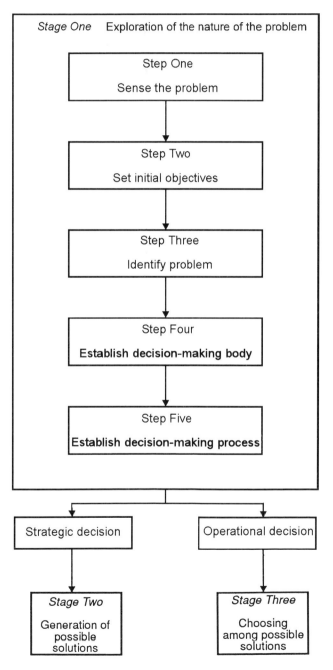

Figure 7.2 Exploration of the nature of the problem stage.

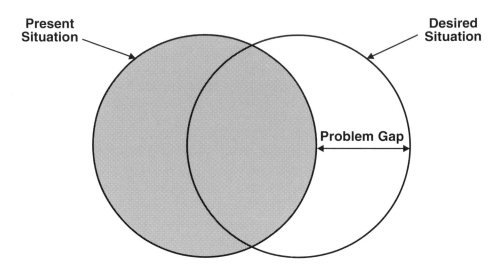

Figure 7.3   The problem gap.

Output

❑   A detected problem gap.

7.2.3 Step 2: Set initial objectives

Step objective

❑   To indicate what would constitute an effective and efficient solution.

Step rationale and context

The setting of objectives provides the end point to which the decision-making process can be channelled towards. When setting objectives, the facilities manager should ensure that there is:

❑   a criterion against which the desirability of subsequent courses of action can be measured;
❑   a standard for evaluating performance once the decision has been implemented;
❑   the basis for self-evaluation by the decision maker on their performance, acting as a benchmark for improvement for future decisions;
❑   flexibility within the decision-making process, to the extent that it is able to respond to ongoing changes.

In the absence of objectives, the decision-making process will tend to produce solutions which are without focus and, more likely than not, at cross-purposes with the general direction of the organisation.

The importance of coherence between higher and lower objectives was illustrated when the London Underground facilities management decided to introduce a computer-aided drawing system. The organisation, in response to cuts in funding by the Government, had set the *primary objective* of recovering the cost of space more effectively. In line with this policy, the facilities management decided to computerise the property management system, with the medium to long term aim of introducing a charging policy for space occupation. However, the *initial objective* set was to ensure the CAD system satisfied the primary objective of recovering space cost, through improving space efficiency via greater accuracy in planning.

Tasks

❏   Formulate objectives that are specific, verifiable and attainable.

Tools

❏   Decision objective checklist.

A fruitful method for generating good quality objectives is to consider proposed objectives against a 'SMART' checklist, (see Table 7.1). The facilities manager, by working through the checklist, can carry out a critical analysis of the usefulness of any objectives proposed. A worked example is shown in Table 7.10.

Input

Relevant information is required about the problem and its environment in order to formulate initial goals. For example, a facilities manager, when deciding on a furniture policy, may work towards the general objective of optimising the organisation's accommodation assets to meet the organisation's business needs, over time, in the most cost effective fashion. However, in order to concentrate this broad goal into 'SMART' objectives, he may require information from:

❏   the external environment; say from a benchmarking exercise to assess what other similar organisations are doing;
❏   the external/internal environment boundary; such as the likely organisational regroupings, with their associated churn, in the short to medium term;
❏   the internal environment; say existing organisational performance standards on shelving, screens, socket outlets, pedestals and work surfaces.

Table 7.1 'SMART' checklist

Decision objective checklist	Date	
Problem description		
Proposed objective		
Problem characteristics	**Comments**	☑
Specific – is the proposed objective sufficiently clear to avoid ambiguity and uncertainty?		
Measurable – does the proposed objective enable its performance to be evaluated?		
Attainable – is the proposed objective realistically attainable?		
Relevant – is the proposed objective consistent and linked to other organisational objectives and processes?		
Trackable – does the proposed objective enable progress towards its accomplishment to be monitored?		

Output

❑   Defined solution objectives.

7.2.4 Step 3: Identify problem characteristics

Step objective

❑   To correctly identify whether a sensed problem is strategic or operational.

Step rationale and context

Once the facilities manager has sensed that there is a problem, the next task is to categorise the problem. The way in which problems are categorised affects subsequent decision-making performance. Perhaps the most important variation between problems is whether the problem requires a *strategic* or *operational* decision for their solution.

Strategic decisions are concerned with matters which relate the facilities management function to the external business environment. They tend to be long term in their effects and direct the facilities management function towards the maintenance of primary objectives. Strategic decisions tend to be ill-structured in nature, with the uncertainty and ambiguity created by the external business environment making them complex and open-ended. In contrast, *operational decisions* interpret a facilities management function's strategic objectives into manageable terms for short-term decision making. Operating decisions tend to be well structured, repetitive and routine, with specific and concise organisational procedures formulated for handling them.

The significance of differentiating between these two basic categories of decisions became apparent, for example, when an organisation made a review of the provision of drinks within its headquarters. Up to this point a tea trolley service had always be used, but it was assessed that the service cost approximately £25 000 per annum. This traditionally operational matter was elevated to that of a strategic problem, with concern being expressed over such issues as:

❑   was the present arrangement good value for money?
❑   how did the service's cost and quality compare with its competitors?
❑   could organisation-wide lessons be learnt from this problem?

The facilities manager, in this particular case, was faced with uncertainty over the effectiveness and efficiency of providing a vending service, in addition to being concerned over the social impact on the staff of stopping the tea trolley service.

Another example is an organisation which has recently decided to change an earlier decision to outsource its catering function, and keep it in-house. This turn around was initiated by the facilities management who, upon reflection, decided that the catering function was of strategic importance, due to the nature of the primary business, and could be a source of competitive advantage if it was kept in-house.

Tasks

❑   Define the problem as being strategic or operational in nature.

Tools

❑   Decision type diagnostic checklist.

A useful way for the facilities manager to differentiate operational from strategic decisions, is to consider the perceived problem against the checklist shown in Table 7.2. A worked example is shown in Table 7.11.

Input

Relevant information is required about the sensed problem to complete the decision type diagnostic test. In the case of the outsourcing problem, information was needed to determine the relationship between the catering function and the core strategy of the organisation. In this particular case, the facilities manager had to collect information on the present and future nature of the core business of his organisation, along with information concerning the present and projected role of the catering function.

Output

❏   Problem defined as being either operational or strategic. If the problem is strategic, go on to the next step. If it is operational, go on to Stage 4: Step 1A.

Table 7.2   Decision type diagnostic checklist

Decision type diagnostic checklist							
Problem description							
Problem characteristics	**Operational**			⇔			**Strategic**
Rarity – How frequently do similar problems occur?	Not rare						Very rare
	Notes:						
Radicality of consequences – How far is the solution of the problem likely to change things within the organisation?	Not radical						Very radical
	Notes:						
Seriousness of consequences – How serious would it be for the organisation if the chosen solution of the problem went wrong?	Not serious						Very serious
	Notes:						
Diffusion of consequences – How widespread are the effects of the decision likely to be?	Not widespread						Very widespread
	Notes:						
Endurance of consequences – How long are the effects of any decision likely to remain?	Not long						Very long
	Notes:						
Precursiveness – How far is the solution of the problem likely to set parameters of subsequent decisions?	Not precursive						Very precursive
	Notes:						
Number of interests involved – How many parties, both internal and external to the organisation, are likely to be involved in the solution of the problem?	Few parties						Many parties
	Notes:						
Summary							

7.2.5 *Step 4: Establish decision-making group*

Step objective

❑   To establish the optimum decision-making group with respect to the nature of the problem and the organisational situation.

Step rationale and context

Once the facilities manager has sensed and defined a strategic problem, the next stage is to determine the *optimum decision-making group* with respect to the type of problem which is being confronted. It is suggested that a productive way of determining the most appropriate decision-making group is to decide on the level of *participation* to be given to others in the decision-making process. The facilities manager can either be *autocratic* in nature; making decisions within his area of authority, issuing orders to people, and monitoring their performance to ensure compliance with his instructions. For example, when planning an office environment, the facilities manager can assume the role of the expert, by virtue of his educational training and understanding of people, and design an environment which will satisfy the people and their needs. This approach is based on the notion that it is undesirable for the eventual users to participate in the planning of the environment, since they get in the way and do not have the necessary experience. Furthermore, participatory decision making makes the project much more expensive and time consuming.

In contrast, the facilities manager can provide for opportunities for those impacted by a decision to *participate* in the decision-making process; forming groups in order to share problems with them and encourage them to arrive at mutually agreed solutions to problems. In the case of planning an office environment, the facilities manager can stimulate participation in the belief that people need to participate in planning their own environment to be satisfied. Through participation in the decision making process, users have a feeling of control over their environment and is the only way users' values can really be taken into account.

The reader will readily appreciate that these two contrasting decision-making styles form a *participation continuum*. It is useful to break down this continuum into five alternative managerial decision making styles:

❑   *Autocratic 1, (A1):*   The manager makes the decision himself using information available to him at the time.
❑   *Autocratic 2, (A2):*   The manager obtains necessary information from others, then takes the decision by himself. The manager may or may not tell the others what the

problem is when getting the information from them. The role of the others is purely as providers of information, rather than as generators or evaluators of alternative solutions.

❑ *Consultative 1, (C1):* The manager shares the problem with relevant people individually, getting their ideas without bringing them together as a group. Then the manager makes the decision, which may or may not reflect the others' inputs.

❑ *Consultative 2, (C2):* The manager shares the problem with others as a group, collectively obtaining their ideas and suggestions. Then the manager makes the decision, which may or may not reflect the others' influence.

❑ *Group 1, (G1):* The manager shares the problem with other people as a group. The group generates and evaluates alternatives and reaches a mutually agreed solution. The manager does not try to influence the group, and is committed to accepting and adopting any solution which has the support of the whole group.

The task for the facilities manager is to identify which of these styles is appropriate for a given situation.

Tasks

❑ Conduct a situational analysis of the problem.

Tools

❑ Situational leadership analysis.

The facilities manager can select the most suitable level of participation within the decision body for a given problem by using a checklist. The checklist comprises seven 'problem attribute' questions, each of which requires a simple Yes/No response.

The questions are as follows:

❑ *Question A* – Is there a quality requirement such that one solution is likely to be preferable to another?
❑ *Question B* – Do you have sufficient information to make a high quality decision?
❑ *Question C* – Is the problem operational in nature?
❑ *Question D* – Is the acceptance of the decision by others critical to effective implementation?
❑ *Question E* – If you were to make the decision by yourself, is it reasonably certain that it would be accepted by others?

❑ *Question F* – Do others share the organisational goals to be obtained in solving this problem?

❑ *Question G* – Is conflict among others likely for the proposed solution?

By answering these questions, the facilities manager can diagnose a situation fairly quickly and accurately, and generate a prescription concerning the most effective decision body.

The simplest way to diagnose the appropriate decision body is through the use of a decision tree as shown in Figure 7.4. The questions A–G, (above), are arranged at the top of the figure. To use the tree, the facilities manager selects the problem which has been sensed, and enters the decision tree on the extreme left hand side at 'state the problem' and asks the first question: Does the problem possess a quality requirement ? The answer, yes or no, denotes a path that leads to another question identified by the letter immediately above the box. The process continues until the facilities manager encounters a terminal node, (that is, an endpoint on the tree), designated by a number called the problem type. At this point, all seven questions have been asked, and decision processes that threaten either decision quality or acceptance have been eliminated. What is left over is the *feasible set*.

For some problem types there is only one alternative remaining in the feasible set. However, the majority of feasible sets have more than one suitable decision process. The basis for choosing among alternatives in the feasible set lies upon a *time-efficient/time-investment continuum*. The time efficient bias promotes the premise that more participative methods are slower than those that are less participative and use up more time on the part of each of those involved in the decision. Consequently, the most autocratic choice within the feasibility set is selected. At the other end of the continuum. the time-investment bias promotes the idea that participation has beneficial organisation development consequences. The facilities manager should use his judgement to choose the appropriate point along this continuum for a given problem.

For example, when managing people through change, one of the most important tasks which the facilities manager is involved in at an early stage is to assess the level of participation to be given to those people being impacted by the change (see Chapter 6 on managing people through change for a fuller discussion of this issue). A worked example of a decision body flow-chart analysis is shown in Figure 7.9.

Inputs

Relevant information is required about the problem to complete the situational analysis of the problem. For example, when deciding upon the level of participation to be given to employees undergoing an office refitting, the facilities manager consulted the upper management of the client group, as well as drawing upon previous managing people through change experiences.

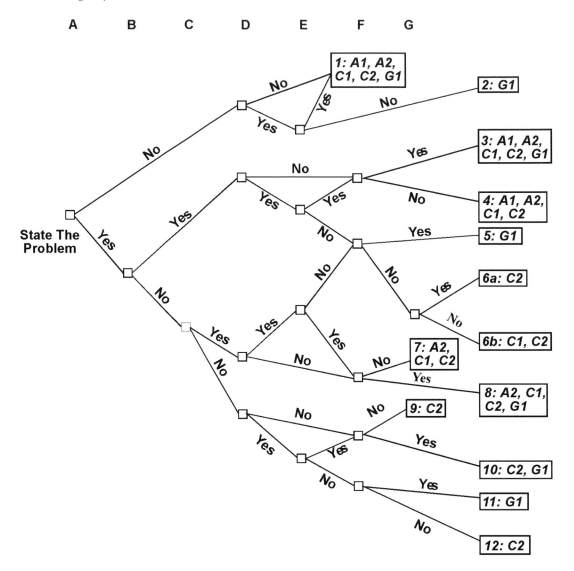

Figure 7.4   Decision body flowchart[2].

Outputs

❑   A problem which has been allocated an appropriate decision body.

7.2.6 Step 5: Establish decision-making process plan

Step objective

❑   To produce and agree an outline plan for the decision making process as a whole.

Step rationale and context

Planning is essential for good decision making. It provides the basis for integrating and coordinating all the tasks within the decision making process. In particular, planning allows the manager to firstly collect and arrange relevant information, secondly to identify and establish effective communication routes, and thirdly to provide a programme of tasks which establishes intermediate and final deadlines that can be worked towards. For example, the reader will appreciate that the tasks to be carried out in a user needs evaluation, (see Table 3.6, Facilitation tasks), is basically a decision-making workplan. The *preparation* phase can be viewed as being synonymous with the exploration of the nature of the problem stage; while the *evaluation generic core* phase can be considered as being the same as generation of possible solutions stage; and, finally the *sort data and respond* phase can be perceived as being the choosing among possible solutions stage.

Tasks

❑ Identify key organisational resources required for the decision-making process.
❑ Establish a plan of work for the decision making process.

Tools

Decision-making worksheet
The worksheet, shown in Table 7.3, allows the facilities manager to record the description of the problem, the anticipated outcome of the decision-making process, who is involved, and key information requirements and sources.

Decision-making process plan
Table 7.4 allows the facilities manager to easily plan how the decision-making process will be carried out–what needs to be done, who will do it, and when it has to be done by. The implementation, follow-up and control stages have been included for completeness.

Inputs

Relevant information is required about the availability of organisational resources, such as people and time, to complete the decision-making process plan. For example, when formulating a disaster planning procedure for a large office block, the facilities manager carefully took into consideration the availability of short-term resources at any given time, so that a contingency element could be built in to allow for resource variations.

Outputs

❑   A plan which provides direction for the remaining stages of the decision-making process.

Table 7.3   Decision-making worksheet

Decision-making worksheet
Problem description
Anticipated output
Assigned by   Date assigned Assigned to (1) Person responsible for output (2) Others involved/assigned
Key input information
Suggested sources of information
Further comments

Table 7.4 Decision-making process plan

Decision-making process stages	Who	Man-days	Calendar date →
Exploration of the nature of the problem			
Generation of alternative solutions			
Evalution of alternative solutions			
Implementation of chosen solution			
Follow-up and control			

Referenced notations

A:	D:	G:
B:	E:	H:
C:	F:	I:

7.3 Stage 2: Generation of Possible Solutions

7.3.1 Introduction

The objective of this stage is to search for information which can be processed into a range of possible solutions. The emphasis of this stage is on effective and efficient information collection, and on creative, idea-generating techniques. Figure 7.5 shows the steps in the generation of possible alternatives stage.

7.3.2 Step 1: Collection and analysis of information

Step objective

❑   To gain a better understanding of the problem context.

Step rationale and context

There is a tendency for managers to skip from the setting of initial objectives to the generation of possible solutions. However, this short cut prevents the decision maker from gaining an improved understanding of the reasons for making the decision in the first place. The aim of this step is to address the problem within a wider context, providing a firm and balanced platform from which to generate possible solutions. This process involves two interacting activities: firstly, the collection of information around the problem area; and secondly, the analysis of this information.

Tasks

❑   Collect information related to the problem.
❑   Interpret information.

Tools

❑   Systematic fact finding and analysis technique.

This technique takes the form of a checklist, shown in Table 7.5, which aims to integrate the collection of information and its analysis. The purpose of the 'what', 'how', 'where', 'who' and 'how many' questions is to identify all the significant issues which should be considered when generating possible solutions. The first 'why?' question is aimed at generating the major reasons why things are the way they are. The follow-up 'why?' question asks the decision maker why those major reasons have been put forward. A worked example is given in Table 7.12.

Input

❏ Output from Stage One: exploration of the nature of the problem.

Output

❏ A problem statement placing the problem in context with its environment.

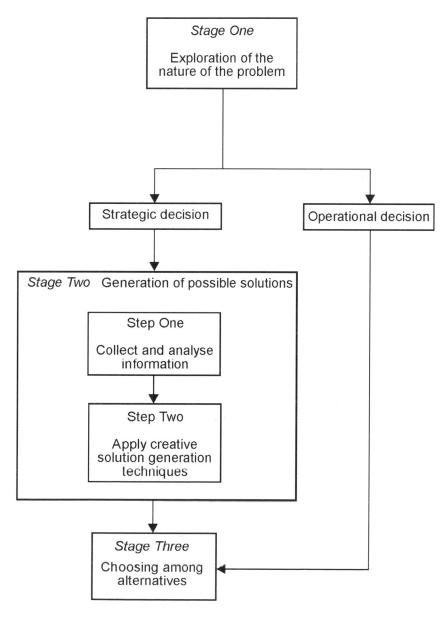

Figure 7.5. Generation of possible solution stage.

Table 7.5   Systematic fact finding and analysis checklist

Systematic fact finding and analysis checklist		Date Problem description		
What activities are carried out?	⇒	*Why?*	⇒	*Why?*
How are things done?	⇒	*Why?*	⇒	*Why?*
Where are things done?	⇒	*Why?*	⇒	*Why?*
Who carries out activities?	⇒	*Why?*	⇒	*Why?*
How many times done?	⇒	*Why?*	⇒	*Why?*
Summary				

7.3.3 Step 2: Apply creative solution generation techniques

Step objective

❑   To produce a range of creative possible solutions.

Step rationale and context

Ideally, managers would be able to generate all the possible alternatives in order to select the optimum solution. However, rather than optimise, managers generally follow a process of *compromising* where they cease to generate possible solutions after they encountered the *first* alternative which meets some minimum standard of satisfaction. Such common managerial practices tend to severely limit the search for solutions. This is particularly undesirable for strategic decisions, where there are few or no precedents. The aim of this step, therefore, is breakout from these potentially rigid procedures and to infuse creativity techniques into the generation phase of the decision-making process. This has the effect of looking at problems from new angles, thereby improving the chances of generating better possible solutions.

It will be seen that the managerial tools discussed try to get away from the traditional 'round the table' meetings. Although such meetings set out to generate and refine ideas, in practice this rarely happens. Instead they often serve as a playing field for organisational politics which are preoccupied with irrelevant issues or delegatable detail.

Tasks

❑   Apply creative techniques to generate innovative possible solutions.

Tools

SCAMPER attribute checklist

This technique, shown in Table 7.6, is essentially very simple and quick, and is perhaps most useful in situations where facilities managers want to develop basic ideas. The first stage for the facilities manager is to identify and pick out the major attributes of the problem under consideration. Each of these attributes in turn is then considered against a SCAMPER checklist of idea-spurring questions: Substitute? Combine? Adapt? Modify? Put to other uses? Eliminate? and Reverse?

Nominal group technique

The nominal group technique allows individual judgements to be effectively pooled within a group, and is particularly appropriate for strategic problems, where there is uncertainty about the nature of the problem and possible solutions. The ideal group size is 5–9, with sessions lasting a maximum of 60–90 minutes.

Part 1: Opening statement

The opening statement sets the tone for the whole session, and should include the following components:

❑   the importance of the generation stage of the decision-making process should be noted;
❑   the group should be informed of the session's overall goal and how the results will be used;
❑   the four basic steps of nominal group technique should be briefly summarised, (see Parts 2–5 below).

Table 7.6 SCAMPER attribute checklist

SCAMPER attribute checklist								Date
Problem description								
Problem attribute	Substitute?	Combine?	Adapt?	Modify?	Put to other uses?	Eliminate?	Reverse?	Attribute summary

Part 2: Individual generation of ideas in writing

Ensure that all group members have a written copy of the problem question. The facilities manager should read the question aloud to the group and ask them to respond to it by writing their ideas in brief statements. This stage of proceedings should be done in silence and be around 4–8 minutes in duration.

Part 3: Round-robin recording of ideas

The facilities manager should explain that this phase is designed to map the group's thinking. The facilities manager should instruct one person at a time to orally present one idea from their list without discussion, elaboration or justification. This process continues until the group feels it has enough ideas.

Group members should be encouraged to discuss on others' ideas and to add new ideas, even though these items may not have been written down during Part 2.

Ideally, the facilities manager should:

❏ record ideas as rapidly as possible;
❏ record ideas in the words used by the group member – the advantages of using the words of the group member are:
  – an increased feeling of equality and member importance,
  – a greater identification with the task,
  – the group feels its ideas are not being manipulated by the group recorder;
❏ record the ideas on a flip-chart, numbering the items in sequence.

This stage provides an opportunity for all the group members to influence the group's decisions. The benefits of round-robin recording are:

❏ equal participation in the presentation of ideas;
❏ an increase in problem-mindedness;
❏ the separation of ideas from specific people;
❏ the increase in the ability to deal with a larger number of ideas – this is because people are more able to deal with a larger number of ideas if ideas are written down and displayed;
❏ a tolerance of conflicting ideas;
❏ the encouragement of 'hitchhiking' – hitchhiking is the notion that ideas listed on the flip chart by one member may stimulate another member to think of an idea not written down on the worksheet during the silent period;
❏ the provision of a written record and guide.

If the facilities manager feels that the level of inhibition within the group may be such that it will discourage people to generate ideas, he may ask for the written lists to be passed in anonymously. The facilities manager then writes down one idea from each list in the same round-robin fashion.

Part 4: Serial discussion of the listed ideas

The facilities manager should explain to the group the objective of this stage is to clarify the meaning and intent of the ideas presented. Each idea should be read out in sequence, and comments should be invited. The members should discuss their thoughts on the importance, feasibility and merits of the ideas. Members may note their agreement or disagreement to an idea, but the facilitator should pacify arguments in order to save time. As soon as the logic of the idea is clear, the next idea should be discussed. The meaning of most of the ideas will be obvious to group members, and discussion should be kept to the minimum. The facilities manager should allow around two minutes an idea.

The facilities manager should encourage the list of ideas as group property. Anyone can clarify or comment on any item. Within reason, new and/or amended items can be included, along with duplicated ideas being combined. However, the facilities manager should discourage the amalgamation of too many ideas into a single idea. Some group members may be trying to establish consensus through this process, and the precision of the original ideas may be lost.

Part 5: Voting

Each group member should receive five 'postcards'. The members should select the five most important ideas and write one in the centre of each card. They should record the item's sequence number in the upper left hand corner. There should be a time limit of around five minutes for this stage, and it should be completed in silence.

When all the group members have completed their five cards, the rank-ordering process should begin. The process should be as follows:

(1)   Each individual should spread their cards out in front of them so that they can see all the cards at once.
(2)   They should decide what they consider to be the most satisfactory solution to the problem from these five cards, and write '5' on it. Turn the card over.
(3)   They should decide what they consider to be the least satisfactory solution to the problem from the remaining four cards, and write '1' on it. Turn the card over.
(4)   They should decide what they consider to be the most satisfactory solution to the problem from the remaining three cards, and write '4' on it. Turn the card over.
(5)   They should decide what they consider to be the satisfactory solution to the problem from the remaining two cards, and write '2' on it. Turn the card over.
(6)   The final card should be numbered '3'.

After this has been collected, the facilities manager should collect the cards and shuffle them together, (to communicate to the group that no one is going to pay attention to how each individual voted). The vote should be recorded on a pre-prepared tally sheet in front of the group.

The facilities manager should then lead a discussion about the voting pattern. For example, if there is a polarisation between two extremely contrasting potential solutions, try to find out why. This helps the group achieve a sense of closure and accomplishment. If time permits, the group can further clarify the items and vote again.

Input

❏   The problem statement from the 'collection and analysis of information' step.

Output

❏   A range of possible solutions.

7.4 Stage 3: Choosing Among Possible Solutions

7.4.1 Introduction

The objective of this stage is to evaluate possible solutions against predetermined criteria in order to arrive at an optimal solution. This requires, firstly, the identification of the evaluation criteria and secondly, a comparison of the alternatives using the selected criterion. Figure 7.6 shows the steps in the 'choosing among possible solutions' stage.

7.4.2 Step 1: Identify evaluation criteria

Step objective

❏   Identify the principal criteria on which the possible solutions will be compared.

Step rationale and context

It is important for the facilities manager to determine what criteria should be used to carry out the evaluation phase. The better a decision maker can distil the more important criteria from the less important ones, the better the final choice will be.

The objectives established in the 'exploration of the nature of the problem' stage provide the basis for selecting the criteria for evaluation. It is prudent, however, to reconsider these objectives at this stage, in view of the specific possible solutions being considered. The evaluation criterion should reflect the:

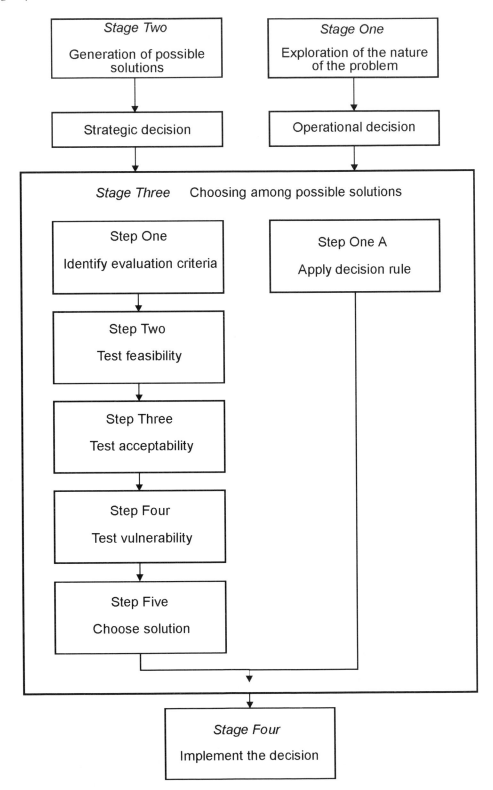

Figure 7.6   The choosing among possible solutions stage.

❑ *feasibility* of each solution;
❑ *acceptability* of each solution;
❑ *vulnerability* of each solution.

The *feasibility* of an alternative is whether there are sufficient physical, human and financial resources available within the organisation to implement it successfully. The *acceptability* of an alternative is a measure of what return is likely from choosing that alternative. The final criterion, *vulnerability* of an option indicates the level of risk associated with an alternative. These criteria elements, and their relationship with each other, are shown in Figure 7.7, and will be discussed in Steps 2–4 below.

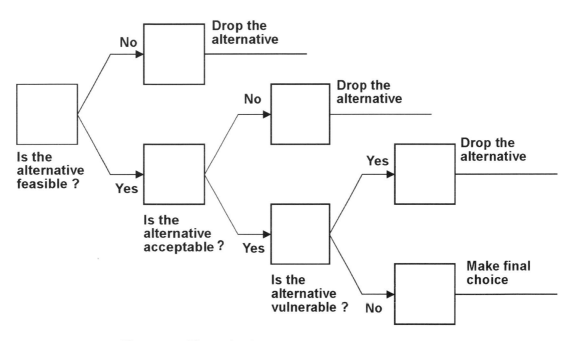

Figure 7.7 The evaluation process.

Tasks

❑ Define evaluation criteria.

Tools

Evaluation criteria checklist
This checklist, shown in Table 7.7, aims to encourage the decision maker to reconsider the initial objectives in light of the information and understanding gleaned from the decision-making process to this point. The facilities manager should record the initial objectives in the left hand column, and then question these objectives, with the question 'Why?', in the middle column. Based upon this process of reflection, the objective should then be represented as an evaluation criterion in the right hand column. The decision maker should read Steps 2–4 below before carrying out this procedure. A worked example is given in Table 7.13.

Table 7.7   Evaluation criteria checklist

Evaluation criteria checklist		Date Problem description		
Initial objectives	$\Rightarrow$	**Why?**	$\Rightarrow$	**Evaluation criteria**
Summary				

Input

❑   Output from Stages 1 and 2.

Output

❑   A set of performance parameters against which possible solutions can be evaluated.

7.4.3 Step 1A: Apply decision rule

Step objective

❏   To work through decision rule to arrive at solution.

Step rationale and context

It has been seen that operational problems are characterised by being routine in nature, (see Stage 1: Step 3). Repetition of a decision situation provides both the opportunity and incentive to develop a decision rule which instructs the decision maker what solution to choose. All the decision maker has to do is feed the required information into the decision rule to determine the appropriate solution.

This process has the potential advantages of reducing the managerial input required in the decision making process, as well as producing good quality, consistent solutions. An obvious example where this 'automatic' decision-making process is in the event of a disaster. The facilities manager will want to develop decision rules for forecastable activities which will need to be carried out, leaving him to concentrate his efforts on unforeseen events which may occur.

Tasks

❏   Collect required information for decision rule.
❏   Work through decision rule.

Tools

Not applicable.

Input

❏   Problem characteristics, (Stage One: Step 3), and decision rule input information.

Output

❏   A chosen solution ready for the implementation stage.

7.4.4 Step 2: Test feasibility

Step objective

❑   Assess availability of resources required for each possible solution.

Step rationale and context

The facilities manager, when evaluating the feasibility of a possible solution, should compare the required levels of resources required by the alternative with the actual resources available. If the resources required by a possible solution are not readily available, the proposed solution is not feasible. The three important elements when assessing the resource requirements of an option are: skills, capacity, and the 'degree of fit'.

Every potential solution option will require a collection of *skills* to be present within the organisation, so that it can be successfully implemented. If a possible solution requires a course of action which is similar to other activities within the organisation, then it is likely that the necessary skills will already be present. If, however, the implementation of the solution will require a completely new set of activities, then it is necessary to identify the required skills and to match these against those existing in the organisation.

Similarly, each possible solution will need a *capacity* requirement of resources, such as finances, space, human resources, and so on. These capacity requirements need to be determined to estimate the resources necessary to implement the solution.

Finally, possible solutions cannot be evaluated in isolation, but have to be assessed in context with existing organisational activities. The *degree of fit* of an option indicates the extent to which the organisational consequences of a solution being implemented are compatible with other organisational activities. This notion is particularly relevant in outsourcing (see chapter 4) where it is agreed that the user's environment toward facilities management outsourcing is first as important, if not more important, than purely 'economic arguments'.

Tasks

❑   Determine the required technical or human skills which are required to implement the option.
❑   Determine the required capacity resources which are required to implement the option.
❑   Determine the option's *'degree of fit'*.

Tools

Feasibility checklist
A helpful way of evaluating the feasibility of a proposed solution is to consider it against the checklist shown in Table 7.8. A worked example is shown in Table 7.14.

Table 7.8   Feasibility checklist

Feasibility checklist	Date Proposed solution
Evaluation criterion	**Response**
Skills requirements	
Capacity requirements	
Degree of fit	
Summary	

Input

❑   Evaluation criterion, (Stage 4: Step 1), and range of possible solutions, (Stage 3).

Output

❑   Two sets of possible solutions. One set consists of solutions which are not feasible and are thus rejected. The other set consists of the solutions which are feasible and are ready to be tested for their acceptability.

7.4.5 Step 3: Test acceptability

Step objective

❑   Assess the extent to which the possible solution satisfies the objectives.

Step rationale and context

The degree to which a possible solution complies with the decision objectives can be evaluated on their operational and financial impacts.

The assessment of the *operational impact* of each alternative should be based on the following:

(1) *Technical specification.* Does the proposed solution increase the chance of the service or product which the operation generates being closer to what the internal/external client wants?

(2) *Quality.* Does the proposed solution reduce the likelihood of errors occurring in the creation of services or products?

(3) *Responsiveness.* Does the proposed solution shorten the time internal/external clients have to wait for their services or products?

(4) *Dependability.* Does the proposed solution give an increased chance of things occurring when they are supposed to occur?

(5) *Flexibility.* Does the proposed solution increase the flexibility of the operation, either on terms of the range of things which can be achieved or the speed of changing what can be achieved?

Financial evaluation involves predicting and analysing the financial costs to which an option would commit the organisation, and the financial benefit which might accrue from the decision.

Tasks

❑ Determine the operational impact of the option.
❑ Determine the financial impact of the option.

Tools

Acceptability checklist
A beneficial method of evaluating the acceptability of a proposed solution is to consider it against the checklist shown in Table 7.9. A worked example is shown in Table 5.5.

Input

❑ Evaluation criterion, (Stage 4: Step 1), and range of possible solutions, (Stage 4: Step 2).

Output

❑ Two sets of possible solutions. One set consists of solutions which are not acceptable and are thus rejected. The other set consists of the solutions which are acceptable and are ready to be tested for their vulnerability.

Table 7.9 Acceptability checklist

Acceptability checklist	Date Proposed solution
Evaluation criterion	**Response**
Operational impact ❑ Technical specification ❑ Quality ❑ Responsiveness ❑ Dependability ❑ Flexibility	
Financial impact	
Summary	

7.4.6 Step 4: Test vulnerability

Step objective

❑ Assess the level of risk associated with a possible solution.

Step rationale and context

The risk inherent in any alternative can be the result of the facilities manager's inability to predict any of the following:

❑ the internal effects of an option within the organisation;
❑ the environmental conditions prevailing after the decision is taken.

Although it is unrealistic to expect accurate predictions of such variables, it is helpful if the decision maker can assess the broad range of risk for a few critical evaluation factors.

Tasks

❑ Determine the risk inherent in an option.

Tools

Downside risk analysis
Perhaps a simple, but nonetheless powerful, method of assessing risk is to assess the worst possible outcome of an evaluation factor for the possible

solution. Once this has been stated, the facilities manager then asks the question, 'Would the organisation be prepared to accept such a consequence?'. For example, even though the expected payoff of option B, (shown in Figure 7.8), is greater than option A, the downside risk of option B might be too great a risk for the organisation to bear.

When considering risk, the facilities manager should be aware of the *risky shift phenomenon* where groups tend to choose more risky options than would otherwise be chosen if the decision was being taken by an individual. Although the cause of this phenomenon is not fully understood, it is generally considered to be the product of:

(1) *Diffusion of responsibility.* When acting individually, decisions generally tend to be more heavily influenced by considerations of what happens if the potential solution goes wrong. However, when individuals feel that the risk element is shared throughout the group, they will be more prone to accept more risk than would otherwise be acceptable.

(2) *Leadership of the group by high risk takers.* There is a tendency for individuals who have a naturally high tolerance of risk to gravitate towards leadership roles within the group, thereby enabling them to be in a position to guide the group towards the more risky potential solutions.

(3) *Peer pressure.* It has been observed that individuals may feel under pressure to adopt higher risk solutions than they would personally like, in response to a perceived stigma attached to be unduly cautious or conservative.

To counteract such forces the facilities manager may wish to adopt some of the following precautions:

❑ assign one group member to be a 'devil's advocate' to promote constructive criticism within the group;
❑ ensure that group leaders suppress their personal preferences at the beginning of the discussion;
❑ periodically bring in people external to the group. They should be encouraged to question the group's assumption's;
❑ allow a follow-up meeting to allow individuals a period of reflection.

Input

❑ Evaluation criterion, (Stage 4: Step 1), and range of possible solutions, (Stage 4: Step 3).

Output

❑ Two sets of possible solutions. One set consists of solutions which are too vulnerable, and are thus rejected. The other set consists of the solutions which are all feasible, acceptable and exhibit tolerable risk. From this latter set the final choice is made.

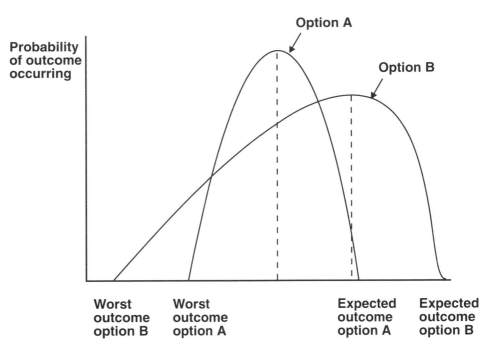

Figure 7.8 Downside risk distribution.

7.4.7 *Step 5: Choose solution*

Step objective

❑ To choose a solution for implementation.

Step rationale and context

Ideally, the choice step will result in the selection of the solution with the highest possible payoff. However, the facilities manager will no doubt be painfully aware that the evaluation of alternatives rarely produces one clear solution, and ultimately the solution chosen will be based on individual judgement, or group consensus. No matter what solution is chosen, the facilities manager should remember that it can often be made to work through effort and skill in its implementation.

Tasks

❑ Choose option to be implemented through group consensus.

Tools

Modified nominal group technique
By modifying the nominal group technique, the facilities manager can pool

individual judgements, and work toward a consensus of what the chosen solution should be. The process should start off at Part 4: serial discussion of the listed ideas, with the list of ideas being replaced by the short list of possible solutions which have passed through the evaluation steps. The voting phase will be aimed at making a final choice, rather than a short list of possible solutions.

Input

❑   Final output of evaluation process, (Stage 4: Step 4).

Output

❑   A chosen solution ready for the implementation stage.

7.4.8 How to implement, follow-up and control a decision

At this stage the facilities manager will have a solution which is ready for the implementation, follow-up and control stages. These final stages close the problem-solving cycle, (see section 7.1.5.).

The *implementation* stage involves the required planning and carrying out of activities so that the chosen solution actually solves the problem. Insufficient managerial care with the implementation stage is a primary reason why often good solutions fail. In particular, managers should be wary of:

❑   the tendency not to involve those people impacted by the decision within the implementation stage, often leading to employee resistance to the decision, (see Chapter 6 on managing people through change);
❑   the tendency not to provide appropriate resources for the implementation phase. Many implementations are less successful than they could have been because of inadequate resources, such as time, staff, or information.

The *follow-up and control* stage involves the facilities manager making sure that what actually happens is what was intended to happen. To enable the smooth running of this stage, the facilities manager should set up the infrastructure in advance for the collection of the information necessary to monitor the implementation programme.

Case Study: Decision making

The decision-making process has been presented within this chapter as having three sequential stages: the exploration of the nature of the problem, the generation of possible solutions and the choosing among possible solutions. This case study aims to illustrate this sequence, and points of interest within it.

Description of the organisation

This example of a decision making process took place in a management company who had recently taken charge of the management of a residential estate of some 500 dwellings from the original developer. The management company consists of six directors who are in charge of formulating policy on all aspects of the running of the estate. The company employs a managing agent whose role is to implement the directors' policy. All the work carried out on the estate (such as the maintenance and repair of the structure and fabric of the estate, along with the cleaning and upkeep of communal facilities such as gardens, car parking, intercoms, gymnasiums and laundry areas), is contracted out.

Initially, the management company were bogged down in developing administrative regulations and procedures. On reflection, many of the directors felt that many of their earlier decisions were rushed, ill-considered and reactionary in nature. The management company wanted to inject some sort of structure into their decision making, in the hope that better quality decisions would be generated. Towards this aim, the directors used this book as a guide to good decision making, adapting and building upon it to form processes more suited to their organisation and culture.

Exploration of the nature of the problem

Sensing the problem

A problem gap between the actual and desired performance of the *day-to-day maintenance* function was sensed by the directors. The problem was identified through two channels. Firstly, it was observed that there was an upward pressure on day-to-day maintenance expenditure. This was not readily obvious as the budgeting categories combined planned and day-to-day maintenance. Secondly, there was an increase in the number of complaints from leaseholders about the speed and quality of repairs being carried out.

The first action taken by the management company was to set up a sub-committee to investigate how information was being processed and presented by the managing agent. The medium- to long-term aim was to develop a management information system that focused on critical areas, and placed directors in a position where they could sense problems at the *opportunity* stage, rather than the *crisis* stage.

Setting initial objectives

The setting of initial objectives was undertaken by the directors using the SMART checklist. The directors felt that the checklist helped them focus on the critical elements of the problem, generating both direction and content for the remainder of the decision-making process. Previously, the directors tended to work towards extremely vague objectives, and were subsequently prone to 'managerial meandering'. Table 7.10 shows the management company's decision objective checklist.

Table 7.10   Decision objective checklist: an example

Decision objective checklist	
Problem description	*A gap between the actual and desired performance of the day-to-day maintenance function.*
Proposed objective	*Day-to-day maintenance should be: (1) of a high quality; (2) cost effective; (3) carried out within an appropriate time limit; (4) integrated with the planned maintenance policy; (5) easy to manage.*
Problem characteristics	**Comments**
Specific – is the proposed objective sufficiently clear to avoid ambiguity and uncertainty?	*Although they are qualitative in nature at the moment, it is envisaged they are specific enough to be getting on with. It is noted that objectives (4) and (5) have ramifications for the planned maintenance, finance and administrative functions. These other areas will be addressed simultaneously, in the anticipation of creating synergy between the functions.*
Measurable – does the proposed objective enable its performance to be evaluated?	*The bottom line cost of the repairs is envisaged as being measurable, along with the speed they are carried out. 'Hard' evaluation of objectives (1), (4) and (5), are seen as difficult. The quality issue in particular must be clarified within the eventual solution.*
Attainable – is the proposed objective realistically attainable?	*Not withstanding the fact that the objectives are a bit vague at the moment, it is anticipated that the objectives are attainable.*
Relevant – is the proposed objective consistent and linked to other organisational objectives and processes?	*All the objectives are extremely relevant to the core mission of the management company: to maintain and preferably enhance the asset value of the leaseholder's property.*
Trackable – does the proposed objective enable progress towards its accomplishment to be monitored?	*It has been identified that there must be changes in the management information system if the progress of these objectives is to be monitored. Again, concern is expressed that the objectives (4) and (5) were difficult to monitor. Intuition to the fore!*

Identifying problem characteristics

This stage of the decision-making process was perceived as being especially useful by the directors. In particular, it stimulated discussion about the trade-off between short-term operational decisions and medium- to long-term strategic decisions. The directors felt the main lesson learnt from this stage was the critical importance of injecting context into any solutions generated. Table 7.11. shows the management company's decision type diagnostic checklist.

Table 7.11 Decision type diagnostic checklist: an example

Decision type diagnostic checklist			
Problem description *A gap between the actual and desired performance of the day-to- day maintenance function.*			
Problem characteristics	**Operational**	⇔	**Strategic**
Rarity – How frequently do similar problems occur?	Not rare	√	Very rare
	Notes: *This is the first time that a day-to-day maintenance policy is being formulated. It is hoped the exercise will not have to be repeated on a regular basis.*		
Radicality of consequences – How far is the solution of the problem likely to change things within the organisation?	Not radical	√	Very radical
	Notes: *Day-to-day maintenance, and its interaction with planned maintenance, is the critical variable for the overall success of the estate. Good maintenance will enhance the estate, as well as keep a downward pressure on the leaseholders' service charge.*		
Seriousness of consequences – How serious would it be for the organisation if the chosen solution of the problem went wrong?	Not serious	√	Very serious
	Notes: *See above.*		
Diffusion of consequences – How widespread are the effects of the decision likely to be?	Not widespread	√	Very widespread
	Notes: *As highlighted in the initial objectives, it has been identified that the day-to-day maintenance policy will have ramifications for other managerial areas such as finance, administration and planned maintenance.*		
Endurance of consequences – How long are the effects of any decision likely to remain?	Not long	√	Very long
	Notes: *Adequate day-to-day maintenance, in conjunction with an effective planned maintenance programme, will reduce maintenance costs in the medium to long term.*		

Table 7.11   Continued

Precursiveness – How far is the solution of the problem likely to set parameters of subsequent decisions?	Not precursive				√	Very precursive
	Notes: *It is hoped that the formulation of an effective day-to-day maintenance policy will limit the range of problems in the future to those of a technical matter, rather than those of a managerial nature.*					
Number of interests involved – How many parties, both internal and external to the organisation, are likely to be involved in the solution of the problem?	Few parties				√	Many parties
	Notes: *It is envisaged that the final solution will be based on input from the directors, leaseholders, the contractors.*					

Summary
The formulation of a day-to-day maintenance policy is definitely extremely important for the estate and is strategic in nature.

Establishing a decision-making group
The directors felt that the eventual decision-making group was intuitively obvious from the outset. However, they did feel the exercise was useful, in that it established the need to explicitly consult the leaseholders about the day-to-day maintenance policy.

Using the situational leadership analysis outlined in section 7.2.5, the directors came up with the following answers, shown in Figure 7.9:

A.   Is there a quality requirement such that one solution is likely to be preferable to another? *Yes.*

B.   Do you have sufficient information to make a high quality decision? *No.*

C.   Is the problem operational in nature? *No.*

D.   Is the acceptance of the decision by others critical to effective implementation? *No.* (Although a willing acceptance of the final solution by the managing agent would be useful, it is not essential).

F.   Do others share the organisation goals to be obtained in solving this problem? *No.* (The directors suspect that the managing agent, and contractors will, in the short term, resist any solution that will make them more accountable for their actions). It should be noted therefore, that question G does not have to be asked in this particular case.

From this analysis, the resultant feasible set was C2. In other words, the directors would consult other parties, such as contractors and the managing agent. However, the final decision would be made by the directors alone, and may or may not reflect the others' opinions.

Establishing a decision-making plan
The management company drew up a plan, in particular highlighting critical milestones. This stage proved useful in maintaining a sense of tension throughout the decision making process.

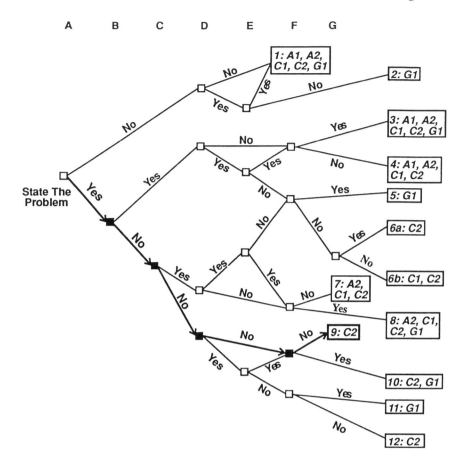

Figure 7.9   Situational leadership analysis flowchart.

Generation of possible solutions

Collection and analysis of information

Information was gathered from two sources: the managing agent and the leaseholders. The directors viewed the former source as corresponding to the *actual* state of affairs, while the latter source indicated the *desired* state of affairs.

The information collected from the managing agent fell into the following topics:

(1)   specifications;
(2)   tendering arrangements;
(3)   contract supervision and control;
(4)   managing agent/leaseholder interface;
(5)   managing agent/management company interface;
(6)   interaction between planned and day-to-day maintenance.

The information collected from the leaseholders fell into the following areas:

(1)   leaseholder/managing agent interface;

(2) perceived quality of maintenance carried out;

(3) perceived priority of work that should be carried out.

From this information a comprehensive picture could be developed. The directors felt that the systematic fact finding and analysis checklist was a useful way of breaking down, and simplifying the analysis of the problem. It became clear that although the problem symptoms manifested themselves at the contractor and managing agent level, the actual cause was at a management company level. Table 7.12 shows the management company's systematic fact finding and analysis checklist.

Application of creative solution generation techniques

In order to stimulate the generation of creative solutions, the nominal group technique was applied. The directors felt that previously meetings tended to revert to a general discussion about the nature of the problem, rather than how to solve it. Although the process of using the nominal group technique was felt to be 'silly' by all of the directors initially, in reflection there was a consensus of opinion that it was a useful way of reaching meaningful solutions quickly.

The process outlined earlier in this chapter was followed. The opening statement was defined as:

'What should be done in order to ensure a well targeted day-to-day maintenance which provides a good quality, cost effective and responsive service?'

In this particular incidence, all the solutions put forward at the final voting stage were aspects of, or permutations of, a measured term contract, (MTC).

Choosing among possible solutions

Identifying evaluation criteria

This stage was separated from the generation phase, in an explicit effort to allow reflection, and not to get 'carried away', and rush headlong into a decision. Firstly, the generation phase was reviewed, and the notion of a MTC was clarified so that all the directors had a consistent understanding of the possible solution to be evaluated. It was agreed that a MTC was where contractors tendered for the right to carry out all work of a certain type for an agreed period.

The directors moved onto developing the evaluation criteria. Many of the directors felt that they had covered similar ground when they set the initial objectives. However, they did feel that the exercise was a suitable moment to reflect on the decision-making process to date, and to make sure that the decision-making process was on the right path for the remaining stages. Table 7.13 shows the management company's evaluation criteria checklist.

Table 7.12   Systematic fact finding and analysis checklist: an example

Systematic fact finding and analysis checklist		Date Problem description *Day-to-day maintenance*		
What activities are carried out?	⇒	*Why?*	⇒	*Why?*
A vast range of day-to-day repairs are carried out. Many of the repairs which have been carried out were on building elements which were due for replacement/refurbishment on the planned maintenance programme.		*Lack of integration between day-to-day maintenance and planned maintenance.*		*Lack of direction and policy from the management company.*
How are things done?	⇒	*Why?*	⇒	*Why?*
Generally speaking, the sequence of events is as follows: a leaseholder reports a problem, the managing agent comes out and inspects the defect, and if needs be contacts a regular contractor to carry out the required works. There are rarely any specifications, tendering arrangements or contract supervision. In addition, response times are often extremely slow.		*Lack of procedures and regulations laid down by the management company, allowing the managing agent free range to carry out shoddy, expensive repairs.*		*Lack of direction and policy from the management company.*
Where are things done?	⇒	*Why?*	⇒	*Why?*
Not applicable.				
Who carries out activities?	⇒	*Why?*	→	*Why?*
Contractors carry out all the repairs. No information is demanded from the contractors to show they are members of any trade associations, have sufficient insurance cover, financial background and so on.		*Lack of procedures and regulations laid down by the management company, allowing the managing agent to employ contractors on the basis of convenience, rather than on quality, cost effectiveness, and timeliness*		*Lack of direction and policy from the management company.*
How many times done?	⇒	*Why?*	⇒	*Why?*
Not applicable.				
Summary *The present problems are a result of a lack of planning, co-ordination and control of the managing agent by the management company.*				

Table 7.13   Evaluation criteria checklist: an example

Evaluation criteria checklist		Date Problem Description *Day-to-day maintenance*		
Initial objectives	⇒	**Why?**	⇒	**Evaluation criteria**
Quality		*Good quality throughout the repair process is essential.*		*The solution should promote good quality at all stages of the repair process.*
Cost-effectiveness		*Cost-effectiveness is essential if a downward pressure on service charges is to be maintained.*		*The chosen solution should maximise competition, but not at the expense of compromising service quality.*
Responsiveness		*Repairs should be carried out as quickly as possible in order to limit the amount of damage, and to satisfy the leaseholders.*		*The chosen solution should enable an appropriately quick and reliable repair service.*
Integration with planned maintenance		*Through the integration of the planned and day-to-day maintenance programmes, maintenance costs can be reduced, and the repair service better targeted.*		*The chosen solution should enable repair activities to be accurately targeted to create synergy with the planned maintenance program.*
Manageability		*The policy should allow the management company to monitor the performance of both the managing agent and the contractor.*		*The chosen solution should be easy to organise and control by the management company.*
Summary *The chosen solution should be predominantly geared towards quality of service and ease of management company control, rather than bottom line cost.*				

Testing feasibility, acceptability and vulnerability

Once the evaluation criteria had been established, the directors then tested the feasibility of introducing a MTC. The directors were somewhat concerned that they were only evaluating one possible solution. To partially address this shortcoming, they split up into two groups, one half arguing for the solution, while the other half played the 'devil's advocate', and argued against it. This arrangement was repeated for testing both acceptability and vulnerability. Tables 7.14. and 7.15. shows the management company's feasibility and acceptability checklists respectively.

When testing vulnerability, the directors felt that the main risk involved was being locked into a contract with a contractor for one year. However,

Table 7.14 Feasibility checklist: an example

Feasibility checklist	Date Proposed solution *Measured term contract*
Evaluation criterion	**Response**
Skills requirements	*Management company: The MTC would facilitate easier and more consistent control for the directors. There is confidence that no new skills were required.* *Managing agent: Concern is expressed whether they have sufficient skills to carry out their envisaged new tasks. On balance, however, it is decided that it is more important to fit the managing agent to the task, rather than the other way round. The situation will be closely monitored, and if the performance of the managing agent is found to be lacking, a replacement will be found.* *Contractor: Concern is expressed whether one contractor will have sufficient expertise for the large number of building trades required. However, taking into account that all specialist maintenance functions are carried out under separate service contracts, there is sufficient confidence that one contractor will be capable of carrying out the basic repairs required of him.*
Capacity requirements	*It is felt that there are sufficient resources to develop the MTC. In fact, even if additional resources are required on the short term, it is felt that they will be quickly recouped in the medium term.*
Degree of fit	*It is felt that the MTC would considerably contribute to the overall effectiveness of the running of the estate, and could be easily integrated with other functions, in particular planned maintenance.*

Table 7.15 Acceptability checklist: an example

Acceptability checklist	Date Proposed solution *Measured term contract*
Evaluation criterion	**Response**
Operational impact	
• Technical specification	*By having a MTC, a detailed specification can be drawn up of likely work items. This will form part of the initial contract documentation, therefore will be enforceable.*
• Quality	*The specification can clearly define expected standards of material and workmanship, with reference to appropriate British Standards and Codes Of Practice.*

Table 7.15   Continued

• Responsiveness	*Work items within the Schedule of Rates can be prioritised in response times, e.g. 24 hours, 48 hours, one week and so on.*
• Dependability	*The terms of the MTC will stimulate the contractor to be dependable, to avoid the risk of liquidated damages.*
• Flexibility	*The MTC will tend to 'lock' in a contractor for the duration of the contract. It is appreciated that this cannot be avoided. On the plus side however, a long-term relationship may be developed in both the client and the contractor's interests.*
Financial impact	*The financial implications of a MTC can be grouped into three main areas. Firstly, it enables more accurate cash flow predictions. Secondly, it promotes lower unit costs. Thirdly, in the medium to long term, (if the repairs can be better targeted, and be of an appropriate quality), savings can be made.*

they felt the risk was acceptable for two reasons. Firstly, there would be break clauses in the contract if gross incompetence and so on was being displayed. Secondly, they felt that the tendering arrangements would tend to filter out potentially troublesome contractors, with the tender requesting references, details of past/current contracts, previous years' audited accounts, insurance arrangements, health and safety policy, and so on.

The final choice to begin developing a MTC was not taken immediately after the evaluation, but was taken in the following meeting. Again, this was an explicit effort to allow a period of reflection.

7.5 Conclusion

In conclusion, one of the directors summed up the use of combining theory, experience and judgement when making decisions when he said:

'I can't see us using these techniques all the time. I thought some of them were a bit contrived to say the least. But saying that (although I'm not sure if it was the techniques themselves, or the fact we were just made to think about what we were doing generally), at the end of the day we seemed to have produced better policies. I think that we will eventually drop them in their present form, but translate the concepts behind them into more tailor-made decision making procedures.'

7.6 References

1. Elbing, A.O. (1970) *Behavioral Decisions in Organizations*. Scott, Glenview, p.14.
2. Adapted from Vroom, V.H. & Jago, A.G. (1988) *The New Leadership: Managing Participation in Organizations*. Prentice Hall, Englewood Cliffs, New Jersey.

Further Reading

Chapter 5

Daniels, A. & Yeates, D. (1984) *Basic Systems Analysis*. Pitman, London.
Daylon, D. (1987) *Computer Solutions for Business: Planning and Implementing a Successful Computer Environment*. Microsoft Press, Redmond, Washington.
Higgins, J.C. (1985) *Computer-based Planning Systems*. Edward Arnold, London.
Hoskins, T. (1986) *The Electronic Office*. Pitman, London.
Mingay, S. & Peattie, K. (1992) IT consultants – source of expertise or expense? *Information and Software Technology,* **35** (5), 341–9.
Otway, H.J. & Peltu, A. (eds) (1983) *New Office Technology: Human and Organizational Aspects*. Pinter, London.

Chapter 6

Adams, J. D. (ed.) (1975) *New Technologies in Organization Development: 2.* University Associates, California.
Beckhard, R & Harris, R. T. (1977) *Organizational Transitions: Managing Complex Change*. Addison-Wesley, Reading, Massachusetts.
Beer, M. (1986) *Organization Change and Development: A System View.* Goodyear, California.
French, W. L. & Bell, C. H. (1984) *Organization Development: Behavioral Science Intervention for Organization Improvement.* Prentice-Hall, Englewood Cliffs, New Jersey.
Mirvis, P. H. & Berg, D. N. (1977) *Failures in Organization Development and Change: Cases and Essays for Learning.* Wiley, New York.
Neilsen, E. H. (1984) *Becoming an OD Practitioner.* Prentice-Hall, Englewood Cliffs, New Jersey.
Ottawat, R. N. (ed.) (1979) *Change Agents at Work.* Associated Business Press, London.
Thakur, M., Bristow, J. & Carby, K. (eds) *Personnel in Change: Organization Development Through the Personnel Function.* Pitman, Bath.

Chapter 7

Bass, B. M. (1983) *Organizational Decision Making.* Irwin, Homewood, Illinois.
Baumol, W. J. & Quandt, R. E. (1964) Rules of thumb and optimally imperfect decisions. *The American Economic Review,* **54**, 23–46.
Cooke, S. & Slack, N. (1991) *Making Management Decisions.* Prentice-Hall,

Hemel Hempstead, England.

Gray, E.R. & Smeltzer, L.R. (1989) *Management: The Competitive Edge.* Macmillan, New York.

Harrison, E. F. (1981) *The Managerial Decision-Making Process.* Houghton Mifflim, Boston.

Hickson, D.J., Butler, R.J., Cray, D., Mallory, G.R. & Wilson, D.C. (1986) *Top Decisions: Strategic Decision-Making in Organizations.* Basil Blackwell, Oxford.

Huber, G.P. (1980) *Managerial Decision Making.* Scott, Glenview.

Kuhn, R.L (1988) *Handbook for Creative and Innovative Managers.* McGraw-Hill, New York.

Mintzberg, H., Raisinghani, D. & Theoret, A. (1976) The structure of 'unstructured' decision processes. *Administrative Science Quarterly,* **21**, 246–75.

Summers, I. & White, D.E. (1976) Creativity techniques: toward improvement of the decision process. *Academy of Management Review,* **1** (2), 99–107.

Van de Ven, A. & Delbecq, A.L. (1971) Nominal versus interacting group processes for committee decision-making effectiveness. *Academy of Management Journal*, 14, 203–12.

Index